Letts STUDY GUIDE

AGE 11-14
KEY STAGE 3

ENGLISH

John Barber

- A clear introduction to the new National Curriculum

- Topic by topic coverage, with lots of diagrams and illustrations

- Activities and projects, designed to encourage active learning

- Frequent questions to test your knowledge

- Index and glossary of terms

- Sample National Test questions and answer plans

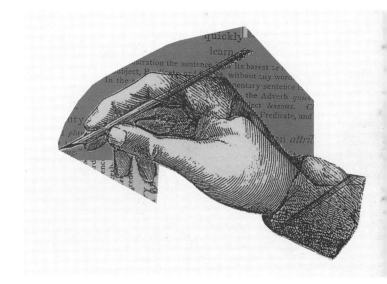

First published 1991
Reprinted 1991, 1992, 1993, 1994, 1996 (twice), 1997, 1998
Revised 1995

Text: © John Barber 1991

Illustrations: Michael Renouf, Judy Stevens, Artistic License
Cover: Veronica Bailey

© BPP (Letts Educational) Ltd
Aldine House, Aldine Place
London W12 8AW
0181 740 2266

British Library Cataloguing in Publication Data
A CIP record for this book is available from the British Library.

ISBN 1 85758 340 X

The extracts in this book are from the following works. Every effort has been made to trace copyright holders and the author and publishers wish to thank those who gave permission for the use of copyright material, and will gladly receive information enabling them to rectify any reference or credit in subsequent editions.

Material from the National Curriculum is Crown copyright and is reproduced by permission of the Controller of HMSO.

Text
p8 from *Five Green Bottles* by Ray Jenkins; p15 from *The Glass Cupboard* by Terry Jones, reprinted by permission of Pavilion Books from 'Fairy Tales' by Terry Jones; p30 from *A Story Like the Wind* by Laurens van der Post, reprinted by permission of the Hogarth Press; p33 from *Taking the Train* by Philippa Bignell, reprinted by permission of HMSO for the Science Museum; p34 from *A Tale of Two Cities* by Charles Dickens; p35 from an article from *The Times* by Arthur Reed, 22 January 1976; p37 from *Holiday Memory* by Dylan Thomas, reprinted by permission of Dent from 'Quite Early One Morning' by Dylan Thomas; p38 from *Ping-Pong* by Gareth Owen; p39 from *Man and Society*, reprinted by permission of Mitchell Beazley; p44 from *Boy* by Roald Dahl, reprinted by permission of Jonathan Cape and Penguin Books Ltd; p51 from *The Hollow Land* by Jane Gardam, reprinted by permission of Julia McRae Books; p52 from *Charlotte's Web* by E B White, copyright © 1952 J White, reprinted by permission of Hamish Hamilton Children's Books; p54 from *Witches' Loaves* by O Henry; p58 from *The Fun They Had* by Isaac Asimov; p60 from *The Three Raindrops* by Terry Jones, reprinted by permission of Pavilion Books from 'Fairy Tales' by Terry Jones; p62 from *Something Borrowed* by Harry Secombe from 'Argosy' Vol XXIX; p65 from *Mrs Beer's House* by Patricia Beer, reprinted by permission of Patricia Beer; p66 from *Banana Boy* by Frank Norman, copyright © 1969 by Frank Norman, reprinted by permission; p69 from *Behind The Wall* by Colin Thubron, reprinted by permission of William Heinemann Ltd; p71 from *The Winner's Tale* from an article from *The Independent* by Gavin Patterson, 25 November 1989, reprinted by permission of *The Independent*; p72 from *A Pennine Journey* by Alfred Wainwright, © A Wainwright 1986, reprinted by permission of Michael Joseph Ltd; p73 from *Kilvert's Diary* by the Rev Francis Kilvert, reprinted by permission of Jonathan Cape; p75 from *Passing of the Third Floor Buck* by Keith Waterhouse, reprinted by permission of Michael Joseph Ltd; p78 from *Carrington: Letters and Extracts from her Diaries* by Dora Carrington, edited by D Garnan, reprinted by permission of Jonathan Cape; p79 & 80 from *The Letters of D H Lawrence* by D H Lawrence; p79 from *The Bronte Letters* edited by Muriel Spark; p79 from *The Letters of E B White* edited by D L Guth; p81 from *The Prose Works of Sir Philip Sidney* by Sir Philip Sidney, edited by A Feuillerant, reprinted by permission of Cambridge University Press; p83 from *Corn Dolly Legends*, reprinted by permission of the *Cambridge Weekly News*; p84 *A Mite Disturbing* from an article from *The Indy*, 26 October 1989, reprinted by permission of *The Indy*; p89 from *Black Beauty* by Anna Sewall; p91 from *This Time Next Week* by Leslie Thomas; p93 from *The Tyger* by William Blake; p94 from *Snake* by D H Lawrence; p96 from *Night Mail* by W H Auden, reprinted by permission of Faber and Faber Ltd from 'Collected Shorter Poems 1927-1957' by W H Auden; p98 from *Father Says* by Michael Rosen, reprinted by permission of Andre Deutsch Ltd from 'Mind Your Own Business' by Michael Rosen; p99 from *Song of the Wagondriver* by B S Johnson; p99 from *Wind* by Ted Hughes, reprinted by permission of Faber and Faber Ltd from 'The Hawk in the Rain' by Ted Hughes; p100 from *Half Asleep* by Gareth Owen; p101 from *The Dis-satisfied Poem* by Grace Nichols; p101 from *The Choosing* by Liz Lochhead, reprinted by permission of Polygon Books from 'Dreaming Frankenstein and Collected Poems' by Liz Lochhead; p102 from *Tich Miller* by Wendy Cope, reprinted by permission of Faber and Faber Ltd from 'Making Cocoa for Kingsley Amis' by Wendy Cope; p103 from *Thaw* by Edward Thomas, reprinted by permission of Myfanwy Thomas and Faber and Faber Ltd from 'Collected Poems' by Edward Thomas; p103 from *I Love Me Mudder* by Benjamin Zephaniah, reprinted by permission of Hutchinson from 'The Dread Affair' by Benjamin Zephaniah; p104 from *Childhood* by Frances Cornford; p104 from *Demolition* by Anne Stevenson, reprinted by permission of Oxford University Press from 'The Fiction-Makers' by Anne Stevenson; p105 from *Men on Allotments* by Ursula Fanthorpe, reprinted by permission of Peterloo Poets 1978 from 'Side Effects' and Peterloo Poets and King Penguin 1986 from 'Selected Poems'; p106 from *Clown* by Phoebe Hesketh; p107 from *Last to Go*, from *A Slight Ache* by Harold Pinter, reprinted by permission of Faber and Faber Ltd; p109 from a letter by John Mortimer, from the Royal Society of Literature's *Letters No 1, Autumn 1992*; p112 from *The First Casualty of War is Truth* from an article from *The Indy*, 16 August 1990, reprinted by permission of *The Indy*; p116 from *Selling us a Stereotype* from an article from *The Indy*, 6 September 1990, reprinted by permission of *The Indy*; p123 from *Charlie and the Chocolate Factory* by Roald Dahl, reprinted by permission of Unwin Hyman Ltd and Penguin Books Ltd; p125 from *Matilda* by Roadl Dahl, reprinted by permission of Jonathan Cape and Penguin Books Ltd; p125 from the *East Cambridgeshire Town Crier*; p126 from *Is there life beyond television?* from an article from *The Sunday Times* by Valerie Grove, 10 April 1988, reprinted by permission © Times Newspapers Ltd 1987/88; p126 from an article by Michael Rosen from *The Radio Times*; p128 from *Join the Nepali Pupils*, reprinted by permission of ActionAid from 'Common Cause'; p129 from *Sorrows, Passions and Alarms* by James Kirkup; p130 from Homework, an HMI Booklet, reprinted by permission of the controller of Her Majesty's Stationery Office; p130 from *Native Ground* by Philip Callow, reprinted by permission of Heinemann; p132 from *The Eagle of the Ninth* by Rosemary Sutcliff, reprinted by permission of Oxford University Press; p133 from *Roman Wall Blues* by W H Auden, reprinted by permission of Faber and Faber Ltd from 'Collected Shorter Poems 1927-1957' by W H Auden; p133 from *The Hidden Minting Kit made Counterfeit Roman Coins* from an article in *The Independent* by David Keys, reprinted by permission of *The Independent*; p136 from *There's a Poet Behind You* by Grace Nichols; p136 from *A Traveller's Life* by Eric Newby; p137 from *Little Things* by Sharon Olds; p143 from *Flowers for Algernon* by Daniel Keyes; p144 from *A Kestrel for a Knave* by Barry Hines, © 1968 by Barry Hines, reprinted by permission of Michael Joseph Ltd; p146 from *A Traveller's Life* by Eric Newby; p 148 from *The Bear* by Frederick Brown © Oxford University Press 1964, reprinted from 'Every Man Will Shout' (1964) by permission of Oxford University Press; p148 *Mac* from 'Children as Poets', edited by Denys Thompson; p149 from *Memories* from 'Children as Poets', edited by Denys Thompson; p149 from *Bonfire* by Clare Tawney, reprinted by permission of Jonathan Cape from 'Fire Words' edited by Chris Searle; p149 from *Getting Home* by Neil Hoggan, reprinted by permission of M Elizabeth Thompson; p150 from *Library Checking* by Harriet Levine, reprinted by permission of M Elizabeth Thompson; p151 from *One Hundred Famous Haiku*, selected and translated by Daniel C Buchanon, reprinted by permission of Japan Publications Trading Co Ltd; p151 from *Collector's Column* by Oliver Pritchett, reprinted by permission of NatWest Dimensions; p153 from *Painting as a Pastime* by Winston Churchill, reprinted by permission of A & C Black; p155 from *Lalita's Way* by Soraya Jintah; p169 from *Matilda* by Roald Dahl, reprinted by permission of Jonathan Cape and Penguin Books Ltd; p169 from *The BFG* by Roald Dahl, reprinted by permission of Jonathan Cape and Penguin Books Ltd; p170 from *The Twits* by Roald Dahl, reprinted by permission of Jonathan Cape and Penguin Books Ltd; p170 from *George's Marvellous Medicine* by Roald Dahl, reprinted by permission of Jonathan Cape and Penguin Books Ltd; p171 from *Danny, The Champion of the World* by Roald Dahl, reprinted by permission of Jonathan Cape and Penguin Books Ltd; p172 from *My Antonia* by Willa Cather; p172 from *Little House in the Big Woods* by Laura Ingalls Wilder, reprinted by permission of Methuen Children's Books; p176 from *The Day It Rained Forever*, by Ray Bradbury, copyright © 1952, renewed 1980 by Ray Bradbury. Originally published in Esquire magazine, reprinted by permission; p178 from *Retired* by Iain Crichton Smith, reprinted by permission of Iain Crichton Smith; p180 from *Turning Over a New Leaf* from an article from *The Indy*, 1 November 1990, reprinted by permission of *The Indy*; p183 from 'His First Flight' by Liam O'Flaherty, from *The Short Stories of Liam O'Flaherty* by Liam O'Flaherty, reprinted by permission of Jonathan Cape; p184 from *Black Boy* by Richard Wright, reprinted by permission of Ellen Wright and Jonathan Cape.

Photographs
p19 Network Photographers; p21 The Fotomas Index; p29, 84, 176 Hulton Deutsch; p30 The Bodleian Library; p70 Sally & Richard Greenhill; p73 English Heritage.

Printed and bound in Great Britain by Sterling Press, Wellingborough

*C*ontents

Introduction   5
Successful studying at Key Stage 3   5
English in the National Curriculum   5
How to use this book   6

Chapter 1: Speaking and listening   7
First words   7
Conversation   8
Discussion   11
Talking about experiences   13
Talking about something you have made
or done   14
Audience   14
Story-telling   15
Instructions and messages   17
Role-play   19
The English language   20
Speaking and writing   25
Speaking and listening chart   26
Level descriptions   27
Project: Riddles   29
Project: Why did the chicken cross the
road – or getting from A to B!   33
Project: Time off!   37

Chapter 2: Reading   41
How to be a good reader   41
Reading stories   46
Reading autobiography   62
Reading travellers' tales   68
Reading diaries   73
Reading letters   77
Reading to get information   83
Reading poems   91
Watching and reading plays   107
Getting the message across   111
Reading chart   120
Level descriptions   121
Project: Books against the box!   123
Project: Learning   128
Project: The Romans invade   132

Chapter 3: Writing 135

Sketch pad in words 135
From brainstorming to final presentation 137
Ideas for writing 144
Writing stories 154
Playscript 155
Letters 156
Spelling 158
Parts of speech 161
Word games 163
Punctuation 164
Writing chart 166
Level descriptions 167
Project: Write your own story in the style of Roald Dahl! 169
Project:The Wild West 172
Project: Journey into space 175
Project: The world around us 180

Chapter 4: Practice National Test questions 183

Paper 1 183
Paper 2: Shakespeare play 186
Extension Paper 187
Answering the test questions 191

Glossary 195

Index 198

Introduction

SUCCESSFUL STUDYING AT KEY STAGE 3

During Key Stage 3 of the National Curriculum, you will have to study the following subjects:

English, Mathematics, Science, Technology, a modern foreign language (usually French or German), Geography and History.

This stage of your education is very important because it lays the foundation which you will need to embark upon your GCSE courses. The National Curriculum requires you and all 11–14 year olds to follow the same programmes of study, which define the knowledge and skills you will need to learn and develop during your course.

At school, your teachers will be monitoring your progress. At the end of Key Stage 3, your performance will be assessed and you will be given a National Curriculum level. Most students should reach Level 5 or Level 6, some may reach Levels 7 or 8, or perhaps even higher. In English, Mathematics and Science, you will have to take a National Test towards the end of your last year at Key Stage 3. The results of your tests, also marked in levels, will be set alongside your teachers' assessment of your work to give an overall picture of how you have done.

How this book will help you

This book is designed for you to use at home to support the work you are doing at school. Think of it as a companion or study guide to help you prepare for class work, homework, and for the important National Tests. Inside the book, you will find the level descriptions which will be used to assess your performance. We have included them in the book so that, as you near the end of Key Stage 3, you will be able to check how well you are doing.

Also included at the end of the book is a bank of practice questions. These are of the same style and standard as the questions you will face in your National Tests. Attempting these questions in the months leading up to your tests should help you to do as well as you can.

Reading the book, and doing the questions and activities will help you get to grips with the most important elements of the National Curriculum. Before you begin to read the book itself, take a few moments to read the introductory sections on 'English in the National Curriculum' and 'How to use this book'.

ENGLISH IN THE NATIONAL CURRICULUM

The National Curriculum separates English into three Programmes of Study:

❶ Speaking and Listening

❷ Reading

❸ Writing

In **speaking and listening**, you will be developing skills that will enable you to speak confidently in a range of situations and make the most of discussions; talk in a structured, interesting way; and be able to explain how language works. You will also learn to become a better listener by understanding and responding to others, noticing how people use gesture and tone of voice.

Your **reading** habits will be changing as you work through Key Stage 3. Some of your reading will be researching in reference books and multimedia, while you will be looking critically at advertisements, letters, biography, travel writing and television, radio and film, as well as studying and enjoying a wide range of the major poems, short stories, novels, and plays in English.

You will **write** in a range of styles, from book reviews to newspaper articles, from poems to autobiography. You will seek to explain, compare, persuade, entertain and express attitudes and emotions. Your vocabulary will be extended and you will be thinking about the audience you are writing for. As you learn to create and re-draft text, possibly using a word processor, you will be wanting to present your work attractively.

HOW TO USE THIS BOOK

In many subjects, you study a topic, complete it, and then move on to the next topic. English doesn't work quite like that. Speaking and listening, reading and writing all seem to be in use when you are working at English.

When you read a poem, discuss it in groups, and write your response or make a poem of your own on a similar theme, all three areas of English are coming into use.

Before you read this book in detail, browse through it, reading a paragraph or two here and there to get the 'feel' of the book. You will then have a better idea of what the book has to offer. If you know that you are going to be reading a play in school, read the appropriate section to see what advice and help have been given. Though you can continue to use the book in this way, using the index to see if there is a section that will help your work at school or for doing some homework, you will find it worthwhile to work systematically through each chapter, completing the activities you are asked to do. You will find **Now test yourself** and **The young English student at work** sections. And after each chapter you will find longer **Projects**, which usually will be bringing the areas of English together.

Each time you do a specific piece of work, whether it is a discussion or you have read a short story or written a letter, record in on the forms that have been placed after each chapter. It is a good way of keeping track of the work you have done.

Finally, there is a chapter devoted to the National Tests, to give you some practice in writing the kind of answers that you will be expected to produce. One of the tests is entitled Extension Paper. You should only attempt this if you think you are capable of reaching the very highest levels of the National Curriculum.

As you read through the book, you will need to involve other people: friends, parents, family. English doesn't always work in isolation – speaking and listening on your own isn't much fun!

The only **essential** equipment you will need is:

- paper
- pen
- dictionary

but it would be useful to have access to a cassette recorder, a video recorder, and a word processor.

To make your work look its best, you will also want to have scrap paper to jot down ideas and a folder with some file paper, both lined and plain.

I would like to thank: my colleague, Andrew Howard, for once again reading through one of my manuscripts and making helpful comments; my daughters, Emma and Hannah, for reading various parts of the book and for allowing me to use some of their writing; and my wife, Françoise, for her suggestions, support, and secretarial skills.

CHAPTER 1
Speaking and listening

FIRST WORDS

Do you remember the first word you ever spoke? You won't – unless it was recorded on a cassette or tape! And that is rather unlikely because no one would have known that you were about to say your first word and had the recorder switched on in readiness. You may have been told what your first word was, of course, but that's not the same as remembering it.

Kate Baker, a pupil, knows what her first words were:

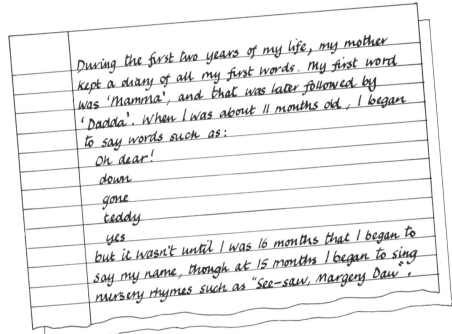

During the first two years of my life, my mother kept a diary of all my first words. My first word was 'Mamma', and that was later followed by 'Dadda'. When I was about 11 months old, I began to say words such as:

Oh dear!

down

gone

teddy

yes

but it wasn't until I was 16 months that I began to say my name, though at 15 months I began to sing nursery rhymes such as "See-saw, Margery Daw".

Shh! She's about to say her first word!

Kate's mother's diaries provide a fascinating and detailed account of Kate's early years.

Long before you *said* your first recognizable word, you *heard* words being used. In fact, not long after you were born you would have heard people talking and 'coo-ing' over you. Gradually, over the days, weeks and months, you were responding to words. A baby isn't very old before he or she is able to recognize his or her mother's voice, though the words used won't be understood for several months.

Now test yourself

* Ask your parents if they remember and can tell you anything about your first words.

* Do you have a young sister, brother, cousin or friend who is one or two years old? If so, try to keep a record – with dates – of the language they use.

Have you ever thought how exciting language is? It can do so much: from asking for cornflakes to talking about a group whose music you enjoy, from telling your sister how much you hate her to listening, to a teacher explaining how to make use of a data base.

During the course of any day you will speak and listen to many words, sometimes amounting to thousands upon thousands. As you speak and listen so much without really giving it any thought, is there any point in reading about it? Yes, because a greater understanding of some of the skills you already use will enable you to sharpen them up and make them even better.

In this book you will find many ideas and suggestions that will help you to do this. These are the Now Test Yourself sections. And in order to help you even further there are exercises and The young English student at work sections. Try as many as you can!

CONVERSATION

Read this extract from *Five Green Bottles* by Ray Jenkins:

An ordinary household. The play is set in the kitchen which is roomy and has access to the hall and living room.

The time is that period of rush between 8 and 8.45 on any weekday morning. Gramp is reading the paper. Kevin is eating his toast. The radio is blaring cheery music. Mother is in the hall – calling upstairs.

MOTHER David! It's eight o'clock. Are you coming down or aren't you? David!
DAVID (*Upstairs*) All right!
MOTHER No 'all right' about it! Do you hear me!
DAVID (*Low*) Keep your hair on.
MOTHER (*Going up a couple of steps*) What did you say?
DAVID I'm combing my hair down.
MOTHER We'll have less of your lip, my lad. And I'm not calling you again. You'll be late.
    And tell that Maureen as well. (*Coming down the steps*) Talk about a house of the dead.
DAVID (*Hammering on a door*) Maureen!
MOTHER (*Shouting*) There's no need to shout!
DAVID (*Singing*) Maureen-O!
MOTHER Maureen, you'll be late! (*Pause*)
DAVID She's died in her sleep.
MOTHER I give up.
(*She comes back into the kitchen.*)
    Nobody can get up in this house – you must get it from your father. If I slept half as much as you lot do there'd be nothing done –
KEVIN The world'd fall to bits –

MOTHER Kevin – get that telescope off the table –
KEVIN I'm looking at tomato cells.
GRAMP This paper's all creased!
MOTHER Don't moan, dad!
GRAMP It's like trying to read an elephant's kneecap!
MOTHER Why have you left that piece of bacon?
KEVIN It's all fat.
MOTHER You don't know what's good for you – it keeps out the cold –
KEVIN Why don't they make coats out of it then?
MOTHER That's enough. And turn that music down for heaven's sake – you can't hear
   yourself think in a din like that.
KEVIN It's supposed to make you feel bright and breezy.
MOTHER You must be joking. Turn it off.
(*The radio is switched off.*)
   Oh! A bit of peace at last!
GRAMP Never had bacon when I went to school. Just bread and jam and a four-mile walk.
KEVIN Aren't you glad you came to live with us then?
MOTHER Kevin, that's enough of that! There's a lot you youngsters today have to be thankful
   for and a full stomach's one of them.
GRAMP Just bread and jam and a five-mile walk.
KEVIN Four, you said.
GRAMP It might've been six if you count the hills. Where's my glasses? I can't read without
   my glasses.
KEVIN The cat's wearing them.
MOTHER Kevin! Oh, I don't know. If it's not one it's the other.
GRAMP The words go up and down without them!
MOTHER (*Patiently*) Where did you have them last, dad?
GRAMP I had them just now.
MOTHER Are you sitting on them?
GRAMP Don't be daft – why should I sit on them?
MOTHER Stranger things have happened. Get up. Come on, get up.
(*Gramp gets up. He's been sitting on them.*)
   There you are. What did I say?
GRAMP Who put them there, that's what I'd like to know!
KEVIN (*Low*) The cat.
MOTHER Do you want any more tea?
KEVIN No, thanks.
GRAMP Look, they're all twisted. You've got to have a head like a corkscrew to get them on
   now!
MOTHER (*Calling*) David! Maureen! I won't tell you again! It's ten past eight already! (*Pause*)
   What were you and David quarrelling about last night?
KEVIN Nothing.
MOTHER Nobody makes a noise like that about nothing. What was it?
KEVIN Nothing.
(*He gets up.*)
MOTHER Where're you going?
KEVIN Get my books.
MOTHER You still haven't answered my question, young man!
KEVIN It was nothing – honest!
MOTHER Talk about blood from a stone. And take this telescope – I've only got one pair of
   hands.
(*Letters come through the front door.*)
   There's the post
(*A door slams upstairs.*)
DAVID I'll get them.
MOTHER Those doors!
KEVIN I'll get them.
MOTHER No, let David do it – it'll be one way of getting him downstairs.
(*David is cascading down stairs.*)
KEVIN It's always him.

9

Perhaps *you* will be familiar with this kind of conversation.

From the time we get up until the time we go to bed, conversation is the commonest form of listening and speaking that we do. Just think of the occasions when you chat: on your way to school when you meet up with friends, between (and during) lessons, at lunchtime, when you arrive home, during the evening – at home, at a youth club, at a friend's home, and so on.

As conversation is such a natural activity, it would be silly to suggest that you have to think all the time about what you should or should not be saying. The easy two-way ebb and flow of words between you and your friends mustn't be seen as difficult or a chore. But perhaps there are situations in which you find yourself having to make conversation:

Now test yourself

Listen carefully to what the other person or people say, so that you will be able to ask questions or make comments that will take the conversation further.

You could see this as a tennis match, with the 'ball' – the topic of conversation – going between you. Try to keep the 'ball' in play for as long as possible before 'serving' another topic.

And why not make a point of starting up at least one conversation a day? Hold conversations with parents, grandparents, uncles, aunts, cousins, neighbours, friends and acquaintances.

WHAT CAN YOU TALK ABOUT?

It is impossible to list a set of topics, as there are endless suggestions that could be made. For example, how much do you know about your parents' childhood and schooldays, about their work, interests and opinions? But remember to be tactful. No one likes to be asked questions in a challenging or aggressive manner.

Also, it's worth remembering to ask *detailed* and *specific* questions in order to get a conversation going. 'Tell me all about your childhood' is less helpful than 'What were your favourite television programmes when you were a teenager?' Start on something specific and then move on to other areas.

One pupil decided to make a note of all the topics that were mentioned during the family's lunchtime conversation. The list included the food they were eating and what they were going to eat the next day; a hospital in Uganda that relied on money and equipment from those living in Europe; the fact that many people took luxuries for granted and turned them into necessities; family arrangements for later in the week; the forthcoming visit of her grandparents; and lots more.

Now test yourself

Take a typical schoolday and, at the end of the day, jot down:

- A list of those you spoke to and listened to.

- The topics you talked about – as far as you can remember.

You'll be amazed at the sheer quantity of topics that have cropped up.

Discussion

You are probably already used to being in small groups in school to discuss a science experiment, a history topic, or a poem, for example. This kind of talk is a most valuable method of thinking and learning – you each chip in with a comment or two and gradually, as a group, you come to understand what you have been given. In fact, to learn something effectively, you always need to put it into your *own* words. Group discussion helps this process.

The two things you were asked to try out with conversations (listening carefully and trying to take the topic further) are *exactly* what you need if you want to improve your skills of discussion. The main difference between a conversation and a discussion is only the fact that a discussion tends to be focused on one particular aspect. If you are talking about the tropical rainforests of Brazil and then you switch to talking about South American football, you are not focusing on the topic. But such a change would not necessarily be out of place in a *conversation*.

In *discussion*, you should concentrate very hard on the topic. If someone makes a comment you don't understand, ask for it to be repeated or ask the speaker to make it clearer. And if the discussion seems to be going off the point, try to bring it back.

One other thing: don't get such a bee in your bonnet about one of your ideas that you try to force it onto your friends, or insist on talking about it at the wrong moment. What is the wrong moment? When everyone is in the middle of discussing an important or central idea. So, wait for a suitable pause, when the idea seems to have been finished. And be prepared to back up the ideas you put forward. Is there some fact you can use in support, some word or phrase that bears out what you say?

The young English student at work

As you have already seen, you need to involve others in your English work. You can hardly practise discussion by simply reading about it in this book! There now follow some discussion ideas to try out with your family and/or friends.

1. Look at an advertisement in a paper, magazine or on a hoarding and discuss:

(a) The age(s) of the people at whom it is aimed (though this can be difficult – some aim at everyone).

(b) How the picture and words are used to persuade.

(c) What actual information (if any) the advertisement contains and how effective, overall, it is.

(You will find out about advertisements on pages 113 to 117)

2. This is a challenging task. Is there some development, local to where you live and about which there is a disagreement? A plan to build a shopping centre in an agricultural area; a suggested by-pass round your city, town or village (making it safer for pedestrians but not so good for local traders); an estate of new houses; the extending of a row of Victorian houses – the list could go on and on! Local newspapers thrive on such issues. Find out as much as you can and discuss with a friend the reasons for and against such a development going

ahead. Why not act the part of the radio reporter, interviewing people about their views? You could use a portable cassette recorder. This would be helpful afterwards in looking back on how well you carried out your speaking and listening skills.

3. Watch an episode from a soap opera on television and talk about how realistic it is to your experience. Are the characters the sort of people you come across? What is it that makes that particular soap opera popular?

4. If you had a free choice of where to live – anywhere in the world – what sort of place would you choose? Would you like it in all weathers? What problems might there be?

In school, you may be asked to tell the rest of the class about your discussion. If you know in advance that you are going to have to speak, you can make a note or two as a reminder, but, if not, you will just have to trust your memory. Try to give a fair impression of the way the discussion went, not merely saying what *your* contribution was, nor what *you* thought was the most important point. Give only the main views and comments as agreed by the group. If you are asked to chair a discussion, it is your job to make sure that everyone has an opportunity to express his or her opinion and that the discussion focuses on the topic, not getting side-tracked on irrelevant matters.

TALKING ABOUT EXPERIENCES

What do you find exciting? One pupil's quick response was:

- anything new, like a birthday present, particularly when it's a surprise
- going on holiday
- starting a new school
- arriving home after a week on a school trip
- going to a party
- watching a cartoon film
- when a member of the family who has been ill in hospital comes home
- when the whole family meets together

We all like to tell others of those events and visits we enjoy. Seize every opportunity you can. There is a danger, though, that in our enthusiasm we include all the details whether or not they are of interest to our listeners. You may have come across something like this:

'It was on the Saturday morning we went to the castle. No, it wasn't, it was on the Friday. Or perhaps it was the Saturday. It wasn't a very hot day. At least, not as hot as the day before, because that was the day we went to the zoo and it was so hot the cages smelt awful. But the day we went to the castle, which must have been the Saturday now I come to think of it. Don't you lose track of the days when you're on holiday? ...'

If you are asked to talk about a visit or an event, choose the interesting bits and leave out the boring details. Describe your chosen items clearly, explaining how you felt. Don't exaggerate: if you were excited and you say why, that is what matters.

Now test yourself

- Make your own list of events you would like to talk about. Family visit? Circus? Disco?
- Select one event and think carefully about the most interesting or exciting part. What brief details will you need to include as an introduction?
- Make a special effort not to be a bore!

TALKING ABOUT SOMETHING YOU HAVE MADE OR DONE

Now test yourself

Tell a member of the family all about an experiment in science or a maths investigation you did at school. What was its purpose? What steps did you take? What equipment was needed? Were you on your own or with some others? If with others, how did you share the action? What was the result? Was it what you thought it might be?

Would you talk only about the exciting bits?

Now test yourself

Talk to a friend about something you have made. What made you decide on that particular thing? How did you choose the materials? Is it of some use or is it an ornament? Did you get any ideas from books or magazines? What questions might your audience have? What answers might you give to those questions?

AUDIENCE

In the last exercise you may have noticed the word **audience** used. You may think of people sitting in rows of plush seats listening to a comedian or singer or watching a play or film when you hear or read the word. In this book, however, it is used to mean the person or people you are talking to or writing to.

Did you know?

The word *audience* comes from the Latin word *audire* meaning 'to hear'.

Can you work out what *audio* equipment means? *Audio*-visual and *audio*-cassette? And have you ever been for an *audition*? What takes place in an *auditorium*?

The idea of an audience is very important in your English work, because every time you speak or write, you need to take into account the audience: you have to choose the words and phrases that will be understood. If you are telling your six-year-old sister about the scientific experiment you are doing in your science lessons at school, you won't want to baffle her with lots of long scientific words – or perhaps you might if you want to show off! On the other hand, you might want to, or have to, use these long scientific words in your science lessons in order to show your teacher (and yourself) that you have understood what he or she has been trying to teach you.

Judging what is right for your audience is not always easy, but comes with practice. That's one of the reasons why you need to try out as many activities in this book as possible, talking and writing to lots of different people.

S TORY-TELLING

Read this story, which is one of the stories from *Fairy Tales* by Terry Jones. You can read another one of his stories from the same collection on page 60.

THE GLASS CUPBOARD

There was once a cupboard that was made entirely of glass so you could see right into it and right through it. Now, although this cupboard always appeared to be empty, you could always take out whatever you wanted. If you wanted a cool drink, for example, you just opened the cupboard and took one out. Or if you wanted a new pair of shoes, you could always take a pair out of the glass cupboard. Even if you wanted a bag of gold, you just opened up the glass cupboard and took out a bag of gold. The only thing you had to remember was that, whenever you took something out of the glass cupboard you had to put something else back in, although nobody quite knew why.

Naturally such a valuable thing as the glass cupboard belonged to a rich and powerful king.

One day, the King had to go on a long journey, and while he was gone some thieves broke into the palace and stole the glass cupboard.

'Now we can have anything we want,' they said.

One of the robbers said: 'I want a large bag of gold,' and he opened the glass cupboard and took out a large bag of gold.

Then the second robber said: 'I want two large bags of gold,' and he opened the glass cupboard and took out two large bags of gold.

Then the chief of the robbers said: 'I want three of the biggest bags of gold you've ever seen!' and he opened the glass cupboard and took out three of the biggest bags of gold you've ever seen.

'Hooray!' they said. 'Now we can take out as much gold as we like!'

Well, those three robbers stayed up the whole night, taking bag after bag of gold out of the glass cupboard. But not one of them put anything back in.

In the morning, the chief of the robbers said: 'Soon we shall be the richest three men in the world. But let us go to sleep now, and we can take out more gold tonight.'

So they lay down to sleep. But the first robber could not sleep. He kept thinking: 'If I went to the glass cupboard just *once* more, I'd be even richer than I am now.' So he got up, and went to the cupboard, and took out two more bags of gold, and then went back to bed.

And the second robber could not sleep either. He kept thinking: 'If I went to the glass cupboard and took out two more bags of gold, I'd be even richer than the others.' So he got up, and went to the cupboard, and took out two more bags of gold, and then went back to bed.

Meanwhile the chief of the robbers could not sleep either. He kept thinking: 'If I went to the glass cupboard, I'd be the richest of all.' So he got up, and went to the cupboard, and took out three more bags of gold, and then went back to bed.

And then the first robber said to himself: 'What am I doing, lying here sleeping, when I could be getting richer?' So he got up, and started taking more and more bags of gold out of the cupboard.

The second robber heard him and thought: 'What am I doing, lying here sleeping, when he's getting richer than me?' So he got up and joined his companion.

And then the chief of the robbers got up too. 'I can't lie here sleeping,' he said, 'while the other two are both getting richer than me.' So he got up and soon all three were hard at it, taking more and more bags of gold out of the cupboard.

And all that day and all that night not one of them dared to stop for fear that one of his companions would get richer than him. And they carried on all the next day and all the next night. They didn't stop to rest, and they didn't stop to eat, and they didn't even stop to drink. They kept taking out those bags of gold faster and faster and more and more until, at length, they grew faint with lack of sleep and food and drink, but still they did not dare to stop.

All that week and all the next week, and all that month and all that winter, they kept at it, until the chief of the robbers could bear it no longer, and he picked up a hammer and smashed the glass cupboard into a million pieces, and they all three gave a great cry and fell down dead on top of the huge mountain of gold they had taken out of the glass cupboard.

Sometime later the King returned home, and his servants threw themselves on their knees before him, and said: 'Forgive us, Your Majesty, but three wicked robbers have stolen the glass cupboard!'

The King ordered his servants to search the length and breadth of the land. When they found what was left of the glass cupboard, and the three robbers lying dead, they filled sixty great carts with all the gold and took it back to the King. And when the King heard that the glass cupboard was smashed into a million pieces and that the three thieves were dead, he shook his head and said: 'If those thieves had always put something back into the cupboard for every bag of gold they had taken out, they would be alive to this day.' And he ordered his servants to collect all the pieces of the glass cupboard and to melt them down and make them into a globe with all the countries of the world upon it, to remind himself, and others, that the earth is as fragile as that glass cupboard.

Now test yourself

- Record 'The Glass Cupboard' on cassette and, playing it back, see how interesting you think you made it.

- Try reading it aloud, or telling it in your own words, to a friend or member of the family.

'ARE YOU SITTING COMFORTABLY ... ?'

Do you still get excited when you hear 'Once upon a time ...?' We all love to hear a good story, however young or old we are. All those people who sit night after night watching soap operas and films on television are gripped by the power of stories.

Years and years ago, before most people could read or write – centuries before radio and television – the story-teller was highly honoured; he provided one of the main means of entertainment. People would gather round, eager to hear a story or two.

Whether you are reading a story aloud or telling it in your own words, you need to make it interesting for your audience.

Below is a list of four things which are important when reading a story. If you can think of other things which you feel ought to be included in the list, write them on the dotted lines provided. Then in the column on the right hand side, number the ideas in the order you think the most important. Call the most important idea '1', the next one '2' and so on.

Lift your head up frequently and look your listeners in the eye.

....

Change the speed at which you speak, speeding up and slowing down according to what is happening in the story.

Change your voice for each character in the story (for example: gruff and stern, whining, gentle, sullen, enthusiastic).

....

Make sure your audience is comfortable and ready to listen.

....

I SAY, I SAY, I SAY!

What are you like at telling jokes? Are you the sort of person who makes a mess of the punchline? Telling jokes is a useful way of practising story-telling. Try them on your family and friends.

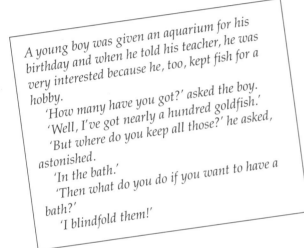

A young boy was given an aquarium for his birthday and when he told his teacher, he was very interested because he, too, kept fish for a hobby.
'How many have you got?' asked the boy.
'Well, I've got nearly a hundred goldfish.'
'But where do you keep all those?' he asked, astonished.
'In the bath.'
'Then what do you do if you want to have a bath?'
'I blindfold them!'

The other day I said to my sister, 'Does that teacher of yours like you?'
'I think she must do,' she said. 'She writes kisses all over my exercise books!'

INSTRUCTIONS AND MESSAGES

Look at the passage that follows. How familiar is it to you?

> 'Go and tell your sister that, if she doesn't stop watching that video now and get ready and go to the shop to get a packet of rice, a pound of tomatoes and three or four onions, before it closes for lunch, then she'll not have any lunch. And there's that letter, took she said must get the post – the first post must have gone a long time ago. And there's another thing: I'm fed up with her lounging around when she's on holiday. It might be a holiday for her, but it's never a holiday for me. You can tell her that, too!'

Have you got all that?

There cannot be many days when we do not either listen to or give instructions and messages. Even when we are toddlers, we are instructed not to touch this, not to touch that. Perhaps you have been stopped in the street and asked the way to the station or to a shop. No doubt at school, you have been asked to give someone a message.

What's the best way to listen to instructions?

❶ Listen carefully to each stage.
❷ Mentally number each stage.
❸ Repeat the instructions aloud stage by stage.

④ Ask questions about any stage that is unclear.
⑤ Go through the complete sequence in your mind.

By following these five 'rules', the passage in the speech bubbles on the previous page might come out like this:

- stop watching video
- if shop closed, no lunch
- buy three things (rice, tomatoes, onions)
- letter to post
- lounging around – mother angry

Do *you* agree with this list? Is anything necessary or important missed out? And could any of these stages have been left out?

Now test yourself

- Now you have seen how to listen to and remember instructions, work out your own rules for **giving** instructions, filling in the empty spaces below:

1 ....

2 ....

3 ....

4 ....

5 ....

- Talk about your list of rules with a friend, having asked your friend to make a list also. Are the lists very different? Or are they similar? Which rule would you say is the most important?

Now it's time to have a go at practising giving instructions and messages. Remember, practising using real life situations is obviously better than only reading about it in this book, so make the most of any occasion you come across, whether it is directing a stranger to the station, teaching a younger brother or sister how to make something, or letting a friend know all the details of a proposed outing.

Now test yourself

Try instructing a friend how to tie a tie or do up shoelaces – but using words only, hand gestures not allowed! See how difficult it is!

R OLE-PLAY

We practise imitating other people, or playing various roles, from quite an early age. You only have to watch young children playing for a short time to see them being a doctor, teacher, parent; it seems to be a natural instinct.

How do we know how to speak and behave as if we were someone else? Probably without realizing it, we pick up clues all the time. We watch a journalist interviewing the Prime Minister on television or a policeman moving someone on – and we gain some idea of how people use language and gestures in communicating with each other.

The purpose of role-play, of placing yourself in imaginary situations, is to make demands on the language you use. It helps you to stretch your powers of persuasion and argument and the range of words you use. It can also prepare you for situations in which you may find yourself.

The young English student at work

QUITE A CHARACTER

Here is a game for two or more players. You will need:

1 20 or more pieces of card (or thick paper) approximately 7cm × 5cm.
2 An octagonal piece of fairly thick card.
3 A cocktail stick or pointed, used match.
4 Dice, watch for timekeeping and pen or pencil.

On each card write down an occupation or a character. To make it look particularly neat, you could use transfer letters or a stencil. Include some of the following:
postman/woman; teenager; housewife; shop assistant; teacher; refuse collector; bus driver; factory worker; farmer; grandparent; architect; engineer; computer operator; waiter/waitress; dentist; garage mechanic; vet. Make up others – as many as you wish. Leave one card blank.

On the octagonal card, write some places for the action and conversation:

Cafe Fair Station Shop Park Museum
Jumble sale School

Pierce the centre with a cocktail stick or used match so that you can spin the card like a top.

How to play

1 Shuffle the cards and place them face down on the table.
2 Each player throws the dice for the order of play; the highest number starts.
3 Each player in turn takes a card and prepares 'character' details: age, sex, name, residence, family, hobbies, personality, etc. If a player picks the blank card, the player invents the whole 'character'. (Allow about five minutes preparation time for this. HINT: The more thoughts you pack into your preparation, the easier you'll find the game!)
4 The players introduce their 'characters' to each other as fully as possible, using the language and gestures suitable for the 'characters'.
5 The opening player spins the setting card to determine where the action takes place.
6 The second player begins the action by starting up a conversation with the other player(s), keeping as close to the 'character' as possible.
7 When a player says or does anything out of 'character', s/he is 'out'.

The young English student at work

ROLE-PLAY PROJECT

If you wish to spend some time on a project that will help you to exercise your speaking and listening skills (particularly if you ask a friend to join in), and that will also enable you to make use of your creative talents, have a go at making puppets. You can use either puppets on strings made out of balsa wood or cardboard, or you could make glove puppets.

Sets and props – and a theatre, complete with stage – would be better still.

Why not put on a production of one of the following:

– a scene from your favourite story

– a scene from a book you are reading at home or at school

– a scene from a situation you have seen on the television, heard on the radio, or read about in a newspaper

Write and act out your own scripts, then move on to short scripts written by other people.

Try to gain as much experience acting, in class or in a school or local drama club, as possible.

Remember: plays on the page are nothing unless they are acted out.

THE ENGLISH LANGUAGE

Did you know?

Have you any idea how many people in the world speak English? Nobody knows exactly, of course, but a recent estimate was 750 000 000, and that's a lot of people! About half that number speak it as their native language; that is, the language they first learnt from their family. There are three-and-a-half times as many native speakers of English in the USA as there are in the UK.

What is English? Like most languages it's rather a mixture. Words from other languages keep slipping in until they, too, become accepted as part of the English language.

Read the following paragraph. Why do you think some of the words are in italics?

After I had drunk a *lager* in the *restaurant*, I went to the *disco* and had a *coffee* with *sugar*. My friend, who had just come from *judo*, had a *chocolate yoghurt* and then a cup of *tea*. A *tycoon* in a fashionable *anorak* entered, together with the *thug* I had seen on his *yacht*. One had a *brandy*, the other a *vodka*.

You have probably guessed – not one of the 15 words in italics was originally English.

The words originally came from:
Turkish Arabic Aztec Dutch Russian Japanese French Hindi
They are not in order and some are represented more than once.

Now test yourself

Look up the words in the dictionary and find out their origin.

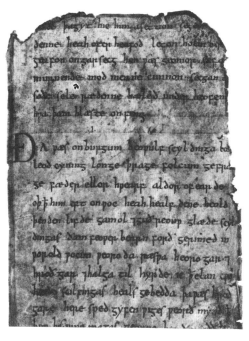

Until the Angles, Saxons and Jutes came invading in the 5th century, the language spoken in this country was basically Celtic (the language still spoken by some Scots, Welsh, and Cornish). The invaders brought a language which developed into what became known as *Old English*. You may have heard of *Beowulf*, a poem about a strong and courageous warrior. That was written in Old English.

The Norman Conquest in 1066 brought a whole new range of words and, because the Normans conquered and ruled the country, the words of governing and justice infiltrated the language:

justice
law
government
parliament
master

are just some of the words derived from Norman French. The masters ate *beef*, *pork*, and *mutton* (boeuf, porc, mouton in French); the *cow*, *pig*, and *sheep* (cu, picga, sceap in Old English) were looked after by the servants.

Other languages have also had an influence on English, but by and large it's true to say that Modern English comes from a mixture of Old English and Norman French.

And because English comes from two rather different languages, it has different sets of spelling rules. Once you know that and see how words are built up, you will probably find you are more sympathetic to spelling.

Mainly from the 17th century onwards, explorers went out to other countries taking English with them, so doing exactly what the Angles, Saxons, Jutes and Norman French had done. That's why English is spoken in America, Australia, New Zealand, India, parts of Africa, Malaysia and several other countries.

STANDARD ENGLISH

Standard English is the name given to the language you will find in newspapers, books, formal letters and reports; it is the language of law courts and schools, television and radio (apart from drama programmes). In most cases, when your teacher marks your work, Standard English is likely to be the language used. It derives from the language of the East Midlands which tended to be the language of trade and government.

Why is Standard English used? Simply, because it is the form of the language understood throughout the English-speaking world. If you pick up an English newspaper in Delhi or New York, Montreal or Sydney, you will read Standard English.

Though there is broad agreement about what Standard English is, language isn't something that remains static and unchanging; language lives. In the past, some people have wanted to make the rules of English resemble the rules of Latin. But Latin is a dead language – no one actually speaks or writes it as an everyday language – and it is only one of the languages from which English is derived.

Here are two pieces of English from the past. See whether you think there has been much of a change over the centuries. Chaucer, who was writing in English six hundred years ago, wrote like this:

Bilfil that in that seson on a day,
In Southwerk at the Tabard as I lay
Redy to wenden on my pilgrymage
To Caunterbury with ful devout corage,
At nyght was come into that hostelrye
Wel nyne and twenty in a compaignye,
Of sondry folk, by aventure yfalle
In felaweshipe, and pilgrimes were they alle,
That toward Caunterbury wolden ryde.

Now test yourself

Once you have read through the extract, underline all the words that are exactly the same as modern English. Next, underline all those words that you recognize, but are spelt slightly differently, perhaps with a missing letter (like season or adventure), an additional letter (like Canterbury or hostelry), or with a different letter or two (like night or fellowship). Are there many words left? Note them below::

....

....

....

Two hundred years after Chaucer, we have Shakespeare:

CAPULET
Hang thee, young baggage, disobedient wretch!
I tell thee what: get thee to church o' Thursday,
Or never after look me in the face.
Speak not, reply not, do not answer me.

Apart from *thee*, there isn't a single word that you wouldn't use. The language is getting very close to modern English. What would we say these days instead of 'Speak not, reply not'? By the way, Capulet is talking to his daughter about the marriage he has arranged for her without even telling her.

Now test yourself

Say Capulet's lines aloud. Which line do you find the easiest to say? And which do you enjoy saying the most?

One of the ways in which changes in language occur is by the introduction of new words. Every job will have its own words; games have to have a set of words (*offside, stumps, checkmate*); in school you may have a *tutor* who gives you *detention* for *truanting*, and so on. The world of electronics has brought many words into the language.

Now test yourself

Look at a computer magazine. Underline words that you think are recent and then check to see if you can find them in your dictionary. Or words brought about by situations or events in the world news. 'Glasnost' and 'ayatollah' came into current use in English only in the 1980s.

DIALECT

Do you have a dialect? That's an unfair question because we all have a dialect. Dialect refers to the words we use and the way we use them, depending on where we live or have been brought up. It mustn't be used instead of *accent* – that's something different. There are many dialects in English, each region tending to have its own.

For example, in which part of the United Kingdom would you hear 'Look after the wee bairn!' and what would a Londoner say instead?

Here is a poem by D H Lawrence written in his native Nottinghamshire dialect. Read it through, preferably aloud:

THE COLLIER'S WIFE

Somebody's knockin' at th' door
　　Mother, come down an' see!
– I's think it's nobbut a beggar;
　　Say I'm busy.

It's not a beggar, mother; hark
　　How 'ard 'e knocks!
– Eh, tha'rt a mard-arsed kid,
　　'E'll gie thee socks!

Shout an' ax what 'e wants,
　　I canna come down.
'E says, is it Arthur Holliday's?
　　– Say Yes, tha clown.

'E says: Tell your mother as 'er mester's
　　Got hurt i' th' pit –
What? Oh my Sirs, 'e never says that,
　　That's not it!

Come out o' th' way an' let me see!
　　Eh, there's no peace!
An' stop thy scraightin', childt,
　　Do shut thy face!

'Your mester's 'ad a accident
　　An' they ta'ein' 'im i' th' ambulance
Ter Nottingham.' – Eh dear o' me
　　If 'e's not a man for mischance!

Wheer's 'e hurt this time, lad?
　　– I dunna know,
They on'y towd me it wor bad –
　　It would be so!

Out o' my way, childt! dear o' me, wheer
　　'Ave I put 'is clean stockin's an' shirt?
Goodness knows if they'll be able
　　To take off 'is pit-dirt!

23

An' what a moan 'e'll make! there niver
　　Was such a man for a fuss
If anything ailed 'im; at any rate
　　I shan't 'ave 'im to nuss.

I do 'ope as it's not so very bad!
　　Eh, what a shame it seems
As some should ha'e hardly a smite o'
　　　　　　　　trouble
　　An' others 'as reams!

It's a shame as 'e should be knocked about
　　Like this, I'm sure it is!
'E's 'ad twenty accidents, if 'e's 'ad one;
　　Owt bad, an' it's his!

There's one thing, we s'll 'ave a peaceful
　　　　　　　　　　'ouse f'r a bit,
　　Thank heaven for a peaceful house!
An' there's compensation, sin' it's accident,
　　An' club-money – I won't growse.

An' a fork an' spoon 'e'll want – an' what
　　　　　　　　　　　else?
　　I s'll never catch that train!
What a traipse it is, if a man gets hurt!
　　I sh'd think 'e'll get right again.

What are the ways in which this poem differs from Standard English?

ACCENT

This is the way we pronounce words. Though accent very often goes with dialect, it isn't the same.

You may hear people referring to BBC English or RP, short for Received Pronunciation. Apparently, the name derived from the 19th century when some people used an accent that was well *received* in society circles, and so it has become associated with a person's social class. But don't worry if you don't speak with an RP accent; only an estimated three per cent of the population do so!

S PEAKING AND WRITING

There are a number of interesting differences between speaking and writing. In **speech** you can:

- pause, perhaps using some 'ums' and 'ers' while you think
- start, stop and start again – like this:

  'I was going to the shops the other day when I … Yes, please, no sugar … when I met one of my old friends from school … No, I'd better not, I'm slimming – or trying to … Anyway, I was so surprised, I forgot to buy the jar of marmalade I'd gone out for.'

- use gestures and facial expressions to back up and give force to what you are saying
- make use of the situation without having to explain everything: 'Half please!' may be all you need to say to a bus conductor
- use slang more frequently and easily

In **writing**, you have the opportunity to:

- think more carefully
- organize the order in which you want to present what you write
- take more trouble to use precise words
- go back over your work to see whether it is right for your audience and for its purpose, whether the language is right for the context, and whether everything is correct
- make sure your thoughts and ideas are fixed – you may not remember exactly what you said
- let other people know what you think when you cannot be with them or cannot telephone them

SLANG

Slang refers to the popular and informal language often used by certain groups of people (young people at school, for example) and which tends to be looked down on by those not in the group.

'I said to that twit over there, "Look here, you wimp, you may think you're really cool, but I hate your guts." By the way, lend us a quid, mate.'

Underline the words here which you would regard as slang.

> ### Now test yourself
>
> In a notebook or on a piece of paper, write down the answers to the following questions:
> - How often do you use slang?
> - On what occasions?
> - Do you ever use it in written work?
> - If so, for what purposes?

S PEAKING AND LISTENING CHART

Use this page to write down your speaking and listening activities. Bearing in mind the advice given in the chapter, together with any comments by a teacher, parent, or friend, try to judge how well you did and what you need to do to improve. After each activity, look at the description of the various levels and see which description best fits what you achieved.

Date	Activity	What I did well	Where I need to improve

LEVEL DESCRIPTIONS: SPEAKING AND LISTENING

At the start of Key Stage 3 the majority of pupils will have reached at least Level 4 in Speaking and Listening. By the end of Key Stage 3 most pupils should be within the range of Levels 4–7. Levels 5–6 are the target for 14-year-olds. Level 8 is the standard reached by very able pupils.

   Use our checklist to assess the Level reached, by ticking the skills that have been mastered.

LEVEL 4

☐ Talk and listen with confidence in an increasing range of contexts.
☐ Talk is adapted to the purpose: developing ideas thoughtfully, describing events and conveying opinions clearly.
☐ In discussion, careful listening, making contributions and asking questions that are responsive to others' ideas and views.
☐ Appropriate use of some of the features of standard English vocabulary and grammar.

LEVEL 5

☐ Talk and listen confidently in a wide range of contexts, including some that are of a formal nature.
☐ Talk engages the interest of the listener with the beginnings of variance in expression and vocabulary.
☐ In discussion, close attention paid to what others say, questions asked to develop ideas and contributions made that take account of others' views.
☐ Begin to use standard English in formal situations.

LEVEL 6

☐ Adaptation of talk to the demands of different contexts with increasing confidence.
☐ Talk engages the interest of the listener through the variety of its vocabulary and expression.
☐ An active part taken in discussion, showing understanding of ideas and sensitivity to others.
☐ Usually fluent in the use of standard English in formal situations.

LEVEL 7

☐ Confidence in matching talk to the demands of different contexts.
☐ Vocabulary used precisely and talk organized to communicate clearly.
☐ In discussion, significant contributions made, evaluating others' ideas and varying how and when to participate.
☐ Show confident use of standard English in situations that require it.

LEVEL 8

☐ Maintain and develop talk purposefully in a range of contexts.
☐ Structure what is said clearly, using apt vocabulary and appropriate intonation and emphasis.
☐ Make a range of contributions which show perceptive listening and sensitivity to the development of discussion.
☐ Show confident use of standard English in a range of situations, adapting as necessary.

EXCEPTIONAL PERFORMANCE

☐ Select and use structures, styles and registers appropriately in a range of contexts, varying vocabulary and expression confidently for a range of purposes.
☐ Initiate and sustain discussion through the sensitive use of a variety of contributions.
☐ Take a leading role in discussion and listen with concentration and understanding to varied and complex speech.
☐ Show assured and fluent use of standard English in a range of situations and for a variety of purposes.

PROJECT: RIDDLES

What goes on four legs in the morning, on two legs in the afternoon, and three in the evening?

In mythology, the Sphinx, a monster with a woman's head, lion's body, serpent's tail and eagle wings, throttled and devoured on the spot those who could not answer the riddle. Oedipus solved it, causing the Sphinx to dash herself to pieces in the valley below where she was installed. The answer is Man, because he goes on all fours as a baby, stands firmly on his two feet as a youth, and leans upon a stick in old age.

The Anglo-Saxons, who settled in England from the middle of the 5th century, were fond of making riddles about a whole host of subjects. They appear to have loved these word-games just as much as people today enjoy such word-games as crossword puzzles, anagrams, I-spy, hangman and the jokes inside Christmas crackers.

The riddle is a guessing game. It must be difficult or mysterious at first, for if it is too simple, it is no fun. The riddle helps people to look at something familiar with a fresh eye, giving snippets of description which can be pieced together.

There are nearly a hundred riddles in one of the very few books of Anglo-Saxon literature that remain: the so-called *Exeter Book*. Unfortunately, this book is in a poor state; with cuts and circular brown stains, it appears to have been used as a beer mat and cutting board!

Here are two riddles from the *Exeter Book*, in translation:

My garment is silent when I tread upon the earth,
dwell in my house, or ruffle the waters.
Sometimes my clothing and this high wind
lift me above the homes of men;
the strength of the clouds carries me
far and wide over the people. My adornments
resound loudly, sound melodiously,
sing out brightly, when I, a travelling spirit,
am resting neither on land nor sea.

It is generally agreed that this refers to a swan.

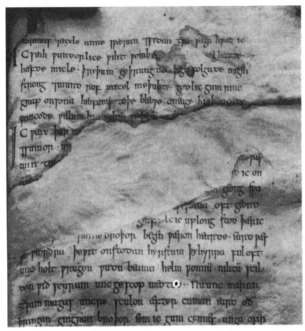

A page from the *Exeter Book*

An illuminated manuscript from around the same time

The next riddle probably has roots in folk mythology of the time. In it, the moon is shown to be waging war against the sun because of its light. But when the moon is about to exert her influence, the sun appears and chases the moon away; a pleasing 'explanation' of night and day.

> I saw a wonderful creature
> bringing plunder between her horns,
> bright air-vessel cunningly adorned,
> plunder homewards from the military expedition;
> she wanted to build a bower in her stronghold,
> construct it with skill, if it were possible.
> Then appeared a wonderful creature over the mountain top
> –he is known to all dwellers on earth–
> who rescued the plunderer and drove the wanderer home
> against her will; she departed west from there
> bearing hostility; she hastened onwards.
> Dust rose to the heavens, dew fell on the earth,
> night went forth. No one afterwards
> knew where the creature went.

François, a thirteen-year-old boy in Laurens van der Post's novel *A Story Like the Wind*, has a very important secret. The story is set in Africa. Xhabbo, a man he has rescued from a horrible death, is undertaking a long and dangerous journey. But a game of riddles forces François to think of something else:

> It mattered less than ever to him that the Matabele boys and girls of his own age were far better at the game than he was. All he cared about was that they should go on playing and make so much noise that no one could hear the sounds of the night outside.
>
> In fact the whole evening was so important to him that he never forgot the riddles put to them all that night. There was, for instance, 'Bamuthi's: 'What is it that always stands and never sits down?'
>
> François could not think for the life of him what 'Bamuthi was after but one of 'Bamuthi's smallest young daughters immediately screamed in a voice of silver 'Old Father, what a stupid riddle! Of course it's a tree!'
>
> And 'Bamuthi had to join in the laughter raised by the whole hut against him, since he was old enough after all to have known of something more intelligent. Now a far more difficult one followed immediately from his eldest son whose voice was just breaking, and who seemed to speak on two different levels of sound simultaneously, causing his sisters to snigger slyly behind their hands.

'Riddle-di, riddle-di-me, I give you a billy goat who grazes with a herd of white goats. Although the goats move about a great deal they manage to munch in the same place.'

That caused a long silence. By the light of the fire in the centre of the hut, François could see one pair of large, glittering black eyes look in vain to another for guidance and in the end 'Bamuthi had to supply the answer, restoring some of his lost honour by saying, 'Surely it can only be the tongue and the teeth'.

Another riddle which caused a great deal of mind searching was, 'There are things in the world that fall from the tops of mountains without breaking themselves. What can they be?'

The answer, of course, was waterfalls, as they all should have known, since they lived so near to the greatest waterfall on earth, the Smoke that Thunders.

One that François liked best came from 'Bamuthi's eldest daughter, who asked shyly, 'What is it that no one can see but goes in and out, round and about, hither and thither, all over the earth, making the dead alive and the living awake?' The answer, of course, was the wind.

Even Ouise-Johanna was to show a surprising inventiveness and produce a riddle which certainly could not have come out of any Bantu tradition and was as modern as any riddle in the bush could be. 'Can any of you tell me who is that quiet, patient, lovable little fellow who dresses so warmly during the day but is left bare during the coldest of nights?'

No one, not even 'Bamuthi, could supply the answer, and a triumphant Ouise-Johanna, her round face glowing like a full moon, was declared to be the great princess of riddles when she answered, once the noise of clapping which the people of Osebeni used to show approval, had ended, 'A clothes peg.'

There was only one riddle which for a moment took François out of that warm, friendly atmosphere of the crowded hut. That was when one of the other Matabele herdsmen asked, 'Could any of you tell me the name of the longest snake in the world?'

When the answer came – a road – François found himself thinking, 'And the longest of the long snakes of the world is the track which Xhabbo is walking out there in the dark.'

When he was back safely in his room with Hintza, his dog, the light extinguished and, tired as he was, trying to sleep, this vision of a road, or rather one of those unending footpaths and tracks of the Dark Continent, wriggling westwards like a snake through the bush and out across the great desert, stayed vivid in his imagination, so much so that he found himself sitting up from time to time listening as carefully as he had ever listened before to the sounds of the night.

Project Action

1. Make up some riddles, imitating the style of the short poems used here, for:
   – a television set
   – a BMX bike
   – a felt-tip pen
   – a dustbin.
2. Write an alternative riddle for one of the subjects that cropped up during the evening François spent with the Matabele boys and girls: tree, tongue and teeth, waterfalls, wind, clothes peg, road.
3. Telling riddles was a way of happily passing the evening. In what ways does your family relax in the evenings? Imagine yourself as an adult looking back on the present time and write a piece of autobiography. You could begin:

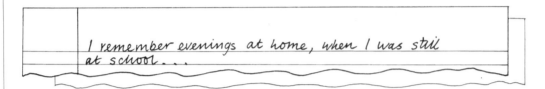

I remember evenings at home, when I was still at school...

4. Have you ever had to keep an important secret which caused you to worry, as François had? How did you come to have the secret? What happened?
   Write down your experience as it stands or use your experience as the basis for a short story.
5. Read *A Story Like the Wind* and, if you enjoyed it, another novel by the same author – and also set in Africa: *Flamingo Feather*.

PROJECT: WHY DID THE CHICKEN CROSS THE ROAD – OR GETTING FROM A TO B!

Transport – getting people and goods from A to B – could well be considered man's oldest technology, for it is probably over 20 000 years ago that man began to use tree trunks, hollowed out to form crude canoes, and simple rafts made from bundles of reeds. Travel by rivers and canals was the most important way of transport – particularly of large loads – right up until the middle of the last century, when the railway system gradually took over. Railways had advantages: they had the ability to go up and down gradients without having to use a system of locks; and branches and spurs could be built to serve almost every town.

Here are some aspects of travel by train in Victorian times:

> It is hard to imagine the changes brought to Britain by the railways. Before they were built, ours was a farming nation with the beginnings of industry, a land where things moved slowly if at all. The railways brought factories, trade, fast-growing cities, and wealth. And, to ordinary people, for the very first time, they brought the opportunity to travel.

Bound by the iron strands of the railway, Britain was unified as never before. Goods, fashion, news and ideas were carried far and wide, and regional differences began to disappear. Among the first to go was local time; in 1840 the Board of Trade suggested that timetabling would be simpler, and services safer, if all trains ran by London time. Station clocks were set accordingly, and the result became known as 'Railway Time'. The introduction of the electric telegraph brought complete accuracy; from 1852, daily signals were transmitted at noon from Greenwich so that station clocks could be synchronized. It was confusing for passengers to have to remember the difference between Railway Time and local time. Because it made life so much easier for everyone, standard time soon came into general use.

The earliest trains had no heating, and winter journeys were miserable for all, even those wealthy and wise enough to bring blankets and brandy. In the early 1850s the Great Northern Railway had an idea that was rapidly copied all over the country. This was the introduction of footwarmers – flat, oblong tins filled with hot water.

Neither did the earliest trains have any lighting. Oil pot-lamps, introduced in the 1840s, barely improved the situation. The clumsy contraptions, designed to hang in slots in the roof of each carriage, were kept at main stations to be cleaned and tended by a lampman. At dusk, he filled them with oil, lit up and mounted the roof of each incoming train to drop the lamps into position. Fuelled by rape-seed oil, pot-lamps were apt to smother passengers with evil-smelling fumes. At best, they gave a feeble light, and that only during evening travel; there was still no daytime lighting in tunnels. Despite these drawbacks, pot-lamps could still be seen in trains on small or remote lines in the early years of this century.

Lack of good lighting prompted the introduction of an amazing variety of gadgets for passengers to buy for themselves. Most were simple candle-lamps; some had suction pads to fix to the window of the carriage, others sported hooks which clipped into the upholstery, and some were designed to hang from the overhead rack. All these lamps folded up so that they could be carried in pockets, and many contained small compartments to hold matches or spare candles. They provided only a faint flickering light by which to read, but even this was welcome in the gloom that prevailed in railway carriages until the arrival of gas and electric lighting.

In the 1860s, coal-gas lighting appeared on several lines, notably on the London underground. The gas was carried on the carriage roofs in concealed containers. It provided a brighter light than the old pot-lamps, but few companies were impressed by the rather precarious and inconvenient method of carrying it. In the late 1870s gaslit trains became much more widespread with the use of compressed oil-gas stored in cylinders beneath the carriage floors. The lamps still had to be specially lit as the day grew dark. Although gas brought a dramatic improvement in railway lighting, it proved to be a major fire-hazard when accidents occurred. However, once companies had gone to the expense of installing gas-lighting, they were far from keen to tackle its replacement, and it remained in use well into this century.

Despite the vast changes that have been made, the pattern of longer journeys probably remains much the same today as it was in the earliest days of travel. The whistle blows and the train slips out of the station: having settled themselves comfortably, scanned the newspapers and glanced at the scenery, railway travellers almost invariably turn their thoughts to food.

Railway refreshments came in for criticism almost from the start. The most common grumble was that hot food, particularly soup, was so scalding when served that it could not be consumed before the train was off. The quality of the soup was also open to question: Dickens calls it 'brown hot water stiffened with flour'. Other items on sale included sandwiches and pies, as well as a range of cakes and buns, all in varying degrees of freshness. Again, Dickens takes a jaundiced view, describing 'glutinous lumps of gristle and grease called pork pie ... sponge cakes that turn to sand in the mouth' and 'brown patties, composed of unknown animals within'.

Philippa Bignell *Taking the Train*

Roads were even more flexible than railways and cost less, but until late in the 19th century, roads were marred by ruts, bumps and potholes. These slowed vehicles down and caused damage and accidents. At one time it became accepted practice to take carts to pieces and use teams of men to carry them – and the goods – over the worst sections of road!

Here is Charles Dickens, writing in *A Tale of Two Cities*, about the Dover mail coach going on its journey from London:

He walked uphill in the mire by the side of the coach, as the rest of the passengers did; not because they had the least relish for walking, but because the hill, and the harness, and the mud, and the mail, were all so heavy, that the horses had three times already come to a stop. Reins and whips, coachman and guard, did their best to keep the team going.

With drooping heads and tails, they mushed their way through the thick mud, floundering and stumbling, as if they were falling to pieces.

There was a steaming mist in all the hollows, and it roamed up the hill, like an evil spirit. A clammy and intensely cold mist, it made its slow way through the air in ripples that followed and overspread one another. It was dense enough to shut out everything from the light of the coach-lamps except for a few yards of road.

All three passengers, plodding up the hill by the side of the mail, were wrapped to the cheek-bones and over the ears. Not one of them could have said, from anything he saw, what either of the other two was like.

'One more pull and you're at the top,' said the coachman. 'Joe!'

'Hallo!' the guard replied.

'What o'clock do you make it, Joe?'

'Ten minutes past eleven.'

'My blood!' yelled the coachman, 'and not atop Shooter's Hill yet! Tst! Yah! Get on with you!'

The horses, cut short by the whip, made a decided scramble for it. Once more the Dover mail struggled on, with the boots of its passengers squashing along by its side. They had stopped when the coach stopped, and they kept close company with it.

The last burst carried the mail coach to the summit of the hill. The horses stopped to breathe again, and the guard got down to skid the wheel for the descent, and open the coach-door to let the passengers in.

Dickens was describing a journey towards the end of the 18th century – a far cry from the supersonic age in which we now live. The following article appeared on 22 January 1976 in *The Times*, written in Bahrain by Arthur Reed, air correspondent:

In a meticulously timed operation with Air France, which put dozens of subsonic airlines behind schedule, British Airways launched the supersonic era of civil aviation today.

Their Concorde Alpha Alpha touched down here from London in 3 hours and 37 minutes, clipping 2 hours and 43 minutes off the normal journey time, and arriving 19 minutes before schedule.

The British Airways Concorde appeared at the end of the runway at Heathrow Airport, London, 5 minutes before its scheduled take-off time which was arranged to coincide exactly with the take-off of the first Air France passenger service from Charles de Gaulle Airport, Paris, some 250 miles away. Captain Norman Todd, aged 50, the commander of the 1350 mph airliner, kept Alpha Alpha sitting on the ground while a queue of subsonic jumbo jets built up behind.

Both Pan American and Trans World, two United States airlines which originally took out options to buy Concorde and then cancelled them, were among those who had to wait.

Heathrow air traffic control, who were in contact with their French opposite numbers, gave a countdown at precisely the same moment to both Captain Todd and Captain Pierre Chanoine, in command of the French Concorde bound for Rio de Janeiro by way of Dakar, West Africa. Both commanders opened the throttles and the civil supersonic era was born.

The British Airways Concorde roared down the runway for 35 seconds, watched by thousands of spectators crowding the rails at the airport, before it was airborne at 11.40 am. The engines were throttled back briefly to reduce the impact of the noise on the communities living at the end of the runway, and then Concorde was climbing away at an angle of 25 degrees to its subsonic cruising height across Europe of 25 000 feet.

Over Paris, Captain Todd exchanged good wishes with Captain Chanoine over the radio.

One hour and 20 minutes later, over the northern end of the Adriatic, the 100 passengers on board felt a distinct surge of power as the airliner was accelerated through the sound barrier. Over the cabin address system, Captain Todd announced: 'Ladies and gentlemen, we are now supersonic.'

Twenty minutes later the digital display in the passenger cabin indicated that we were flying at twice the speed of sound to the accompaniment of a round of applause from the 30 passengers who had paid the £676.20 round trip fare and the 70 invited guests.

Unfortunately the display in the rear cabin, where the guest of honour, the Duke of Kent, was seated, stuck at Mach 0.7 (about 460 mph) and no amount of banging of it by passengers could get it working again.

Lunch of smoked salmon, breast of duck and fresh strawberries was served as the Concorde boomed its way over the islands of Crete and Cyprus, then across Lebanon and Syria. Thirty minutes before landing, reverse thrust was applied in flight and we began to descend from our cruising height of 12 miles into Bahrain.

The flight was enriched by the presence on board of a gentleman from Trowbridge, Wiltshire, dressed overall in a fancy dress of white and purple and with his face painted silver. Mr Bob Ingham, aged 50, the manager of a plant hire company, said his outfit represented the age of Aquarius. He changed into it in a lavatory at the airport and then had some trouble in convincing the strict security guard that he was a bona fide passenger.

Project Action

1. Think carefully about the various journeys you have undertaken (bus, train, boat, plane, bicycle – on foot). Describe, in as much detail as you can, what was for you the most interesting or the most frightening.

2. Having read the article about the earliest passenger trains, list the differences between trains in Victorian times and those of today.

3. Research:
   What had the 'Beeching Axe' to do with railways?
   What is Mach? Remember the Concorde Alpha Alpha's digital display stuck at Mach 0.7.
   Sub and super are prefixes that have been tacked on to sonic in the Concorde article. What do the prefixes mean? From which language does sonic derive?
   Look in an atlas to trace the routes travelled by the two Concordes.
   Who wrote *The Worst Journey in the World* and where was it set?

4. Re-read the paragraph concerning Pan American and Trans World airlines and write the newspaper article that might have appeared in the United States about the first two Concordes. Would the report be enthusiastic and full? What might have been omitted?

5. In the early days of air travel, the argument was put forward that, if he had intended us to fly, God would have given us wings. How would you reply to such a comment in the days of supersonic flight? What happened to Icarus?

6. Read the first few pages of *A Tale of Two Cities* Chapter 2, from which the Dover mail description was adapted, and find out what fears possessed the passengers, coachman, and guard – apart from the weather.

P ROJECT: TIME OFF!

Bank holidays are, by tradition, days on which many people pursue leisure activities. Dylan Thomas, in the course of a short story, describes family preparations and a day on the beach:

> August Bank Holiday. A tune on an ice-cream cornet. A slap of sea and a tickle of sand. A wince and whinny of bathers dancing into deceptive water. A sunburn of girls and a lark of boys.
>
> I remember sharing the last of my moist buns with a boy and a lion. Tawny and savage, with cruel nails and capacious mouth, the little boy tore and devoured. Wild as seed-cake, ferocious as a hearth-rug, the depressed and verminous lion nibbled like a mouse at his half a bun, and hicupped in the sad dusk of his cage.
>
> And mothers loudly warned their proud pink daughters or sons to put that jellyfish down; and sand-fleas hopped on the picnic lettuce; and someone had forgotten the salt.
>
> I remember August Monday from the rising of the sun over the town to the husky hushing of the roundabout music.
>
> There was no need, that holiday morning, for the sluggardly boys to be shouted down to breakfast; out of their jumbled beds they tumbled, scrambled into their rumpled clothes; quickly at the bath-room basin they catlicked their hands and faces, but never forgot to run the water loud and long as though they washed like colliers; in front of the cracked looking-glass bordered with cigarette-cards, in their treasure-trove bedrooms, they whisked a gap-tooth comb through their surly hair; and with shining cheeks and noses and tide-marked necks, they took the stairs three at a time.
>
> But for all their scramble and scamper, clamour on the landing, catlick and toothbrush flick, hair-whisk and stair-jump, their sisters were always there before them. Up with the lady lark, they had prinked and frizzed and hot-ironed; and smug in their blossoming dresses, ribboned for the sun, in gym-shoes white as the blanco'd snow, neat and silly with doilies and tomatoes they helped in the higgledy kitchen. They were calm; they were virtuous; they had washed their necks; they did not romp, or fidget; and only the smallest sister put out her tongue at the noisy boys.
>
> And the woman who lived next door came into the kitchen and said that her mother, who wore a hat with cherries, was having 'one of her days' and had insisted, that very holiday morning, in carrying all the way to the tram-stop a photograph album and the cut-glass fruit-bowl from the front room.
>
> This was the morning when father, mending one hole in the thermos flask, made three; when the sun declared war on the butter, and the butter ran; when dogs, with all the sweet-binned backyards to wag and sniff and bicker in, chased their tails in the jostling kitchen, snapped at flies, writhed between legs, scratched among towels, sat smiling on hampers.
>
> There was cricket on the sand, and sand in the sponge cake, sand-flies in the watercress. Children with spades built fleeting castles; wispy young men whistled at substantial young women; uncles huddled over luke-warm ale.
>
> I remember the patient and laborious hobby of burying relatives in sand.
>
> I remember the princely pastime of pouring sand, from cupped hands or buckets, down collars and tops of dresses; the shriek, the shake, the slap …

Dylan Thomas *Holiday Memory*

Bank holidays aren't the only occasions on which we take time off, of course. Sport has figured prominently as a leisure-time activity, though Philip Stubbes, writing four hundred years ago, presents football as a violent way of taking time off:

> As concerning football playing, I protest it may rather be called a friendly kind of fight, than play or recreation; a bloody and murdering practice, than a fellowly sport or pastime. For doth not every one lie in wait for his adversary, seeking to overthrow him and to pitch him on his nose, though it be upon hard stones, in ditch or dale, in valley or hill? Sometimes their necks are broken, sometimes their backs, sometimes their legs, sometimes their arms, sometimes one part thrust out of joint, sometimes another, sometimes their noses gush out with blood,

sometimes their eyes start out, and sometimes hurt in one place, sometimes in another. They have sleights to meet one betwixt two, to dash him against the heart with their elbows, to hit him under the short ribs with their gripped fists, and with their knees to catch him upon the hip, and to pitch him on his neck, with a hundred such murdering devices.

Not all outdoor activities have to be as violent:

THE BOY FISHING
I am cold and alone,
On my tree-root sitting as still as stone.
The fish come to my net. I scorned the sun,
The voices on the road, and they have gone.
My eyes are buried in the cold pond, under
The cold, spread leaves; my thoughts are silver-wet.
I have ten stickleback, a half-day's plunder,
Safe in my jar. I shall have ten more yet.

E J Scovell

Perhaps playing table-tennis is more your idea of leisure:

PING-PONG
Swatted between bats
The celluloid ball
Leaps on unseen elastic
    Skimming the taut net

Sliced		Spun
Screwed		Cut
Dabbed		Smashed
	Point	
	Service	
Ping		Pong
Pong		Ping
Bing		Bong
Bong		Bing
	Point	
	Service	
Ding		Dong
Dong		Ding
Ting		Tong
Tang		Tong
	Point	
	Service	
Angled		Slipped
Cut		Driven
Floated		Caressed
Driven		Hammered
	THWACKED	
	Point	
	Service	
Bit		Bat
Tip		Tap
Slip		Slap
Zip		Zap
Whip		Whap
	Point	
	Service	
Left		Yes
Right		Yes
Twist		Yes

Skids   Yes
Eighteen   Seventeen
Eighteen   All
Nineteen   Eighteen
Nineteen   All
Twenty   Nineteen

                    Point
                    Service

Forehand   Backhand
Swerves   Yes
Rockets   Yes
Battered   Ah
Cracked   Ah

                    SMASHED
                    SMASHED
                    GAME

Gareth Owen

This is what a young people's encyclopedia has to say about leisure:

Leisure is not so much a specific activity as a state of mind. As such it can be experienced while lying on a beach, while working or while vigorously exercising. It describes a person's attitude towards what he or she is doing and the quality of the time spent doing it. The advantage of such a broad and unspecific definition is seen when two people take the 24 hours in a day and try to subtract from them periods they do not consider to be leisure, such as working, sleeping and eating – no two people are found to agree fully about what should be taken out and what should be left in.

However defined, leisure is certainly important both in the life of the individual and for the society of which he is a part. For the individual it may provide relaxation from daily pressures and routines, creative experience such as education or voluntary work that helps to liberate and develop the personality, or entertainment as an antidote to boredom or drudgery. This last element is reflected in the fact that many employers provide leisure facilities such as football pitches, piped music, games rooms and holiday centres, because they believe that these will produce fitter and happier workers. Equally, in many countries government agencies provide facilities for certain types of leisure for the 'good' of people generally.

In many ways leisure is bound up with work. It is easy, although misleading, to think of leisure as the opposite of work, or to define it as time left over after work. But not all human societies make the distinction. Rural life has always involved an integration of the two. The tradition of the artist and the craftsman is also one in which there is little division between work and play.

In assessing our lives we may give priority to work or leisure, or equally to both. Those who say that work is the most important thing in their lives are not necessarily saying that their lives are devoid of leisure-like experiences: perhaps they obtain from work some of the satisfaction others get from leisure. Those who value leisure highly may be in arduous, dull, or otherwise unsatisfying jobs. It is a commentary on the material values of our society that most people prefer additional paid work to more leisure.

People today generally have more free time than they did a few decades ago, although the actual gain is sometimes overstated. Equally, there are now more diverse ways of spending leisure: more facilities, indoor and outdoor, provided by both private enterprise and public authorities. Television, sports centres and holidays abroad (other than for the wealthy) were unknown a few years ago. Leisure is now big business and all too often a business that sells people something that they do not really want or need as part of a convenient package.

Man and Society

Project Action

1. In *Holiday Memory*, Dylan Thomas had made up some words that you won't find in a dictionary. Which words are they? Can you guess what he means by them? Try writing your own 'dictionary definitions' for each of them. Why do you think he made up his own words?

2. Find and read a copy of Dylan Thomas' complete short story. Ask a librarian or teacher for help, if necessary.

3. Is there a particular Bank Holiday that you remember well – not necessarily a Bank Holiday at the seaside, nor in August? What makes it memorable? Write a description or diary entry of where you went and what you did. Perhaps you could make a good short story out of it instead?

4. If you were told you could have 24 hours to do whatever you liked – no expense spared – what would you do?

5. Having jotted down some suitable questions to ask in order to get the topic going, talk to the members of your family about what they regard as leisure. Remember that the encyclopedia said no two people agree fully about what should or should not be classed as leisure. How much time per week would each member of the family estimate was spent on leisure?

6. In his book of poems *Salford Road* (from which *Ping-Pong* is taken), Gareth Owen has a poem called *Boredom*. Here is one of the verses:

Boredom
Is
Trev
Gone for the day
To Colwyn Bay
For a holiday
And me
On my own.

Read the poem and write your own 'opposite' version, beginning:

Excitement
Is

CHAPTER 2

*R*eading

Imagine that you are riding your bike and you come across these two signs:

What will you do?

It is likely that you will make sure your hands are on the brakes and you will probably keep well in to the side of the road. The signs may have caused you to act without really thinking about them, particularly if you are an experienced cyclist, but your eyes will have transmitted *signals* to your brain (whether consciously or not).

Looking at, and responding to, signs is a form of reading. Letters put together to make up words, act as signs, too. For example, when you see the letters t a b l e, that particular combination of letters will *signify*:

A word is simply a sign: it stands for something.

Every day we face an amazing number of signs, both as diagrams and/or pictures (as in road signs, for example) or as words.

Now test yourself

Look around the room you are in at the moment and make two lists: one list of words, the other of signs. (If you have a hi-fi system, there will be several entries for each list. A cooker may have several, too.)

H OW TO BE A GOOD READER

A good way of explaining how to be a good reader is to compare it with the question 'What makes a good cyclist?'

Possible answers to this question might be someone who:

- has complete physical control over the bike, who doesn't wobble
- changes gear by instinct at exactly the right moment, changing to a lower gear when the going becomes more difficult
- reads and responds to road signs and traffic conditions
- enjoys cycling

Now let's answer the question 'What makes a good reader?' in a similar way: Someone who:

- reads the words fluently, without 'wobbling'
- knows when to read difficult bits slowly with concentration, and when to read fast
- responds to clues and varying situations
- enjoys reading

Perhaps that sounds rather too neat and simple, so let us look in more detail at some of the aspects of reading.

TYPES OF READING

What happens when you want to know what is on television? You select *Radio Times, TV Times*, or a newspaper, whatever is available to you. You quickly find

the right day and the time you want to watch. You read to find out what programmes are broadcast on each channel. If you decide that one of the programmes seems a possible one to watch, you may read further details in the form of a 'summary': you'll try to get an overview of the storyline or plot, actors and actresses starring, whether it is part of a serial, and so on. Your reading has therefore been a process of selection. You would certainly not read in detail every single programme entry, because if your chosen programme were about to start, it would probably have finished by the time you had stopped reading.

This type of reading is often called **scanning**. It is the same process you use when you look up your friend's telephone number in the telephone directory or a word you are not sure about in the dictionary. You would not start at the beginning unless your friend's surname was 'Abel' or the word was 'aardvark' (described in the dictionary as 'a large, burrowing, African mammal with a long snout and ears, feeding on termites and ants'!)

Now test yourself

In addition to looking up a television programme, a telephone number and a word, think of another two situations for which you might use scanning as a reading technique:

1 ....

2 ....

The young English student at work

You have been given the following research project by your teacher:

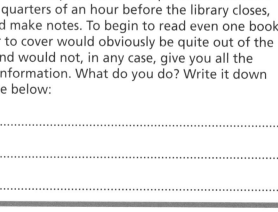

Imagine that you are a journalist working on the South Wales Gazette in the 19th century. There has been a serious mining accident. Find enough information about the geographical, historical, social and technical background to write a newspaper article about the incident.

The best place to find this information is, of course, the library.

Consulting the library catalogue, you discover several books that could help. But there is a problem. You have only three quarters of an hour before the library closes, to read and make notes. To begin to read even one book from cover to cover would obviously be quite out of the question and would not, in any case, give you all the necessary information. What do you do? Write it down in the space below:

....

....

....

The answer? You *scan* the contents pages, looking at the chapter headings and sub-headings for particular, relevant information. Search for any clues you can find. Having chosen the sections that seem most appropriate, your eyes *skim* the text paragraph by paragraph, searching for useful details. **Skimming** means looking over the whole text, getting some general idea of what it is about, training your eyes to pick out only the important words and phrases without reading every word; it helps you to save valuable time and effort. Once you have found the most relevant paragraphs, you then have to read more closely and **intensively**, of course.

Did you write something along these lines?

But how do you know when to **scan**, to **skim**, or to **read intensively**? The answer is: when you know *why* you are reading. For any assignment involving reading – whatever the subject – ask yourself, right at the very beginning, what your purpose is, and that will suggest the kind of reading necessary.

If you are sprawled on your bed reading this extract from Roald Dahl's *Boy*, for example, what sort of reading do you think you will be doing?

My four friends and I had come across a loose floor-board at the back of the classroom, and when we prised it up with the blade of a pocket-knife, we discovered a big hollow space underneath. This, we decided, would be our secret hiding place for sweets and other small treasures such as conkers and monkey nuts and birds' eggs. Every afternoon, when the last lesson was over, the five of us would wait until the classroom had emptied, then we would lift up the floor-board and examine our secret hoard, perhaps adding to it or taking something away.

One day, when we lifted it up, we found a dead mouse lying among our treasures. It was an exciting discovery. Thwaites took it out by its tail and waved it in front of our faces. 'What shall we do with it?' he cried.

'It stinks!' someone shouted. 'Throw it away.'

Thwaites hesitated. They all looked at me.

When writing about oneself, one must strive to be truthful. Truth is more important than modesty. I must tell you, therefore, that it was I and I alone who had the idea for the great and daring Mouse Plot. We all have our moments of brilliance and glory, and this was mine.

'Why don't we,' I said, 'slip it into one of Mrs Pratchett's jars of sweets? Then when she puts her dirty hand in to grab a handful, she'll grab a stinky dead mouse instead.'

The other four stared at me in wonder. Then, as the sheer genius of the plot began to sink in, they all started grinning. They slapped me on the back. They cheered me and danced around the classroom. 'We'll do it today!' they cried. 'We'll do it on the way home! *You* had the idea,' they said to me, 'so *you* can be the one to put the mouse in the jar.'

Thwaites handed me the mouse. I put it into my trouser pocket. Then the five of us left the school, crossed the village green and headed for the sweet shop. We were tremendously jazzed up. We felt like a gang of desperados setting out to rob a train or blow up the sheriff's office.

'Make sure you put it into a jar which is used often,' somebody said.

'I'm putting it in Gobstoppers,' I said. 'The Gobstopper jar is never behind the counter.'

'I've got a penny,' Thwaites said, 'so I'll ask for one Sherbet Sucker and one Bootlace. And while she turns away to get them, you slip the mouse in quickly with the Gobstoppers.'

Thus everything was arranged. We were strutting a little as we entered the shop. We were the victors now and Mrs Pratchett was the victim. She stood behind the counter, and her small malignant pig-eyes watched us suspiciously as we came forward. 'One Sherbet Sucker, please,' Thwaites said to her, holding out his penny.

I kept to the rear of the group, and when I saw Mrs Pratchett turn her head away for a couple of seconds to fish a Sherbet Sucker out of the box, I lifted the heavy glass lid of the Gobstopper jar and dropped the mouse in. Then I replaced the lid as silently as possible. My heart was thumping like mad and my hands had gone all sweaty.

'And one Bootlace, please,' I heard Thwaites saying. When I turned round, I saw Mrs Pratchett holding out the Bootlace in her filthy fingers.

'I don't want all the lot of you troopin' in 'ere if only one of you is buyin',' she screamed at us. 'Now beat it! Go on, get out!'

As soon as we were outside, we broke into a run. 'Did you do it?' they shouted at me.

'Of course I did!' I said.

I felt like a hero. I *was* a hero. It was marvellous to be so popular.

Well? You won't be scanning or skimming, nor are you likely to be searching for information. So what will it be? It will be **recreational**; that is, for enjoyment.

This may sound a rather simple way of treating reading. After all, when you start reading a novel, for example, you may have to read intensively to 'get into' it before you can truly call your reading recreational. And even reading about conditions in a South Wales coalmine during the last century may also become recreational! The secret is to be aware of the various reading styles and be flexible, to be able to 'change gear' when necessary, to return to the example of the good cyclist.

Let's take as an example the reading of this book. You will possibly use all four reading skills at various times, depending on what your aim is:

1 You may **scan** the index to see if a type of English work has been covered by the book.

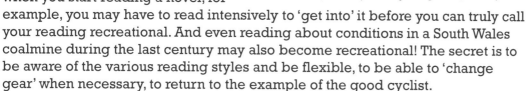

2 You may **skim** part of one of the units to see if it offers clues or tips to help with a project you have undertaken.

❸ You may then **read intensively** to gain the maximum information.

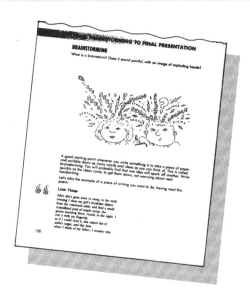

❹ Getting absorbed by one of the stories or extracts, you may read for **recreation**.

Little Things

After she's gone away to camp, in the early evening I clear my girl's breakfast dishes from the rosewood table, and find a small crystallized pool of maple syrup, the grains standing there, round, in the night. I rub it with my fingertip
as if I could read it, this raised dot of amber sugar, and this time
when I think of my father, I wonder why

Now that you've seen the different ways and methods of going about reading, let's have a look at a variety of reading material.

R EADING STORIES

THE STORY-TELLER'S DECISIONS

Here are four possible beginnings for a story:

1

> It was one of those bright days early in October, that Jane Harris skipped off school for the day. Having watched the charity concert on the television throughout the evening – all in a good cause, for she had played an important part in the school charity collection – she had pushed her science homework to the back of her mind.

As she crossed the bridge that led to the short cut through the park, the flowing water somehow startled her into remembering the physics experiment she should have written up. To her, life seemed unfair. Raising money for the Third World (that was funny, why 'third'? Who were the first and second?) was much more important than copying up notes that she could already read quite clearly. She knew Mrs Rogers wouldn't see it that way, though.

It was easy to avoid being seen. The rhododendron bushes with their broad, thick leaves were perfectly placed, dense here and there, but with convenient peep-holes. There would be half-an-hour of danger, then once school had started, she would be free for the day. She would easily find a sheltered spot, read the Judy Blume her friend, Rosie, had passed on to her, and as she had a packed lunch, she could manage quite well.

The absence note that would be needed tomorrow, how she would make up the day's events when her parents asked her what sort of day it had been, how she would cope when Rosie phoned that evening to ask how she was: these thoughts came to her later, when school had started and it was too late to change her mind.

Mrs Rogers was surprised, when she took the register, to find that Jane was absent. The girl had seemed fit and well in the previous lesson and had written plenty of notes. And had it not been Jane just before the bridge? Mrs Rogers thought she had seen her there after she had dropped her son off at the primary school near the station.

'Have you seen Jane today, Rosie?'

'No, miss, she can't be well,' replied Rosie.

'No, I suppose not, though she seemed as right as rain yesterday,' Mrs Rogers said, half to Rosie, half to herself.

2

I'm normally quite conscientious. My Nan always says you go to school to learn, not to mess around, and I think she's right really.

I had quite enjoyed the science experiment we had done and, as usual, I had put down all the things Mrs Rogers had told us to. We'd had a laugh about my writing 'fizzed' instead of 'effervesced'. I couldn't see why we had to use the longer word. But that was all.

The concert was brill. It wasn't only that, though. When they said how much money people were pledging and kept showing you the telephone numbers so that people with credit cards could just say an amount over the phone, I found it exciting. Somehow I kept thinking of the little girl whose picture I had seen in the paper. Those big, dark eyes had haunted me for a week or so.

I suppose part of skipping off school for the day had been to give my life a bit of excitement. The routine can get a bit dull – day in, day out, the same old things.

It was when I looked down into the water going under the bridge that I remembered I hadn't written up my science homework. The water frothed a bit at the edges and it must have reminded me of the liquid we had heated until it *fizzed*.

3

The Isaac Newton School
BIRCHMINSTER STAFFS ST3 9TY
Telephone: Birchminster 380731
Headteacher: E Shaw M A (Oxon)

Mr and Mrs B Harris   4 October 1995
35 Fielding Road
Birchminster
Staffs

Dear Mr and Mrs Harris

I am sorry to have to inform you that your daughter, Jane, truanted from school yesterday. It appears that she had forgotten to complete her science homework and sought to avoid punishment by absenting herself.

Had it not been for the vigilance of her form teacher, Mrs Rogers, who caught sight of her before school near the park entrance by the bridge, her truancy might not have been discovered.

On being questioned by me this morning, I regret to say, Jane tried to lie her way out of the situation. She is now quite contrite, and I hope there will not be a recurrence of her misdemeanour.

We take a severe view of such behaviour. You will appreciate, I am sure, that she will have to accept an appropriate punishment. She will be detained every break and lunchtime for a week.

I look for your co-operation and support in this matter.

Yours sincerely

E Shaw

E Shaw
Headteacher

4

3 October

Wednesday

Hopped off. Felt free and excited. Park was lovely and calm. Finished Rosie's Judy Blume book. Life in the States seems much better. Got a bit cold at lunchtime – had to jump around to get warm again. Managed to get Rosie on phone just before Mum came home from work. Easy to copy Mum's signature – she'd left a letter on the kitchen table, so it was dead easy. Felt a bit scared but grown-up at the same time. Did the science homework I missed last night. Think I did it quite well.

4 October

Thursday

Bad day. Thought I'd got out of trouble for yesterday, but Shaw's interrogation tripped me up. Don't think I'm the first he's 'broken'! Mum cried when I gave her the letter, Dad shouted and said I couldn't be trusted. Lucky that Shaw didn't mention the forgery – Mum would've brained me.

Now that you have read these beginnings, you will see that a story-teller has to make quite a few decisions. For example, what viewpoint should he or she take, and what format should the story take? The next few pages will help you to look out for some of these decisions when you read stories. You may have to begin each story by reading intensively, but that will probably soon shade into recreational reading. You can enjoy stories perfectly well without going into details about a writer's decisions. However, the purpose in talking about stories in detail is, first, to try to interest you in the way stories are put together (and this will probably help you in writing your own) and, secondly, to help you at the beginning of a book when you feel, perhaps, like giving up.

After all, starting a story is often the most difficult part. How many times have you picked up a book and put it down several times before getting into it?

The following exercise shows how the story-teller can approach a story in different ways and how this can affect the reader's view of the plot and characters.

The young English student at work

1. Look at the list of details below used in extract **1**, then number those details also used in extracts **2**, **3** and **4** in the order that they appear. The first few have been done to get you started.

Extract 1	Extracts	2	3	4
– bright day				
– early October				1
– Jane Harris plays truant		2	1	2
– watched charity concert on TV		1		
– school charity involvement			˙2	
– science homework not done				
– crossed the bridge leading to park				
– water as reminder of homework				
– life seemed unfair: Third World v homework teacher would have different perspective				
– cover from foliage				
– half-an-hour's danger				
– free to read for day				
– packed lunch				
– possible problems: absence note parental enquiry phone call from Rosie?				
– Mrs Rogers at registration: Jane had seemed well Jane had written notes Jane by bridge? son dropped off Rosie questioned				

2. Read through extracts **1** and **2** again. Then, in the space below, note the details in **2** that do not appear in **1**.

....

....

....

....

....

....

....

What do these details *add* to the impression you have of Jane from the first extract? Jot down what you think of her.

....

....

....

Story-teller's decisions: viewpoint

One of the most important decisions a story-teller has to make is that of viewpoint. How is he or she going to present and tell the story?

Look back at extracts **1** and **2**. There is one major difference between them. Can you spot it?

Extract **1** was written by a story-teller who knew everything: both Jane's *and* Mrs Rogers' thoughts and actions were expressed and described. Extract **2**, on the other hand, cannot give any indication of what Mrs Rogers is thinking because it is written as if from Jane's point of view.

When the story-teller's viewpoint is that he or she knows everything – as in **1** – the story can jump from a female teenager in Paris to an elderly man in Singapore, an urchin in the back streets of a big city to a mother pushing her toddler in a pushchair along a country footpath. We sometimes use the word **omniscient** for such an all-knowing author.

Did you know?

Whenever you come across *omni* at the beginning of a word, it means *all*. *Sciens* is the Latin word for 'knowing', so: *omniscient* means 'all knowing'

If *potens* means 'capable', what does *omnipotent* mean? And if the Latin word *vorare* means 'to devour' and an *omnivorous* animal comes along, what is your reaction likely to be?

When an author decides to 'be' the character telling the story – as in **2** – there can only be a certain amount that we can be told; the author has the direct thoughts, feelings, actions, memories of only the one character. Everything we know must come from the conversations, letters, telephone calls, involving the character and others. Stories of this kind are called **first-person narrative**, because, in terms of grammar, 'I' is referred to as the first person.

1 and **2** are the most common story-teller styles you are likely to come across. However, the third and fourth beginnings of our story about Jane show two further ways open to a story-teller.

Extract **3** is in the form of a letter. Some novels have been made up entirely of letters.

> ### Now test yourself
>
> Think up a way of continuing Jane's story using letters. Jane's parents replying to Mr Shaw? Jane's mother writing to Jane's aunt? Jane to her Nan?

By the way, Mr Shaw's letter to Jane's parents takes a very different view of Jane from **1** and **2**, doesn't it?

Jane's journal or diary in extract **4** shows yet another way of telling a story. The most famous books in recent years to make use of this technique are the exploits of Adrian Mole.

> ### Now test yourself
>
> Write Jane's diary entries for 5 and 6 October.
>
> **5 October**
>
> ....
>
> ....
>
> ....
>
> ....
>
> ....
>
> **6 October**
>
> ....
>
> ....
>
> ....
>
> ....
>
> ....

Read these beginnings of stories and see what viewpoint the writer has chosen.

THE HOLLOW LAND

I'm Bell Teesdale. I'm a lad. I'm eight.

All down this dale where I live there's dozens of little houses with grass growing between the stones and for years there's been none of them wanted. They're too old and too far out or that bit too high for farmers now. There was miners once – it's what's called the hollow land – but they're here no more. So the little houses is all forsook.

They have big garths round them, and pasture for grass-letting – sheep and that – and grand hay fields. Maybe just too many buttercups blowing silver in June, but grand hay for all that, given a fair week or two after dipping time.

All these little farm houses for years stood empty, all the old farming families gone and the roofs falling in and the swallows and swifts swooping into the bedrooms and muck trailing down inside the stone walls.

So incomers come. They buy these little houses when they can, or rent them or lease them. Manchester folks or even London folks, with big estate cars full of packet food you don't see round here, and great soft dogs that's never seen another animal.

All down Mallerstang there's becks running down off the fell. It's bonny. Down off the sharp scales, dry in summer till one single drop of rain sends them running and rushing and tumbling down the fell-side like threads of silk. Like cobwebs. And when the wind blows

across the dale these becks gasp, and they rise up on theirselves like the wild horses in Wateryat Bottom. They rise on their hind legs. Or like smoke blowing, like ever so many bonfires, not water at all, all smoking in the wind between Castledale and the Moorcock toward Wensleydale. It's bonny.

And townfolk come looking at all this now where once they only went to the Lake District over the west. Renting and leasing they come. Talking south. 'Why'd they come?' I ask our grandad who's leased the farm house he used to live in (my gran died). 'There's not owt for 'em here. What's use of a farm to them? Just sitting in. Never a thing going on.'

'Resting,' says my grandad. 'They take 'em for resting in after London.'

Well, this family that come to my grandad's house, Light Trees, wasn't resting. Not resting at all. There's a mother and a father and four or five great lads, some of them friends only, and there's a little lad, Harry, and the racket they make can be heard as far as Garsdale likely.

Jane Gardam

From the beginning of *The Hollow Land*, can you say what you think the story is going to be about? Are there any clues for the reader to pick up? Find a copy of the book to read in order to see if you made some sensible guesses.

CHARLOTTE'S WEB

'Where's Papa going with that axe?' said Fern to her mother as they were setting the table for breakfast.

'Out to the hoghouse,' replied Mrs Arable. 'Some pigs were born last night.'

'I don't see why he needs an axe,' continued Fern, who was only eight.

'Well,' said her mother, 'one of the pigs is a runt. It's very small and weak, and it will never amount to anything. So your father has decided to do away with it.'

'Do *away* with it?' shrieked Fern. 'You mean *kill* it? Just because it's smaller than the others?'

Mrs Arable put a pitcher of cream on the table.

'Don't yell, Fern!' she said. 'Your father is right. The pig would probably die anyway.'

Fern pushed a chair out of the way, and ran outdoors. The grass was wet and the earth smelled of springtime. Fern's sneakers were sopping by the time she caught up with her father.

'Please don't kill it!' she sobbed. 'It's unfair.'

Mr Arable stopped walking.

'Fern,' he said gently, 'you will have to learn to control yourself.'

'Control myself?' yelled Fern. 'This is a matter of life and death, and you talk about *controlling* myself?' Tears ran down her cheeks and she took hold of the axe and tried to pull it out of her father's hand.

'Fern,' said Mr Arable. 'I know more about raising a litter of pigs than you do. A weakling makes trouble. Now run along!'

'But it's unfair,' cried Fern. 'The pig couldn't help being born small, could it? If I had been very small at birth, would you have killed me?'

Mr Arable smiled. 'Certainly not,' he said, looking down at his daughter with love. 'But this is different. A little girl is one thing, a little runty pig is another.'

'I see no difference,' replied Fern, still hanging onto the axe. 'This is the most terrible case of injustice I ever heard of.'

E B White

Charlotte's Web is a very popular story, so you may well know it already, but if you don't, what is the likely outcome of Fern's conversation with her father?

The young English student at work

Now you have practised using these extracts, go away and pick up three or four novels from your bookshelves or from the library and have a look at the opening couple of pages. In each case, which viewpoint has the writer decided to use? Use the space below to fill in your answers.

Title of book ....   Title of book ....

Writer's viewpoint ....   Writer's viewpoint ....

....

Title of book ....   Title of book ....

Writer's viewpoint ....   Writer's viewpoint ....

....

Story-teller's other decisions

The viewpoint is only one of several decisions the writer has to take, however. Other decisions include:

1. Who the characters are going to be
2. Where the story is going to take place
3. What is going to happen
4. What the point of telling the story is
5. Where the story is going to start – is it going to be chronological (arranged in the order of time)? Or are there going to be flashbacks?

There now follows an entire short story. Read it through and then think about the various decisions the writer had to make. Write down in the space provided what you think was the author's answer to each decision. Then check to see if you are right!

WITCHES' LOAVES

Miss Martha Meacham kept the little bakery on the corner (the one where you go up three steps, and the bell tinkles when you open the door).

Miss Martha was forty, her bank book showed a credit of two thousand dollars, and she possessed two false teeth and a sympathetic heart. Many people have married whose chances to do so were much inferior to Miss Martha's.

Two or three times a week a customer came in, in whom she began to take an interest. He was a middle-aged man, wearing spectacles and a brown beard trimmed to a careful point.

He spoke English with a strong German accent. His clothes were worn and darned in places, and wrinkled and baggy in others. But he looked neat, and had very good manners.

He always bought two loaves of stale bread. Fresh bread was five cents a loaf. Stale ones were two for five. Never did he call for anything but stale bread.

Once Miss Martha saw a red and brown stain on his fingers. She was sure then that he was an artist and very poor. No doubt he lived in a garret, where he painted pictures and ate stale bread and thought of the good things to eat in Miss Martha's bakery.

Often when Miss Martha sat down to her chops and light rolls and jam and tea, she would sigh, and wish that the gentle-mannered artist might share her tasty meal instead of eating his dry crust in that draughty attic. Miss Martha's heart, as you have been told, was a sympathetic one.

In order to test her theory as to his occupation, she brought from her room one day a painting that she had bought at a sale, and set it against the shelves behind the bread counter.

It was a Venetian scene. A splendid marble palazzo (so it said on the picture) stood in the foreground – or rather forewater. For the rest there were gondolas (with the lady trailing her hand in the water), clouds, and sky. No artist could fail to notice it.

Two days afterwards the customer came in.

'Two loaves of stale bread, if you please.'

'You haf a fine bicture, madame,' he said while she was wrapping the bread.

'Yes?' says Miss Martha, revelling in her own cunning. 'I do admire art and' (no, it would not do to say 'artists' thus early) 'and paintings,' she substituted. 'You think it is a good picture?'

'Der balace,' said the customer, 'is not in good drawing. Der bair spective of it is not true. Goot morning, madame.'

He took his bread, bowed, and hurried out.

Yes, he must be an artist. Miss Martha took the picture back in her room.

How gentle and kindly his eyes shone behind his spectacles! What a broad brow he had! To be able to judge perspective at a glance and to live on stale bread! But genius often has to struggle before it is recognized.

What a thing it would be for art and perspective if genius were backed by two thousand dollars in the bank, a bakery, and a sympathetic heart to – but these were day-dreams, Miss Martha.

Often now when he came he would chat for a while across the showcase. He seemed to crave Miss Martha's cheerful words.

He kept on buying stale bread. Never a cake, never a pie, never one of her delicious tarts.

She thought he began to look thinner and discouraged. Her heart ached to add something good to eat to his meagre purchase, but her courage failed at the act. She did not dare affront him. She knew the pride of artists.

Miss Martha took to wearing her blue-dotted silk waistcoat behind the counter. In the back room she cooked a mysterious compound of quince seeds and borax. Ever so many people used it for the complexion.

One day the customer came in as usual, laid his nickel on the showcase, and called for his stale loaves. While Miss Martha was reaching for them, there was a great tooting and clanging, and a fire-engine came lumbering past.

The customer hurried to the door to look, as anyone will. Suddenly inspired, Miss Martha seized the opportunity.

On the bottom shelf behind the counter was a pound of fresh butter that the dairyman had left ten minutes before. With the bread knife Miss Martha made a deep slash in each of the stale loaves, inserted a generous quantity of butter, and pressed the loaves together again.

When the customer turned once more she was tying the paper round them.

When he had gone, after an unusually pleasant little chat, Miss Martha smiled to herself, but not without a slight fluttering of the heart.

Had she been too bold? Would he take offence? But surely not.

For a long time that day her mind dwelt on the subject. She imagined the scene when he should discover her little deception.

He would lay down his brushes and palette. There would stand his easel with the picture he was painting.

He would prepare for his luncheon of dry bread and water. He would slice into a loaf – ah!

Miss Martha blushed. Would he think of the hand that placed it there as he ate? Would he –

The front door bell jangled viciously. Somebody was coming in, making a great deal of noise.

Miss Martha hurried to the front. Two men were there. One was a young man smoking a pipe – a man she had never seen before. The other was her artist.

His face was very red, his hat was on the back of his head, his hair was wildly rumpled. He clinched his two fists, and shook them furiously at Miss Martha. At *Miss Martha*.

'*Dummkopf!*' he shouted with extreme loudness; and then '*Tausenmier!*' or something like it in German.

The young man tried to draw him away.

'I vill not go,' he said angrily, 'else I shall told her.'

He made a bass drum of Miss Martha's counter.

'You haf shpoilt me,' he cried, his blue eyes blazing behind his spectacles. 'I vill tell you. You vas von *meddlingsome old cat!*'

Miss Martha leaned weakly against the shelves and laid one hand on her blue-dotted silk waistcoat. The young man took the other by the collar.

'Come on,' he said, 'you've said enough.' He dragged the angry one out the door to the sidewalk, and then came back.

'Guess you ought to be told, ma'am,' he said, 'what the row is about. That's Blumberger. He's an architectural draftsman. I work in the same office with him.

'He's been working hard for three months drawing a plan for a new city hall. It was a prize competition. He finished inking the lines yesterday. You know, a draftsman always makes his drawing in pencil first. When it's done he rubs out the pencil lines with handfuls

20

of stale breadcrumbs. That's better than India rubber.

'Blumberger's been buying the bread here. Well today – well, you know, ma'am, that butter isn't – well, Blumberger's plan isn't good for anything now except to cut up into railroad sandwiches.'

Miss Martha went into the back room. She took off the blue-dotted silk waistcoat and put on the old brown serge she used to wear. Then she poured the quince seed and borax mixture out of the window into the ash can.

O Henry

Decision

What is the author's viewpoint?

....

The writer is omniscient, observing Martha and her customer, but particularly knowing her thoughts and feelings.

Decision

How many characters are there?

....

Three. The principal character is Martha, of course, whose feelings we see develop in some detail; the 'artist', as she takes Blumberger to be; and his colleague, whose position in the story is to deliver the surprise ending and explanation.

Decision

What sort of character is Martha?
Write down any of the following words that seem to you to describe her exactly:

kind   cunning   stupid   vain   shy   ingenious   caring   rash

....

....

....

Some of these words seem rather contradictory, saying opposite things. Did you write down some opposites? Can you back up each word you have written down by quoting particular parts of the story?

How do you know what a character is like? There are three obvious ways to find out:

❶ You can listen to what people say about themselves. Do you remember Jane, in extract **2** on page 47, saying:
   'I'm normally quite conscientious'?
❷ You can read what the other characters say about him or her.
❸ The evidence of people's actions and behaviour is the most convincing and reliable source of information.

However, when characters talk about themselves and others, you have to think carefully about what they are saying. If Mr Shaw's only contact with Jane had been over her truancy, for example, 'normally quite conscientious' wouldn't be the words he would use to describe her!

Decision

Where is the story going to take place?

....

....

By setting his story in Martha's bakery, the writer keeps the story neatly together in one place and concentrates our attention on Martha. If the reader had been taken to Blumberger's office for the 'disaster', he or she wouldn't have felt the surprise *with* Martha and, as the story focuses so much on her, that is very important.

Decision

What is going to happen?

....

....

....

....

....

O Henry builds his plot carefully, presenting Martha's growing interest in the 'artist' and the steps she takes to attract him: placing the picture behind the bread counter, taking care over her appearance and complexion. The first time we read the story, we overlook the clue that Blumberger is perhaps not an artist by his comment that the picture is 'not in good drawing'.

The fire-engine which distracts Blumberger's attention, giving enough time for Martha to insert the butter, shows that her action is a spur-of-the-moment decision; she could not have foreseen the fire-engine, she is 'suddenly inspired'. It is also convenient that the dairyman had left the butter ten minutes before.

By giving us Martha's thoughts after Blumberger has left the shop, of whether he would take offence, of his laying down his brushes and palette, of the happy surprise he would have on slicing the loaf, the author builds up *our* hopes, too. The reader's interest mounts until, with a great deal of noise, the angry 'artist' shouts, '*Dummkopf*' and his colleague explains what has happened.

Decision

What is the point of the story?

....

....

Looking beneath the surface of the story, you can see that the author was interested in showing that the reader has to be careful making assumptions about other people. If only Martha hadn't constructed in her mind the circumstances of her 'artist' and found out more about him first, before taking any action, she would perhaps have been luckier in her relationship. It can't be imagined she will have much luck now! Or do you think Blumberger will 'pardon' her?

Decision

Where is the story going to start?

....

....

The structure of the story is simple; the author has handled the time chronologically.

Chronological is made up of two Greek words: *chronos* meaning 'time' and *logos* meaning 'reason'. In your dictionary, look up *chronicle* and *chronometer*.

So, to remind you of what was said on page 48, reading a story intensively by looking at a number of decisions an author has to make can often help the reader to understand and enjoy what a story-teller has produced.

Read this next story, then when you have finished, take some time to think about the writer's decisions.

THE FUN THEY HAD

Margie even wrote about it that night in her diary. On the page headed May 17, 2155, she wrote, 'Today Tommy found a real book!'

It was a very old book. Margie's grandfather once said that when he was a little boy *his* grandfather told him that there was a time when all stories were printed on paper.

They turned the pages, which were yellow and crinkly, and it was awfully funny to read words that stood still instead of moving the way they were supposed to – on a screen, you know. And then, when they turned back to the page before, it had the same words on it as it had had when they read it the first time.

'Gee,' said Tommy, 'what a waste. When you're through with the book, you just throw it away, I guess. Our television screen must have had a million books on it and it's good for plenty more. I wouldn't throw *it* away.'

'Same with mine,' said Margie. She was eleven and hadn't seen as many telebooks as Tommy had. He was thirteen.

She said, 'Where did you find it?'

'In my house.' He pointed without looking, because he was busy reading. 'In the attic.'

'What's it about?'

'School.'

Margie was scornful. 'School? What's there to write about school? I hate school.' Margie always hated school, but now she hated it more than ever. The mechanical teacher had been giving her test after test in geography and she had been doing it worse and worse until her mother had shaken her head scornfully and sent for the County Inspector.

He was a round little man with a red face and a whole box of tools with dials and wires. He smiled at her and gave her an apple, then took the teacher apart. Margie had hoped he wouldn't know how to put it all together again, but he knew all right and after an hour or so, there it was again, large and black and ugly with a big screen on which all lessons were shown and the questions were asked. That wasn't so bad. The part she hated most was the slot where she had to write them on a punch code they made her learn when she was six years old, and the mechanical teacher calculated the mark in no time.

The inspector had smiled after he had finished and patted her head. He said to her mother, 'It's not the little girl's fault, Mrs Jones. I think the geography sector was geared a little too quick. These things happen sometimes. I've slowed it up to an average ten-year level. Actually, the overall pattern of her progress is quite satisfactory.' And he patted Margie's head again.

Margie was disappointed. She had been hoping they would take the teacher away altogether. They had once taken Tommy's teacher away for nearly a month because the history sector had blanked out completely.

So she said to Tommy, 'Why would anyone write about school?'

Tommy looked at her with very superior eyes. 'Because it's not our kind of school, stupid. This is the old kind of school that they had hundreds and hundreds of years ago.' He added loftily, pronouncing the word carefully, '*Centuries* ago.'

Margie was hurt. 'Well, I don't know what kind of school they had all that time ago.' She read the book over his shoulder for a while, then said, 'Anyway, they had a teacher.'

'Sure they had a teacher, but it wasn't a *regular* teacher. It was a man.'

'A man? How could a man be a teacher?'

'Well, he just told the boys and girls things and gave them homework and asked them questions.'

'A man isn't smart enough.'

'Sure he is. My father knows as much as my teacher.'

'He can't. A man can't know as much as a teacher.'

'He knows almost as much I betcha.'

Margie wasn't prepared to dispute that. She said, 'I wouldn't want a strange man in my house to teach me.'

Tommy screamed with laughter. 'You don't know much, Margie. The teachers didn't live in the house. They had a special building and all the kids went there.'

'And all the kids learned the same thing?'

'Sure, if they were all the same age.'

'But my mother says a teacher has to be adjusted to fit the mind of each boy and girl it teaches and that each kid has to be taught differently.'

'Just the same they didn't do it that way then. If you don't like it, you don't have to read the book.'

'I didn't say I didn't like it,' Margie said quickly. She wanted to read about those funny schools.

They weren't even half finished when Margie's mother called, 'Margie! School!'

Margie looked up. 'Not yet, mamma.'

'Now,' said Mrs Jones. 'And it's probably time for Tommy, too.'

Margie said to Tommy, 'Can I read the book some more with you after school?'

'Maybe,' he said nonchalantly. He walked away whistling, the dusty book tucked beneath his arm.

Margie went into the schoolroom. It was right next to her bedroom, and the mechanical teacher was on and waiting for her. It was always on at the same time every day except Saturday and Sunday, because her mother said little girls learned better if they learned at regular hours.

The screen was lit up, and it said: 'Today's arithmetic lesson is on the addition of proper fractions. Please insert yesterday's homework in the proper slot.'

Margie did so with a sigh. She was thinking about the old schools they had when her grandfather's grandfather was a little boy. All the kids from the whole neighbourhood came, laughing and shouting in the school yard, sitting together in the classroom, going home together at the end of the day. They learned the same things so they could help one another on the homework and talk about it.

And the teachers were people.

The mechanical teacher was flashing on the screen: 'When we add the fractions ½ and ¼ –'

Margie was thinking about how the kids must have loved it in the old days. She was thinking about the fun they had.

Isaac Asimov

What do you think Isaac Asimov was driving at when he wrote that story? What is he saying about our lives today?

Here is another of Terry Jones's *Fairy Tales* (you will remember *The Glass Cupboard* on page 15). What points do you think he is trying to make?

THREE RAINDROPS

A raindrop was falling out of a cloud, and it said to the raindrop next to it: 'I'm the biggest and best raindrop in the whole sky!'

'You are indeed a fine raindrop,' said the second, 'but you are not nearly as beautifully shaped as I am. And in my opinion it's shape that counts, and *I* am therefore the best raindrop in the whole sky.'

The first raindrop replied: 'Let us settle this matter once and for all.' So they asked a third raindrop to decide between them.

But the third raindrop said: 'What nonsense you're both talking! *You* may be a big raindrop, and *you* are certainly well-shaped, but, as everybody knows, it's purity that really counts, and I am purer than either of you. *I* am therefore the best raindrop in the whole sky!'

Well, before either of the raindrops could reply, they all three hit the ground and became part of a very muddy puddle.

The young English student at work

Read as many short stories and novels as you can. You may find it easy to select books in a library or bookshop, but if you don't, then ask advice – librarian, teacher, someone who has an idea of what you might like. Try to have a book 'on the go' all the time, so that whenever you have a spare moment, you can enter another world. Read books recommended by friends (Jane Harris had borrowed a book by Judy Blume from her friend) and recommend to others those books you have enjoyed.

KEEPING A RECORD

Do you keep a list of the books you have read, or have you ever jotted down any comments – perhaps about the characters and what they have got up to or how you felt about the story as a whole? In the unit on writing, you can read more about keeping a journal or 'sketch pad in words', but now seems a good place to suggest that you keep a log of your reading. It is fascinating to look back months, or even years, later to see what thoughts you had at the time. You might like to write something like this:

Title: Tree by Leaf
Author: Cynthia Voigt

Outline:
Clothilde's Father, who has recently returned from war, has been disfigured and refuses to stay in the main house with the rest of the family. They are somewhat afraid of "the man in the boathouse", as they call him.
During the term, Nate, Clothilde's elder brother is at boarding school near his Grandfather's house. He stays with the wicked Grandfather having told the family that he is on a cruise with some friends. Grandfather tempts him into running the factory which the SPEER family has owned for a long while.
In an old aunt's will, Clothilde is left Peninsula, the house they are living in. As the family are short of money, there is a fear they will sell it. Clothilde feels angry at the decision and remains cross until one day she meets her Father and he said he wouldn't sell it unless he had to. She has a long talk with her Father and he has a giggle with her. He will consider coming back for the evenings when Deidre, Clothilde's younger sister, is in bed so he won't scare her by his face. Clothilde knew he would come back someday. He did. Clothilde's mother got the flower garden she wanted. It all ends happily.

My Favourite Character:
Clothilde is my favourite character because she takes strong and sure decisions and has a way of reacting that I think I would have if I were in her place. She has a close relationship with her Father that the war has spoilt, but time builds up what was destroyed.

Why I liked this book:
It is an anti-war book about people who treat badly people who have been disfigured in the service of their country. It doesn't come over strongly but is implied in the book.

You do not have to use the same headings as here; you might prefer to select some of the following instead, or as well, and you can vary what you want to say for each book:

1. Characters and what you thought of them.
2. Where the story took place. (There could be several places, of course. You could say if any of the settings were the kinds of places where you would like to spend a holiday.)
3. What the writer seems to have been interested in. (For *The Glass Cupboard*, for example, you might write that Terry Jones was concerned about people's greed, how greed brought about their downfall, and how we have all got to look after the Earth.)
4. Good passage(s). (Perhaps for reading aloud in class if you are asked to talk about a book you have read and enjoyed.)

See also page 120 at the end of this chapter.

R EADING AUTOBIOGRAPHY

Did you know?

Autos is the Greek word for *self*, *bios* is the Greek for *life* and *graphein* is to write, so:

autos + bios + graphein

is a combination of three separate Greek words meaning 'self-written life'. So what is an *autograph*? What do you study when you study *bio*logy? If a car ran on rails or needed to be connected to a cable for its power supply, it couldn't be called an *auto*mobile. Why not?

Someone writing autobiography has to make lots of similar decisions to the story teller:

- when to start (birth, earliest memory?)
- how much description
- which events to focus on
- which people and places to describe, and so on. And when we read, we have to think about the character telling the story. We have to be on our guard and consider the light in which the writer appears. Not all autobiographers show themselves as pleasant people!

What impression of the young Harry Secombe do you have from this story of his childhood in Swansea?

> ### SOMETHING BORROWED
>
> It was a hot Saturday afternoon in July, and Billy Evans and Ronnie Thomas and the gang had gone up Kilvey Hill to look at tadpoles. I was in my 'delicate' phase at the time, after having had a series of childhood illnesses one after the other. I had measles so quickly on top of chicken pox that the spots were fighting each other for space. Now I was getting over jaundice and was only allowed out near the house.
>
> When Joyce Llewellyn came over to me I was reading a book of poetry by Keats which my grandfather had given me. Somehow I felt a kinship with the delicate poet and had also taken to leaping around the front room improvising ballet steps to the music on the radio, while my parents exchanged vaguely worried glances. You might say that I was positively ethereal at this time.
>
> 'Come on, Harry,' said Joyce, showering me with spit. 'We're playing weddings and you're the bridegroom.'
>
> I looked up, startled.

'I've been ill,' I said timorously, knowing the rigours of Joyce's games. 'Besides, my mother says I'm only to play near the front door.'

She tried another tactic.

'Mildred will be awful upset,' she said. 'She's the bride.'

My head swam, and the book dropped from my lap. Mildred Reilly – the girl I worshipped from afar, the girl with the Shirley Temple dimples; whose 'Hello' could send me into a decline.

She was a newcomer to the district and her parents only let her play with us very occasionally. Her dad had a three-wheeled Morgan runabout, in the back of which she sat like a little princess, as they chugged down St Leger Crescent on their regular Sunday outing.

I had caught a chill one Sunday evening waiting in the rain for the car to come home so that I could see her wave to me. She didn't wave either, she was asleep in her mother's arms. If I could have thought of a rhyme for 'Mildred' I would have written a poem about her.

Joyce was irritated. 'Are you coming or not? Tony Rees is over by there – I'll ask him then.'

I was at her side in two strides as she turned away.

'All right,' I said, my voice high-pitched and trembly. 'If it's Mildred, I don't mind.'

'I thought you wouldn't,' said Joyce Llewellyn with an old-fashioned look.

We went across to the Patch where the ceremony was to be performed.

This 'patch' was a square-shaped piece of waste ground which lay helplessly in the middle of our little community of council houses, as if the architect had left a packet of cigarettes on the blueprint and had absent-mindedly worked around it. All the windows of the houses around faced on to it, so parents could keep an eye on us kids who played there.

They had set up a tent made from blankets and an old eiderdown with two broomsticks as the central supports, and a group of chattering girls stood outside it. As we came near, one of them squealed, 'He's coming, Mildred – get back in quick. He mustn't see you before you marry him.'

There was a giggle and a flash of pink and the blanket in front of the tent was secured with a large safety-pin.

Joyce poked around on the ground in a heap of clothes. 'Try these on,' she said, throwing me a pair of striped pants.

Red-faced, my glasses steamed with perspiration, I struggled into them. Ada Bayless snickered slyly. 'Aren't you going to take your other pants off first?' She was a big girl for her age.

I stood upright, clutching the trousers at the waist.

'They're a bit too big,' I stammered, embarrassed and a little frightened by the proximity of so many girls with no other boy for moral support.

Joyce Llewellyn regarded me critically. She was now wearing her idea of a parson's outfit, with her father's stiff collar back-to-front and a homburg rammed down over her stringy red hair.

She bent down and picked up a length of string from among the heap of clothing. Her father was a sailor and the way she trussed me around the waist would have made him a proud man.

'There now, that'll hold 'em,' she remarked with satisfaction.

I fought for breath against the stricture of her reef knots. 'Don't you think you tied it too tight?' I gasped.

'Nonsense, you can't have 'em falling down during the ceremony, and besides, you've gone a much better colour,' my Torquemada replied.

I stood helplessly, near to tears, and wishing I had never been tempted into coming along.

A coat was flung at me. 'Try that for size,' spat Joyce.

I tried it on defeatedly to find that it was a tail-coat which enveloped me in all directions, but before I could take it off Joyce called, 'Are you ready, Harry? Mildred's getting impatient; her mother's coming home from shopping soon.'

At the mention of Mildred's name, I melted. To be near her, to hold her hand, would be worth all this dressing up.

I submitted meekly to being led into position outside the tent, where the girls had set up an old packing case as an altar. Joyce stood in front of me with a tattered copy of *Pears Cyclopaedia* in her hands and behind me the other girls, acting as bridesmaids, sang *Here Comes the Bride* in three different keys.

I could feel the hair rising on the back of my neck as I heard her footsteps behind me. She stopped beside me, and I turned round as far as my string belt would allow to look at her.

Her dress was long and pink and full of holes. Her hat was a cloche-type hat belonging to her mother, and her lips were made up with lipstick which had smudged and she was wearing high-heeled shoes several sizes too big. To me she was the most beautiful creature I had ever seen.

When she put her hand on my arm I shook like a leaf, and I vowed silently that I would die for her; I would fight all the dragons in the world for her; I would see that she had ice-cream every day; she would never go to school if she didn't want to.

'Do you take this woman to be your lawful wedded wife?' intoned Joyce from page 381 of *Pears Cyclopaedia*.

I nodded dumbly. 'Say "I do",' hissed the 'parson'.

'I do,' came croaking from my throat.

'Do you take this man to be your – er – lawfully wedded husband?'

'I do,' whispered my beloved through the gaps in her teeth.

'Where's the ring?' spat Joyce.

'Here it is,' cried Ada Bayless, dropping her end of Mildred's frock and rushing forward with a gold ring. 'Be careful; it's my Mum's and she'll kill me if she finds I've pinched it.'

'Put it on her finger,' I was commanded.

Taking her hot, sticky little hand in mine I placed the ring on her finger where it dangled loosely. My heart was full and the rest of the ceremony was lost in a welter of happiness.

'I now pronounce you man and wife,' declared Joyce Llewellyn in a spray of triumphant spittle, shutting the book firmly. 'Kiss the bride,' she said.

Mildred lifted her cheek demurely and with all the tenderness in my young world I kissed her.

'You're sweating,' said the girl who held my heart in her hands and she rubbed her cheek vigorously where I had kissed it.

'Open the bottle of pop and get the broken biscuits.' Joyce was on the job again. 'Let's have the reception.'

'Let's have some then,' said my bride, leaving my side with an alacrity that hurt. All the other girls crowded around her giggling and chattering, leaving me bewildered and alone. They all crowded into the tent after the pop and biscuits. I stood uncertainly outside, feeling suddenly much older.

Then Mildred came out and offered me a drink from her cup. 'Use the other side,' she said. 'I've got lipstick on.'

Gratefully I accepted, not realizing how thirsty I was, and before I had realized it I had drained the cup.

'You greedy thing,' she cried. 'You're only supposed to take a sip.' She slapped my face. 'I hate you. Old four eyes – old yellow face!' she chanted, turning the knife in the wound. 'You look awfully silly in those clothes,' and, turning on her heels, she went back into the tent.

I couldn't see for tears. I stood biting my lip.

'I've been ill,' I blubbed through the opening in the tent. Her back was turned to me and the other girls all giggled as I stuck my head inside.

'You wait,' I began; then, hearing footsteps behind me, I saw Billy Evans and Bob Jones holding jars of tadpoles.

'Look what we've got,' said Billy, holding his jampot in the air. 'There's about two thousand tadpoles in there at least.'

Then, seeing my strange get-up, Bob Jones said, 'What are you doing? You've been playing with the girls.'

'I haven't,' I said. 'Well, anyway I didn't want to – it's all Joyce Llewellyn's fault.'

'Let's knock their tent down,' said Billy Evans, kicking at the broomstick supporting the back of it.

The girls shouted angrily inside as we pushed the tent over, and Joyce Llewellyn pummelled all three of us as we pulled the blankets over their heads.

'You've spoiled the reception; you've ruined everything,' she cried hysterically, tears streaming down her face.

Mildred, my Mildred, ran sobbing to her house as I shouted, 'Serves you right, serves you right,' with a throat constricted with hatred and love all mixed up together.

Then my mother came out and called me in, and I went to bed early. I didn't have any supper, not because I was refused it, but because I didn't feel like it.

But I had a good breakfast on Sunday morning. It was laver bread and bacon and fried potatoes; and when I saw Mildred Reilly next I stuck my tongue out at her.

Why do you think this episode has importance for the author? He says that it is because *Something Borrowed* brings back vivid memories:

'The "Patch" no longer exists, as an air-raid shelter was built on it during the war. The girl I "married" now has several children and has long since left the district. But it is still all there in my mind's eye. The agony of first love and the cruelty of children to one another, the very fabric of life itself.'

Moments of pain – both physical and mental – and excitement seem to find a prominent place in autobiographies. Sometimes those moments may be trivial and insignificant to others, but very important to the writer.

Here is Patricia Beer writing about the excitement of swimming and the 'agony', for her, of entering the cold sea in Devon:

It was at Straight Point I learned to swim. My father, who nearly always bathed too – my mother never did – gave me a few unsystematic lessons, but I really taught myself at the age of about five. It was a safe beach with no currents, and once I was in the water I was left alone, and in any case my father, without his glasses, could not have told either of us from a dolphin. I first of all discovered how I could support myself, and even move, by a kind of dog-paddle, and on to this I later superimposed a few more or less conventional strokes. I never became a good swimmer in the sense of winning races or displaying beautiful style, but in an unambitious, inelegant way I *was* a good swimmer, if that could mean being thoroughly at home in the water rather than master of it.

I greatly enoyed swimming, but I dreaded the initial getting wet. I was thin and had a poor circulation, and the water always seemed icy, even in August. I was invariably the last to get under, which was psychologically painful too. I knew quite well as I watched my friends and relatives swimming and splashing that the agony of plunging would be less if I could be the first to endure it. We all ran down to the sea together, so I had a perfectly fair chance, but I never managed it. I tried everything: letting the water creep up by millimetres so that my body hardly noticed the encroachment, sprinkling a few drops over my shoulders and chest to anticipate and so lessen the final anguish – nothing worked. I should really like to know whether I was more cowardly and less resolute than the others or whether, in spite of their shrieks and exclamations, they in fact suffered less.

For nine years, Frank Norman lived in Dr Barnardo's Homes. His account of one particular Saturday afternoon is, understandably, well remembered.

One Saturday afternoon I was lying about in the recreation hut, when suddenly a prefect appeared and asked me what I was doing. I told him nothing, though in fact I was hanging about in the hope that someone would come in with a cigarette and give me a puff. 'Well, the second eleven football team are one short,' he said.

'So what,' said I.

'So you can play,' said he.

'You must be joking.'

'No I'm not.'

'But I don't know the rules even.'

'That doesn't matter, it's only the second eleven.'

'I don't know how to play.'

'Look,' he said, losing patience. 'If you don't play I'll smash your face in.'

'Have it your way,' I shrugged. 'But don't blame me if we lose.'

'There isn't anyone else we can get at such short notice,' he said. 'The rest of the boys have gone off to the pictures.' With a faint heart I followed him to the sports room where he kitted me out with boots, shorts and jersey and then escorted me to the football pitch where the other ten boys waited to play against a local village team. Many derogatory remarks were passed by the other members of the Home team as they saw me approaching. The referee blew his whistle and I reluctantly joined the rest of the boys on the field. The stupid game began, the two teams rushing furiously up and down the field kicking the ball to one another and shouting 'Over here, over here!' Now and then the ball would come near me, and though the uppermost thought in my mind was to run away from it I did kick it once or twice, in no particular direction, for all I wanted to do was to get it away from me before I was barged by one of the husky boys from the opposing team. Towards the end of the first half the visitors scored a goal, making them one and us nil. The ball was placed in the centre once more and kicked off. Suddenly out of the blue I saw it bouncing in my direction with about six members of the village team charging after it. Taking a few steps forward I gave it a mighty kick and the next thing I knew there was a mighty roar as spectators and both teams shouted 'GOAL!'

Sheepishly I looked around and saw that I had deftly kicked the ball into *our own* goal mouth. The goalie stood scratching his head with an astonished expression on his face, and there were many threats of 'Wait till we get you after', from my fellow-sportesmen in the Home team. At the end of the first half the visitors were two goals up, one of their own and one of mine.

During the break I kept well out of harm's way at the other end of the field.

At the commencement of the second half, the captain of our side ordered me in no uncertain terms to keep well out of the way and not to touch the ball, unless there was absolutely no other alternative. I willingly complied with his wishes and confined myself to parts of the field where the ball was not. Within fifteen minutes the Home side had scored two goals; their blood was up and they played like tigers – several fouls were incurred. But the referee (a member of the staff) turned a blind eye to them. The visitors retaliated but were unable to score a third goal. I have to own that the Barnardo Boys put on a fine show, especially as they were playing with one man short, for I was contributing nothing whatever to their success.

Several minutes before the final whistle I stood minding my own business in the penalty area of our goal when suddenly I turned to see the ball cannonading in my direction, with all the members of both sides charging after it. Pedro had often told me of the bullfights of his home land, and at the moment I knew exactly how a *torero* must feel when an enraged bull bears down on him. They were all yelling at the top of their voices and I would have fled if I had not been riveted to the spot by fear. A member of the opposite side gave the ball a pulverising kick straight at my face. I put up my hands to protect myself and the ball bounded off them, the force of the kick knocking me to the ground. 'Hand ball!' they yelled in unison. The referee blew his brains out on the whistle and awarded a penalty kick to the villagers. The boys jeered at me and threatened my life as the captain of the other side placed the ball on the penalty spot and thundered the ball into the net. Our goalie had not the slightest chance of saving it for the shot was true and as straight as an arrow.

The whistle blew, indicating the end of the game and perhaps the end of my life. My head bowed in shame, I ambled along behind my fellows to the showers; no one spoke to me as we entered the wash-house, but the atmosphere was electric and I knew that I was doomed. As we took off our football togs two of them came over to me and became insulting. I tried to explain to them that I had been shanghaied into the game, but although they were well aware of that it seemed to make no difference. Without warning one of them took a swing at me, which caught me on the side of the head and sent me sprawling on the floor. Painfully I staggered to my feet hoping that that was going to be the end of it, but no such luck, the great oaf struck me again and once more I hit the deck. Another of the boys, completely unable to contain himself, pounced on top of me and began to pummel my body. Crouching, I covered my face with my hands as best I could but still suffered considerable damage: 'Okay that's enough', said the referee who must have been present throughout the whole of the proceedings, but had not bothered to intervene. The boy stopped hitting me and with a black eye, split lip and multiple bruises I staggered to my feet and wandered away quietly by myself without uttering another word. At tea that evening the assembled boys glanced at me askance but no one said a word.

What impression do you have of Frank Norman here? Do you feel sorry for him or do your sympathies lie with the team? Underline any words or phrases that back up what you think. His decision to include this episode from his life shows its importance for him. Do you think he has remembered it accurately? Would he have remembered the early conversation word for word? And all the other details? Might he have added to his memory? And, if he has, does it matter?

Some time ago, in sorting out some papers of an aunt, following her death, a pupil came across a typewritten piece of autobiography. It wasn't about her aunt because she knew that the facts of her aunt's early life were very different from those written down, and there was no indication of who wrote it; but she thought it must have been a friend. This is the beginning of the account:

60 YEARS ON
Many moons ago, I was born on a farm near Hever, which had been in my Mother's family for over two hundred years. She was the last unmarried daughter left. She met my Father whilst skating on a nearby pond and they fell in love.

Unbeknown to anybody they went to London and were married at St George's, Hanover Square, Registry Office. They returned to the farm for four years. When I was born, they decided to sell up and move to a flat in a London suburb. As for me, I was going to live on a farm owned by an uncle and stay there indefinitely.

I have many happy memories of that three-gabled farm house, standing in solitude down the end of a long lane. I slept in a four-poster bed surrounded by curtains and at the slightest movement, it started up the clanging of the curtain rings. An inquisitive bat sometimes found his way into the open, latticed window, forcing me to hide under the bedclothes until he decided to depart.

Promptly every morning at six, I would hear my Aunt pump up the sparkling water from the well, ready for my Uncle to take to the various animals. I would dress and descend that lovely oak staircase for breakfast, often to find a couple of moorhen's eggs on my plate, which were probably taken from the nest on the nearby pond.

The next job was milking, by hand in those far-off days – an art I learned from my Uncle. The milk was then strained and put into large enamel pans and placed on the stove to be brought nearly to the boil. When cool, the luscious cream would be skimmed off. They made butter. This process was all done by hand, the butter being weighed into half-pound pats and sold to various callers who would often appear carrying yokes to collect a couple of pails of water freshly drawn from the well.

The pond in front of the house always fascinated me and I was not content until my Uncle improvised a fishing rod. With some bait, I managed to catch a fairly large carp. I was so excited and made so much noise, that everybody thought I had fallen in the water. I ended up by catching twenty carp and two tench.

Much to my dismay, my Aunt would not agree for us to eat them and they were finally given to the carter's boy.

At milking time, my Cousin and I would go and collect the cows. On one occasion she was walking rather close to the backside of one of them when it suddenly decided to mess all down the front of her clean frock, which greatly upset her.

When harvesting approached, a number of farmers with their dogs would gather round the last remaining piece of corn and shoot the rabbits as they ran out.

Before Christmas, my Aunt would be busy fattening up the turkeys; pigs would be killed and large portions would be hung up the chimney to be smoked. On Boxing Day, a shooting-party would set out, whatever the weather, and return at dusk with a haul of rabbits. After sharing them out, they would sit down before a well-earned meal, washed down by home-brewed cider.

I stayed at this farm until I was seven years of age, and owing to the fact that the School Board man was checking on me, I had to return to my parents' flat and go to school.

The young English student at work

- Try reading some autobiographies in full. Roald Dahl's *Boy* (from which 'The Great Mouse Plot' on pages 44 to 45 is taken) talks about the bestselling author's schooldays. *Cider with Rosie* is a popular autobiography describing Laurie Lee's country upbringing in the 1920s. Both are easily obtainable.
- Some others to look out for: *Under the Eye of the Clock* by Christopher Nolan, *Testament of Youth* by Vera Brittain, *The Only Child* by James Kirkup, *The African Child* by Camara Laye, *Over the Bridge* by Richard Church, *Grandad with Snails* by Michael Baldwin, *Ring of Bright Water* by Gavin Maxwell, and *My Left Foot* by Christy Brown. And have a look in your school or public library for others.

READING TRAVELLERS' TALES

In many ways, reading accounts of people's travels is like reading autobiography. Travel writing emphasizes the places and people visited more so than autobiography, but they obviously overlap.

Many travellers have been fascinating writers, mainly because of the views they have had about the countries they have visited. But you sometimes wonder if they are speaking the truth. The Roman senator Sidonius Apollinaris, writing about one and a half thousand years ago, said of the Burgundians, who were living in what today is central France, that they:

> are seven feet high, grease their hair with rancid butter, have enormous appetites and speak in stentorian tones.

Now test yourself

- Have a guess at what the last phrase, 'in stentorian tones' means.

- Then look up 'stentorian' in your dictionary. Were you right?

How accurate do you think Sidonius was being?

A few years ago, Colin Thubron, who has written many books about his travels, visited China. Here he describes a hospital:

> Four men lay on wooden stretchers in the Nanjing hospital, while a doctor pressed acupuncture needles into them. He looked bland, matter-of-fact, too young. Tired crescent-moons looped under his eyes. Patients were often treated here if Western medicine miscarried, he said, but if acupuncture failed they would revert to pain-killing drugs.

I stood watching and ignorant, while one by one he turned the men into pin-cushions. They followed him with sultry, half-closed eyes. One man had goitre in the leg and stomach. Another, a wincing youth with long, aesthetic feet and hands, was suffering high blood pressure. They grunted and frowned as the needles went in. The doctor talked of them as if they were absent, and they seemed to conspire in this. They never spoke. The worst had a stone in his kidney – bigger than a soya bean, the doctor said. The man was grinning. He was in much pain. He would receive acupuncture for five days, to expand the ureter, said the doctor, but if the stone was still not released, they'd operate.

What were the chances of success, I asked?

The doctor pointed to a tray scattered with small dark stones. 'There.'

In the last bed lay an old peasant wearing pyjamas and a perforated cap. His toes had almost rotted away, as if from years in the paddy fields. He stretched inert, but followed us with frightened eyes.

'This one had a blood circulation problem.' The doctor touched a needle into the man's groin. 'He was half paralysed. Western medicine couldn't do anything. We've treated him in twenty days, and he's nearly cured.'

I wondered if he were a hysteric. 'Why?'

But the doctor would not guess. He dealt in cures, not theories.

I slipped away and peered into the pharmacy. It was banked with wooden drawers for more than a thousand different herbs, and the air was pungent with hypnotic aromas, like a spice bazaar.

A line of white-jacketed girls was fastidiously preparing mixtures for each patient, assigning them for immersion in tea or soup. As I watched them, I noticed a hole in the wall above their heads. Inside it, a pair of yellow incisor teeth appeared. Nobody took any notice. The next moment a colossal rat came scuttling down the piping. The girl beneath it was mixing herbs with dainty exactitude. It plopped onto the counter and dashed over her hands. I waited for a scream. But she did not emit a sound. She merely glanced up as if at some tiresome pet, then continued sorting herbs with fussy deliberations of her white fingers.

What sort of person is the doctor, according to the writer's description? Does there seem to be any difference between the author's initial reaction and what emerges during the conversation? Did you enjoy the last paragraph? Write down below any of the words or phrases that help to make it lively and easy to visualize.

....

....

And here is Thubron visiting a school in Nanjing:

I gained permission to visit the city's top high school, and nobody pretended it was ordinary. The tuition and maintenance fees together cost two-thirds of an average worker's salary, and the entrance examination was gruelling.

I was met by an official with an anxious, kindly face. A little group of visitors had assembled. His introductory speech stressed the teaching of creativity and independence, parroting the current Party line. 'During the Cultural Revolution we had a wrong policy. The Gang of Four used Revolutionary slogans to lead the students astray. Intellectuals were crushed...' My attention strayed to the cluster of schoolgirls assigned to us as guides. They stood awkwardly together in hideous purple uniforms. The official's voice rose in formal harangue. '... When a nation wishes to develop, it needs intellectuals... the Cultural Revolution, a tragic mistake... a necessary lesson...Gang of Four... pernicious... mistakes...'

We trooped into the schoolyard, and one of the fourteen-year-old girls came alongside me. I was not sure if she was there to guide me or to practise her English. I tested her covertly: 'Do you like your school uniform?'

'This?' Her expression crinkled into laughter. 'It's *terrible*. Don't you think?'

'Yes, it is.' I looked with relief into a brown, puppyish face, rather pretty. I said: 'Your principal talked about discussion groups. I wondered what you discussed.'

'Principal?' She grimaced comically. 'He's not our principal. He's just a yes-and-no man.'

'Propaganda?'

'Yes,' she giggled. 'There's not much political discussion any more. Luckily.'

On the tarmac in front of us several hundred lethargic little boys were drawn up in ranks for drill. They all moved at different times and speeds, listlessly. 'They're much better than usual,' the girl said. 'They must know you're here.'

From our guided tour it was hard to sense anything beyond a mind-crushing discipline, the Confucian respect for rote-learning and inherited wisdom. We were shown into classrooms whose fifty-odd students only raised their eyes from their books when ordered. The teacher's command was absolute. They were all expecting us. Model pupils delivered dead-sounding speeches: 'We think our school is lively and interesting. We all study hard...'

In this wall of formality, the only window was my guide. In her I discovered a vital but homesick girl, who found her teachers too didactic. She loved reading, she said, or just sitting alone in the dusty garden of osmanthus and pines by one of the classrooms. On Saturdays she rushed home to her parents – factory engineers living 20 miles outside the city. Her father was even smaller than she was, she said, and kept her doubled up with laughter all weekend.

As for the school, its occupants seemed frozen in pre-adolescence. Boys and girls were rigorously separated. One or two, she had heard, maintained covert friendships – a little kissing and passing of love-notes – but she was not sure. Her friends did not even talk about clothes fashion. Their worst crimes were chatting after lights-out in the dormitories (for which they were ejected into the corridors).

'What about the food?' I asked.

'Our food? It's horrible.'

'And the teachers?'

She wrinkled her nose.

Yet somehow, I thought, this system had fostered her. Her independence was more eloquent than the official's speech about nurturing it.

We wandered through the empty science-rooms and into a small biology museum lined with stuffed animals and marinated reptiles. We came to a standstill in front of a jar of chicks. They hung blind and long-dead in their amber. When the girl looked at them I thought she might joke: their nakedness was faintly ludicrous. But instead her face glazed into sadness, and she murmured: 'I feel pity for them.'

As she said this, I realized that I was still steeped in a conventional anxiety about Chinese cruelty, and that ever since entering the country I had unconsciously waited for some expression of tenderness, of empathy with pain. And now here it was, absurdly, expressed for bottled birds, and I felt a sharp, unexpected surge of warmth, as if somebody – either she or I – had been absolved. I wanted to hug her.

Instead, a few minutes later, I shook her hand in farewell, and partly because the phoney principal was hovering near us, added formally that I hoped she would build (as the slogans say) a new China. She seemed small and precarious for such construction, but perhaps the time was right.

The official's face is described as 'anxious' and the girls were standing 'awkwardly'. Can you offer any reason why this might be so? There is criticism of the school by both the writer and the girl: the uniform, the bored little boys, the 'mind-crushing discipline', large classes of 50 plus, dull methods of teaching, separation of boys from girls, the food. Does the writer come to any conclusions, though, about there being *some* good in the system?

Now test yourself

- Imagine guiding Colin Thubron round your school during a normal working day. Do you think you can work out some of the questions he might ask, having read these two extracts?

- On a piece of paper or in your notebook, write down what you think these questions might be. Then, after each question, write down what your answer would be.

Gavin Patterson won a student travel writing competition for this essay. He was visiting the Philippines:

 I took two tortuous journeys to get my bags and bicycle upstairs. Zamboanga's Unique Hotel sits atop a busy shipping office and the stairs are permanently blocked by silent, staring squatters awaiting their turn in the queue.

At the reception desk Lourdes was powdering her face while Evelyn chattered aimlessly. My feet were a mess of putrid flesh, begging for a rest. I proudly peeled off my clinging socks and the girls giggled nervously.

I was given my old room off the main hall: a long bare rectangle with a permanently blocked toilet and a tapless basin squeezed into a cupboard-sized cubicle. By the door stood Rey, from Air Force Intelligence, beer bottle in hand. Inside, an old crate of empty San Miguel bottles still lay in the corner, but the bed sheets were new.

I shut the door and lay down to ease the throbbing in my feet. Seconds later, the ever-inquisitive Evelyn burst in, offering help. I asked for medication and she nodded vaguely, giggled and disappeared, leaving the door wide open.

Heavy metal thudded in from Rey's suite next door. He was encamped with two others, together negotiating the surrender of 500 Muslim rebels. Guerrilla leaders arrived for talks throughout the afternoon and Rey brought them to admire my feet.

Evelyn returned with two huge 10 000 unit penicillin pills, crushed one and pressed the powder into my sores, assuring me it worked.

I sat on the bed, feet up, trying to read the newspaper. Looking straight ahead I could see out into the crowded hall. Behind and below through the torn mosquito netting lay the street: a mass of foodstalls, revving motorcycles, and squat men staggering under huge parcels. It led to the docks.

The bellboy arrived to polish my floor with a half-coconut. Lourdes came in to pluck her eyebrows in my mirror. There was a constant stream of visitors: the nosy; the concerned; the indefatigable clutterers. I dozed briefly, only to be woken by a crash as Leon, the hotel owner, tripped over my bicycle and dropped a crate of beer beside the bed.

It was dark: a brownout; the only light a candle on an upturned lavatory bowl. Ignoring his own 'Consumption of alcohol prohibited' signs, he just smiled and began opening bottles. Solitude here is impossible. As the local philosophy goes, if you're alone, you're lonely.

Apart from his bags, bicycle and feet, the writer focuses on the people and the goings-on in the hotel. Would you say he admired/disliked/tolerated them? Can you back up your verdict with any evidence?

Each year, many visitors go to Hadrian's Wall and imagine what life might have been like on a Roman fort. In his book *A Pennine Journey*, Alfred Wainwright describes the scene and his reactions:

I walked slowly through a dead city, along a main street lined with shattered walls. A profound stillness lay over the camp, a silence so intense that I could hear my heart pounding as I went along. The effect of this wholesale devastation is almost overwhelming to the mind. In a way, the scene is awful, horrible.

The ages which have wrought this decay are forgotten; I felt, as I stood there, that I was the sole witness of some terrible catastrophe which had wiped out a community of which I had been a member, that but an hour had passed since it happened and I was still unnerved by the shock …

It is as if an earthquake had overthrown the place, and all the inhabitants had fled in terror. Not long ago this street was a busy thoroughfare, the courtyard a tumult of voices; there was singing and shouting everywhere. Now it was silenced forever; death had stolen in and chilled the very stones. An empire had fallen.

Look at the photograph on page 73 of a Roman fort on Hadrian's Wall. If you hadn't read the extract first, do you think the photo would have conveyed the same feelings?

R EADING DIARIES

Unless they are fictional diaries, like Adrian Mole's, you can feel rather an intruder or eavesdropper reading a diary not intended for anyone else's eyes. Diaries, like those of the Reverend Francis Kilvert who kept a private diary for nine years before his early death towards the end of last century, can offer a fascinating and detailed picture of day-to-day life. Here are some extracts, dating from 1870. The first has little to do with him:

TUESDAY 8 FEBRUARY

From Wye Cliff to Pont Faen. Miss Child in great force. She showed me her clever drawings of horses and told me the adventures of the brown wood owl 'Ruth' which she took home from here last year. She wanted to call the owl 'Eve' but Mrs Bridge said it should be called 'Ruth'. She and her sister, stranded in London at night, went to London Bridge hotel (having missed the last train) with little money and no luggage except the owl in a basket.

The owl hooted all night in spite of their putting it up the chimney, before the looking glass, under the bedclothes, and in a circle of lighted candles which they hoped it would mistake for the sun. The owl went on hooting, upset the basket, got out and flew about the room. The chambermaid almost frightened to death, dared not come inside the door. Miss Child asked the waiter to get some mice for 'Ruth' but none could be got.

WEDNESDAY 9 FEBRUARY

A very cold night and a slight shower of snow fell early this morning. Then it froze all day. The mountains all white. Went up the Cwm to White Ash. Old Sarah Probert groaning and rolling about in bed. Read to her Mark VI and made sure she knew the Lord's Prayer by heart, making her repeat it. Hannah Jones smoking a short black pipe by the fire, and her daughter, a young mother with dark eyes and her hair hanging loose, nursing her baby and displaying her charms.

FRIDAY 11 FEBRUARY

Last night broke the key of my musical box whilst winding up the box. Went down at midnight and tried to turn the broken key barrel with the tongs – unsuccessfully, and the teeth of the comb stuck in the midst of a tune hitched on the spikes all night. Very bad for the box, so I got up early and directly after breakfast ran over to Hay across the fields in a keen white bright frost. Bevan the watchmaker wound up the box, set it right and mended the key. Bought four valentines at Herthen's after searching through a tumbled heap for a long time and ordered some cheese at Hadley's. Coming back the hills were lovely.

The other guests and the staff of the hotel cannot have been too grateful for Miss Child and her owl, not least the waiter requested to get some mice! Are there enough details to suggest what kind of lady Miss Child must have been?

One of the most famous diarists was Samuel Pepys, who kept a diary over a long period of time. He used a cipher so that nobody could read what he had written and, in several cases, it isn't really surprising! Scholars at the beginning of the last century managed to decode it. Here are three very short entries:

1 JANUARY 1662

Waking this morning out of my sleep on a sudden, I did with my elbow hit my wife a great blow over her face and nose, which waked her with pain – at which I was sorry. And to sleep again.

6 JANUARY 1663

Myself somewhat vexed at my wife's neglect in leaving of her scarf and waistcoat in the coach today that brought us from Westminster, though I confess she did give them to me to look after – yet it was her fault not to see that I did take them out of the coach.

1 DECEMBER 1663

At noon I home to dinner with my poor wife, with whom now-a-days I enjoy great pleasure in her company and learning of Arithmetic.

With the information gleaned from these three extracts, what sort of man do you think Samuel Pepys was? And, given the chance, what do you think his wife would have written about him?

The author, Keith Waterhouse, imagines a schoolboy's diary:

MONDAY 1 MARCH

St David's Day. Got up. Went to school. Came home. Had fish fingers. Went to bed. Started to count up to a billion but only got up to 7,643 for the reason that, my father made me stop. He said that if he had to come up to my bedroom once more, that he would strangle me. This man is dangerous.

TUESDAY 2 MARCH

Got up. Had breakfast. Got ticked off by my father for holding my breath. People should not get ticked off for holding your breath, for the reason that, it is a free country. Therefore I hate my father. He thinks he is somebody but he is nobody. Also he have hair coming out of his nose.

WEDNESDAY 3 MARCH

Ember Day. I am going to get my father. He has been asking for it and now he is going to get it. Just because I was sucking bread. He go purple and bangs the table. If he was Run Over I would be glad. He look like a Jelly and also is Smelly.

THURSDAY 4 MARCH

Moon's first quarter 3.01 am. Got up. Went to school. Watched telly. Left roller skate at top of stairs, but it did not work. This only works in comics such as Whizzer and Chips etc ... therefore, comics are stupid. They, the people you are trying to get, do not step on the roller skate and go ker-bam-bam-bam-bam-bam-kkkklunk-splat-aaargh. Instead of this, they just pick up the roller skate and say (This house getting more like a pigsty every day). He is Potty and also Grotty.

FRIDAY 5 MARCH

Today I said I was going to John's house but I did not, I went to the Pet Shop to buy a poisonous snake, but they did not have one. The copper-head, the Rattle-snake, the cobra and the Mamba are among the poisonous snakes to be found in the world. The man in the Pet Shop just laughed and tried to sell me a hamster. I am going to get him after I have got my father.

SATURDAY 6 MARCH

Sun rises 7.35 am. I have got an Idea from watching Telly. It is where they were in a certain foreign country and he, the Tall one invents this special kind of warfare. It comes to pass that this Warfare is something nobody else knows about, therefore he wins it. It is called (long word) warfare. (Long word) warfare is where, they do not fight with guns, tanks, also armoured cars, thus killing them, you fight with a person's mind so therefore he will do what they tell him. It begins with the letter P. This I am going to do to my Father.

SUNDAY 7 MARCH

Second in Lent, first day of Operation Stare. Operation Stare is where, you just look at your father. You do not say anything, you just Look. This was when he was reading the paper, also when he was painting chest of drawers. He did not know I was there until, he saw me. I was just Staring at him. This is operation Stare. It is (long word) warfare. It did not work, as he said (If you nothing to do you can tidy up your room). Another example of the poisonous snake is, the sea-snake. He has spots all on his neck. He is Spotty and also Potty.

MONDAY 8 MARCH

On this important day I invented the art of making yourself cry. You have to pretend that you have a dog. This could be a Sheep-dog or numerous others, it is called Zebadee. You have to pretend that it runs away in the park and, you come to this swamp and it rescues you and die. After you have gone into the swamp to get it out, the (dog). It dies and you are sorry. This can make you cry, but my father just say, (Stop snivelling or I will give you something snivel about).

TUESDAY 9 MARCH

Nothing happened. I am still going to get my Father. I will make him Crack.

WEDNESDAY 10 MARCH

Birthday of Prince Edward. Today I got my Father to think that I could not move my left arm, also that I could not feel anything in it, it was Dead. I thought this would make him sorry and it did. He went all white and call me Son. He pinch my arm and asked if I could feel it, I replied that (I could not.) We had better see Dr Murray!!! he exclaimed, but just as he was helping me on with my coat to go to Dr Murray, he sticks a pin in my arm accidentally on purpose. This hurt me so I said (Oh.) He went all purple and call me Lad.

THURSDAY 11 MARCH

Got up. Decided to Lie Low.

FRIDAY 12 MARCH

Full moon 3.34 am. On this day Operation Blink came into being. You just blink your eyes all the time, it drive him Potty. Also, at the same time you must screw your nose sideways and also make your mouth go down, while you are blinking your eyes. I did this all the time, until my Father Went Out.

SATURDAY 13 MARCH

An unlucky day for my father. On this, the second day of the famous victorious Operation Blink, he take me to see (The Railway Children). I was sick on the bus going, also in the cinema. When we came out, he asked (Are you feeling better now). I replied that I was, therefore, we went on the bus. I was sick. My father does not know it, but, I did it on purpose. I have discovered the art of being sick. It is my secret. I was Sick all over his shoes. The (Railway Children) is a good picture, it better than Rolf Harris. He is cracking.

SUNDAY 14 MARCH

Third in Lent. Operation Blink and Operation Sick are still in being. I said I was going to Get him and I have got him. If you keep sniffling, he does not say anything but you can tell he does not like it, this big Vein stands out in his forehead and sort of goes throb-throb. This is Operation Sniffle. This morning I heard him say to Mr Baker (Are they born like it or what, I don't know what I am going to do with him). This means that I have won. He knew that I was holding my breath all through lunchtime, but he does not say anything, he just Went Out. This also means, that I have won. Today I have started counting up to a billion and have got up to 10 500. I have got to get up to 25 000 before going to bed, or it will mean that I have lost the Battle. He has come back in and, he knows that I am counting up to a billion but, he is just staring at wall and drinking whisky. It is 3.10 pm on Sunday 14 March, the day of Victory. He has cracked, and must sign my Terms.

Did you notice that there were mistakes in the entries? Keith Waterhouse has made mistakes on purpose. Can you think why?

READING LETTERS

In *Night Mail*, a poem you can read on pages 96 to 97, the poet lists types of letters that people receive. It covers a whole variety, but two main categories of letter emerge:

1. **Personal** – thank you letters; 'letters of joy from girl and boy'; invitations; love letters; gossipy, chatty letters from family and friends.
2. **Formal** – 'letters from banks'; bills; job applications; letters from Headteachers to parents of truanting children!

Fewer personal letters are written now than there used to be. A major factor must be the influence of the telephone; it is so much easier and quicker. The telephone is particularly important if you wish to make arrangements, as you don't have to wait a day or so for a reply. And to hear someone's voice, of course, can be exciting.

Before the telephone, however, letters were the obvious way to keep in touch with friends and relations. Letters written a century or so ago can give a fascinating insight into the life and customs of the age. One letter gives an account of a journey from London to the north of England by boat. The journey was supposedly more comfortable than going by horse and coach even though it took four days to reach the Yorkshire coast where the boat anchored. Getting into a little boat from the larger vessel in the darkness – and with a heavy swell – took some nerve. Unfortunately, some presents the writer of the letter had brought as a gift for his sister were lost overboard.

The reason such an event can be recounted nearly two hundred years later is because a letter was written. Though there cannot be many families lucky enough to have any letters that old, it is not uncommon to come across the occasional letter tucked away in a drawer or cupboard.

It can be absorbing and moving to read an old love letter from a husband to his wife away on military service during a war, or even to find out how much it cost to take the family to the zoo forty years ago. When families telephone each other and swap details of their everyday lives, so much that is spoken simply disappears and is forgotten as soon as the telephone receiver is replaced.

What a shame it would be if the art of letter writing were not maintained. When we write a letter, we can say and mean so much more because we have the time to think carefully about what we want to say before we write it down. Those to whom we write can think about the letters, re-reading them as often as they please. If they are special in some way, they can be well worth keeping.

Much more leisure time is available now than it used to be, so is it simply that we have become lazier? Do we not have enough spare time each week to write letters to our families and friends? The excitement of finding a personal letter on the mat amongst the so-called 'junk mail' is surely enough of an incentive for us to write back in reply. If we do not write letters, we can hardly expect to receive any.

Fashions and attitudes change. It used to be considered poor not to reply to a letter the same day that it was received. No firm or business could allow itself the disgrace of a reply being sent later than the following day. Is this still the case?

Computerized communications are at the opposite end of the spectrum from personal letters. During a recent radio broadcast, a man explained how he had received a letter requesting payment for an item for which he had already submitted a cheque. At the bottom of the letter, it stated that the sum due was £00.00. He assumed that this was a rather novel form of receipt. A fortnight later, he was amazed and annoyed to receive a reminder, printed in red, indicating that he had not paid the £00.00. In anger, he telephoned the company. When he was told that, if he sent a cheque for £00.00, it would satisfy the computer, he exploded and wrote a strongly worded letter to the managing director. Needless to say, he did not receive a reply.

If you read almost any letter written last century, such a sequence of nonsensical communications is shown up even more sharply. Family letters written by an old lady, born and brought up in the Yorkshire Dales in the 1860s and 70s, show a delightful turn of phrase. She worked as a maid to a local well-to-do family. She writes to her family explaining the beginning of her working day:

> … I know not why I am so fatigued, for I manage seven hours of sleep before the bell summons me at quarter past six. On rising, I tend to the range (which I have learnt to keep burning by night) so that I can warm some water for my master. I wait without the room, jug in hand, until the clock strikes the first beat of seven of the clock. I knock and enter, averting my eyes from all but the table and bowl …

> *… I know not why I am so fatigued, for I manage seven hours of sleep before the bell summons me at quarter past six. On rising, I tend to the range (which I have learnt to keep burning by night) so that I can warm some water for my master. I wait without the room, jug in hand, until the clock strikes the first beat of seven of the clock. I knock and enter, averting my eyes from all but the table and bowl …*

Her education? At a tiny village school in the Dales until she was barely eleven!

Now test yourself

Write down what you think are the advantages and disadvantages of:
1 Communicating by letter and;

2 Communicating by telephone. Which one comes out on top with more advantages and fewer disadvantages than the other?

Like diaries, letters can give an insight into the people and places described, episodes and activities, the character of the writer and sometimes of the person being written to.

What do you make of this letter sent to Gerald Brenan by the painter, Dora Carrington?

> A BaD, CoLd
>   DuLL letter
> But we live in a
>   BaD DuLL coLD
>   climate
> and I've a cold, Bad, DuLL character
>
> oh to be my Persian cat
> lying snug upon the mat

It is rather like a letter written by the novelist, D H Lawrence:

> Here I am – London – gloom – yellow air – bad cold – bed – old house –
> Morris wallpaper – visitors – English voices – tea in old cups – poor D.H.L.
> perfectly miserable, as if he was in his tomb.

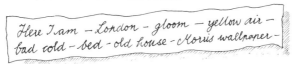

Do you think that there is enough in either of the two letters for you to say what
the writers were like?

Branwell Brontë, brother to the famous novelist sisters – Charlotte, Emily and
Anne, died from drinking too much. Here is a note he sent to someone in the
village of Haworth where they lived:

Sunday, Noon

> Dear John,
>   I shall feel very much obliged to you if you can contrive to get me Five pence
> worth of Gin in a proper measure.
>   Should it be speedily got I could perhaps take it from you or Billy at the lane top,
> or, what would be quite as well, sent out for, to you.
>   I anxiously ask the favour because I know the good it will do me.
>   *Punctually* at Half-past Nine in the morning you will be paid the 5d. out of a shilling
> given me then.–Yours,
>
>   B. B.

Can you point to a word in the first sentence and an idea in the second, which
suggest that his sisters would not approve?

Word ....

Idea ....

The author of *Charlotte's Web*, E B White, writes to an editor:

> Hotel Gramercy Park
> New York
> 1 March
>
> Dear Gene:
> Herewith an unfinished MS of a book called *Stuart Little*. It would seem to be for children,
> but I'm not fussy who reads it. You said you wanted to look at this, so I am presenting it
> thus in its incomplete state. There are about ten or twelve thousand words so far, roughly.
> You will be shocked and grieved to discover that the principal character in the story has
> somewhat the attributes and appearance of a mouse. This does not mean that I am either
> challenging or denying Mr. Disney's genius. At the risk of seeming a very whimsical fellow
> indeed, I will have to break down and confess to you that Stuart Little appeared to me in a
> dream, all complete, with his hat, his cane, and his brisk manner. Since he was the only fictional
> figure ever to honor and disturb my sleep, I was deeply touched, and felt that I was not free to
> change him into a grasshopper or a wallaby. Luckily he bears no resemblance, either physically
> or temperamentally, to Mickey. I guess that's a break for all of us.
> Stop in here for a drink some fine afternoon. We are enjoying room service and would
> like to see you.
> Andy White

Do you think Mr White exaggerates when he uses these phrases: 'shocked and grieved', 'I will have to break down and confess', 'honor and disturb', 'I was deeply touched'? Can you suggest why he might have exaggerated?

Here is another letter by D H Lawrence, but very different from the earlier one:

Villa Igea
Villa di Gargnano,
Lago di Garda, Italy
Friday 6 October 1912

DEAR MAC,

Your books came today, your letter long ago. Now I am afraid I put you to a lot of trouble and expense, and feel quite guilty. But thanks a thousand times. And F thanks you too.

Today it is so stormy. The lake is dark, and with white lambs all over it. The steamer rocks as she goes by. There are no sails stealing past. The vines are yellow and red, and fig trees are in flame on the mountains. I can't bear to be in England when I am in Italy. It makes me feel so soiled. Yesterday F and I went down along the lake towards Maderno. We climbed down from a little olive wood, and swam. It was evening, so weird, and a great black cloud trailing over the lake. And tiny little lights of villages came out, so low down, right across the water. Then great lightnings split out.–No, I don't believe England need be so grubby. What does it matter if one is poor, and risks one's livelihood and reputation. One *can* have the necessary things, life, and love, and clean warmth. Why is England so shabby?

The Italians here sing. They are very poor, they buy two-penn'orth of butter and a penn'orth of cheese. But they are healthy and they lounge about in the little square where the boats come up and nets are mended, like kings. And they go by the window proudly, and they don't hurry or fret. And the women walk straight and look calm. And the men adore children – they are glad of their children even if they're poor. I think they haven't many ideas, but they look well, and they have strong blood.

I go in a little place to drink wine near Bogliaco. It is the living room of the house. The father, sturdy as these Italians are, gets up from the table and bows to me. The family is having supper. He brings me red wine to another table, then sits down again, and the mother ladles him soup from the bowl. He has his shirt-sleeves rolled up and his shirt collar open. Then he nods and 'click-clicks' to the small baby, that the mother, young and proud, is feeding with soup from a big spoon. The grandfather, white-moustached, sits a bit effaced by the father. A little girl eats soup. The grandmother by the big, open fire sits and quietly scolds another little girl. It reminds me so of home when I was a boy. They are all so warm with life. The father reaches his thick brown hand to play with the baby – the mother looks quickly away catching my eye. Then he gets up to wait on me, and thinks my bad Italian can't understand that a quarter litre of wine is 15 centesimi (1¼ d.) when I give him thirty. He doesn't understand tips. And the huge lot of figs for 20 centesimi.

Why can't you ever come? You could if you wanted to, at Christmas. Why not? We should love to have you, and it costs little.

Notice how observant the writer is: the clear description helps us feel what the landscape and weather are like; we feel as if we are present in the room with the Italian family having their supper.

There appears little need for description in the next letter, for in this case – as the writer says – 'few words are best'.

> Mr Molyneux
> Few words are best. My letters to my Father have come to the eyes of some. Neither can I condemn any but you for it. If it be so, you have played the very knave with me; and so I will make you know, if I have good proof of it. I assure you before God, that if I ever know you do so much as read any letter I write to my Father, without his commandment, or my consent, I will thrust my dagger into you. And trust to it, for I speak it in earnest. In the meantime, farewell.
> From Court this last day of May 1578.
> By me,
> Philip Sidney

Mr Molyneux was secretary to Philip Sidney's father when he was Lord Deputy Governor of Ireland. The spelling has been modernized to make it easier to understand; there can be no doubting Philip Sidney's message, though.

Turn back to the Headteacher's letter to Jane's parents on pages 47 to 48.

Notice how a formal letter lacks the chattiness that you often find in a personal letter. For example, the Headteacher writes 'I am sorry to have to inform you …' not 'I am sorry to say…', 'I hope there will not be a recurrence of her misdemeanour' not – 'I hope she won't be naughty again'.

Most formal letters will make a series of statements, perhaps asking you to take some action or asking you to give some information. When you read such a letter, take the letter stage by stage, reading a paragraph at a time, to see what you need to do.

The young English student at work

Imagine that you have received the following letter. In the spaces that follow write down four key statements from the letter.

```
                                    ALPHA ELECTRONICS GROUP
                                    PLOT 3
                                    HAUXMERE INDUSTRIAL ESTATE
                                    FLINTBOURN
                                    CAMBRIDGESHIRE
                                    CB3 7YW

R Thorp                             5 August 1991
8 High View Way
Bridgeton
Northamptonshire
BD1 2XP


        Dear Sir or Madam

        According to our warranty records, you are the proud owner of a
        Radio-Cassette Player Model XVP 347 A.

        I am writing to inform you that our quality control engineers
        have detected a possible source of future malfunction in the
        above-mentioned product.

        In the process of manufacture, the mains cable retaining clip,
        situated within the battery compartment, may have been only
        partially secured. Models within the serial number range 319720
        to 365124 are likely to have been affected. Please note that
        the serial number is printed on a metallic label affixed to the
        underside of the appliance.

        Should your appliance be one of those specified, please return
        it to the retailer for a free safety check.

        We apologize for any inconvenience this may cause.


        Yours faithfully,

        M Lodge
        M Lodge
        Customer Relations Manager
```

Statement ....   Statement ....

....

....

....

Statement ....   Statement ....

....

....

....

R EADING TO GET INFORMATION

There are many occasions when we need to find some information for school, work, or home.

If you want to find out about corn dollies and what they are or why the tower of Pisa leans or about the invisible bugs that enjoy eating your skin, you will look in encyclopedias, magazines, newspapers and books.

Do you always remember what you read? If you happen to be a genius or have a strong interest in the subject you are reading about, you may find it easy to remember a lot of information, otherwise here are some tips to help you:

1. Why do you want the information? If you answer this question, you set out with a purpose, and you are halfway there.
2. Look at each paragraph in turn to see what its topic is. There *should* be one main topic in each paragraph.
3. See if you can work out the reason for putting each topic in the order it appears. Try to find the link of ideas.
4. Do something with the information. Jot down one or two notes of interest or talk about it to someone else.

In addition to thinking about these hints as you read this extract from *Corn Dolly Legends*, look out for a word from which we get our name for breakfast foods.

> Have you ever seen a corn dolly? They are the intricately woven straw decorations often seen in churches at this time of the year – and often in homes as an everlasting decoration.
> Perhaps you've made one or something similar with drinking straws?

The corn dolly's origins are hidden in legend and mythology surrounding the annual grain harvest.

In some parts of the country, farmers still leave a whole row of wheat standing in the fields at the end of the harvest in the belief that they will have bad luck if it is cut.

Legend had it that Ceres, the ancient goddess of all that grows on the earth, hides in the corn.

Other customs included the reapers – the people who harvested the corn – beating down the last row of corn shouting 'knock her into the ground'. They believed they were driving Ceres into the earth ready for the next year's harvest.

It is from these beliefs that there grew the tradition of saving the last stalks of corn from a field and making them into the shape of a woman decorated with coloured ribbons.

This figure – the corn dolly – was taken to the farmhouse and displayed on the wall during any harvest festivities as they are today.

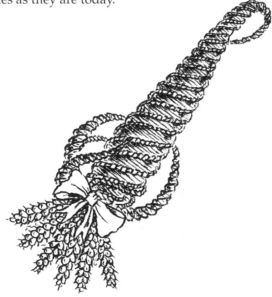

Did you spot the word for breakfast foods? What was it? ....

If you are thinking of going to Pisa as a tourist, which bits of information are you most likely to remember from this entry in an encyclopedia?

The tower of Pisa is the bell tower of the cathedral of Pisa in Tuscany, Italy. It leans because, when the building was half completed, the soil under one half of the circular structure began to subside and the tower tipped.

Work on the tower was begun in 1173, but was discontinued for a century after the subsidence. However, in 1275 architects devised a plan to compensate for the tilt. Two storeys were built out of line with the others and closer to the vertical in an effort to alter the tower's centre of gravity.

But the leaning has continued to increase gradually throughout the centuries. Pumping to keep water away from the surrounding ground and the injection of cement grout into the foundations and the surrounding subsoil have been tried in recent years, but without success.

The tower, which is one of the most unusual in existence, is Romanesque in style and made of white marble. It is cylindrical in shape and has eight storeys.

The tilt is about 17 feet, or more than 5 degrees from the perpendicular. The tower continues to increase its tilt by about a quarter of an inch each year.

Don't read the next article just before going to bed!

A MITE DISTURBING: THE BUGS THAT BREED ON YOUR SKIN

MORNING: You stumble, bleary eyed, out of what you think is an empty bed. But settling down for breakfast under the duvet are about two million eight-legged creatures with serrated claws. No, these aren't the huge, hairy, bloodsucking bed bugs endemic in some countries, but tiny (so tiny they weren't discovered until 1965) harmless dust mites that live only in beds and carpets. However clean your house, they'll always be there – using it as a restaurant, toilet, love nest and cemetery.

You pull on a pair of jeans. As you do so, millions of dry skin flakes are brushed off your body – the tighter the clothing the greater your loss of skin – and are whizzed off into the air. In fact you'll lose enough to fill a suitcase in your lifetime, but you won't even notice losing it.

This is what the dust mites eat. There is never any shortage. The skin flakes float down like magic carpets to the waiting hordes below – it is like a permanent food shower.

After a heavy night, your mouth feels terrible, so you head off for the bathroom. A quick brush of your teeth and a swill of mouthwash might improve the taste in your mouth but it won't do much to remove the hundreds of millions of bacteria, viruses and fungal growths that populate your gob.

Indeed, you'll be adding a few more horrors that have gathered on your toothbrush overnight. Don't panic, however, these are tiny compared even to the dust mite. They're not going to do anyone any harm.

What you should be worrying about is what goes into your toothpaste. About 40 per cent of what you're paying for is water; there's chalk – exactly the same stuff used by teachers on blackboards – to grind away the gunge; titanium oxide (that's the whitener used in paint), antifreeze, seaweed and paraffin oil to give it a bit of substance; to get that foaming effect we expect from toothpaste, a dash of detergent is added; and then to make the whole revolting concoction taste fresh, a double dose of peppermint gets mixed in at the end. Well, almost at the end, for without one essential ingredient your tube would be teeming with bacteria in seconds, and that ingredient is formaldehyde, an extremely strong disinfectant used in mortuaries and abattoirs. Yummy!

You're late. You race down to the kitchen and grab a glass of milk. Luckily it's fresh, so there will only be a couple of million bacteria in it. Give them a few days, and they'll have reproduced so rapidly that jelly-like, zeppelin-shaped bacteria will have started to form, attaching themselves to each other as though they were all joining a New Year's Eve conga.

Before long, they will have turned into those big sour lumps that rise to the surface of your tea like icebergs and plop out onto the cornflakes.

Back to the kitchen and, unbeknown to you, placing the glass of milk on the table has caused a flurry of movement. For the kitchen table, like the fridge, sink and work surfaces, not to mention your face and hair, is covered in the most common of household bacteria, the pseudo-monades. Unlike mites, they're not like real creatures but more like blobs with a tail, and so tiny you wouldn't even be able to see a pile of one hundred thousand of them.

They use their tails to hang from things like your nostrils, and whirl them like outboard motors to propel themselves away from danger. These pseudo-monades are nifty. Travelling at speeds of 0.0001 miles per hour might not seem much to us, but for them it's seven body lengths a second. Even Carl Lewis would have trouble keeping up with that.

There's just time to put on a smidgeon of lipstick, but then again you might change your mind if you knew what went into it. Mostly acid needed to burn into the contour of your lips; food shortening, soap and castor oil to make it spread; petroleum wax solidifies it all into what we see as the 'stick'. Then there's the perfume to make it all smell nice, and food preservatives to stop it going off. And if that's not enough to make you throw up, there's one last ingredient – fish scales, scraped off the floors of fish factories and mixed with ammonia, which give that essential sparkle to a girl's smile.

AFTERNOON: It's been a hard day at school, but it's your turn to do the hoovering. The house is covered in what we call dust – a cocktail of insect corpses, sand, sea salt and skin flakes – and buried deep down beneath it all are millions of dust mites.

To a dust mite, a vacuum cleaner feels like being hit by Hurricane Hugo. But, for them, being sucked into the bag is like being transported to dust mite Heaven. For here they have acres of delicious skinflakes to feed on and the warmth to breed in large numbers.

They certainly have the last laugh. For the speed and strength of the vacuum not only sucks things up, it also shoots bits out through the tiny holes in the Hoover bag. Not the mites themselves because they are too big, but the mites' excrement. A cheerful note; as you vacuum, you are being sprayed with millions of tiny pellets.

You sit down for a well-earned bowl of ice cream. Ice cream is basically aerated fat, but the salesmen think, quite rightly, that nobody would want to eat that. So they add sugar, and a sort of glue – which is made by boiling down the bits of animals that no one wants, like the udders, nose, tail and rectal skin. Then they add a touch of flavouring, because rectal skin ice cream wouldn't sell as well as chocolate chip.

All the while a host of globular green creatures, a fraction of a millimetre small, are grazing on the sugar produced from the leaves of the roses on the table through suction tubes. At the same time, they are spraying a foaming liquid out of their bottoms, which in its turn goes to feed the tinier yeast creatures that live inside the rose leaf.

EVENING: It's time for the evening's ablutions. By the end of the day there are millions of bacteria clinging to your body's every crevice. About 8,000 per square inch on your legs, and 40 000 per square inch on your chest. What they really like is your face. For the holes in your skin are like pop-up toasters, constantly ejecting the salt, nitrogen compounds and grease that bacteria thrive on.

Special bacteria live on your forehead, about 72 million of them. They're protected by the surface grease and are even happier under a layer of make-up. Water will not do much to shift these harmless things, it'll just move them from one part of the face to another. What will get rid of many of them though is face cream. But then again, you might well feel a mixture of paraffin, beeswax, and sheep sweat is an awful lot worse.

And anyway, these blobs' reproductive system is much less fussy than with us humans. In 10 minutes, they'll have doubled their population by merely splitting in half, putting paid to most of your efforts at washing them off.

Just one more bleary look in the mirror, and something else is looking back at you. Giants compared to bacteria, these are the eyelash mites that live with their heads and eight legs buried in the base of your eyelashes. Asleep all day, it's now time for them to wake up. For at night as you dream, they crawl out and mate on your unsuspecting eyelids.

Using the information in the article, note down any details about cosmetics that you could use in the course of conversation with friends!

Have you ever wondered how years came to be counted? Who decreed that 1066 was the number of the year in which the Norman Conquest took place? And would every country in the world know the year as 1066? Read this article from a history book and find out:

Historians often need to be much more accurate than just giving the name of a period during which something happened. They use the number of the year. For instance, Columbus discovered America in 1492. But 1492 years from when? When did people start to count from?

Christian countries all use a system of counting years which starts from the birth of Christ. They have used this method since AD 525 when Dionysius Exiguus, a monk, worked out how many years had passed since Christ's birth. We should say that Columbus discovered America in AD 1492. AD stands for Anno Domini, which is the Latin for 'In the year of our Lord'. So Columbus arrived in America 1492 years after the birth of Christ. History, of course, does not begin with the birth of Christ, so we also count the years backwards from that point. Something which happened 10 years before the birth of Christ is said to have happened in 10 BC ('Before Christ'). Ten years before 10 BC was 20 BC. The bigger the number when the date is BC the earlier it happened – 800 BC was a long time *before* 80 BC.

There are other ways of counting years. In the countries where Islam is the main religion, for example, they start counting their years from Muhammad's flight from Mecca. This happened in the year we call AD 622, so in Islamic countries the number of the year is not the same as ours. The Jewish calendar starts further back than the Christian one, and the year that we call AD 2000 will be the Jewish year 5760 and the Islamic year 1420.

One last word is important before we leave the ways historians count the years, and that word is *century*. A century is 100 years. We say that we live in the 20th century. That means we live in the 20th set of 100 years after the birth of Christ. However, the date of years in the 20th century does not start with '20' but with '19'. The year 1966 was not in the 19th century, but in the 20th century. The year 150 is in the second century because it is in the second set of 100 years after the birth of Christ. The first century was all the years up to 100.

How much of this information was new to you?

If you wanted to fly your kite, play tennis or have your first rock-climbing lesson, you might be interested to know how much wind was expected. The force of wind is measured by a scale devised by Admiral, Sir Francis Beaufort, who lived from 1774 to 1857. (He was born in which century? Look back to the article on page 86, if you are in doubt!)

THE BEAUFORT WIND SCALE

Symbol

0	Calm		Smoke rises vertically
1	Light air		Smoke moved by wind; wind does not move weather vane
2	Light breeze		Wind felt on face; leaves rustle; weather vanes begin to move
3	Gentle breeze		Leaves and small twigs are in constant motion; wind extends light flag
4	Moderate breeze		Loose paper blows about; dust is raised; small branches are moved
5	Fresh breeze		Small trees in leaf begin to sway; ripples appear on expanses of water
6	Strong breeze		Large branches sway; umbrellas used with difficulty; whistling heard in telegraph wires
7	Moderate gale		Whole trees sway; blustery; difficult to walk against the wind
8	Fresh gale		Wind breaks twigs off trees; very difficult to walk
9	Strong gale		Slight structural damage; chimney-pots and slates dislodged from roofs
10	Whole gale		Trees torn up by roots; considerable structural damage
11	Storm		Causes great damage, but doesn't happen very often
12	Hurricane		Countryside is devastated; occurs mainly in tropical areas

---

Which number on the scale do you think would be the most suitable for flying a kite? ....

Up to which number would playing tennis be acceptable? ....

The shipping forecast on the radio talks of 'Moderate breezes'. In your notebook draw the symbol which shows these.

Now test yourself

- Look at the weather details in today's newspaper. Are Beaufort Scale symbols used? Can you tell from these alone what the weather is going to be like?

- Listen to the shipping forecast on the radio (BBC Radio 4 forecasts throughout the day). Can you spot the numbers from the Beaufort Scale being used (for example, 'Gale force 10, imminent')?

USING A DICTIONARY

One of the most frequently used books for getting information will be your *dictionary*, which can help you find out:

❶ The spelling of a word.
❷ How you should say it.
❸ Where the word has come from.
❹ Whether it is a noun, verb, adjective, and so on.
❺ What the word means.
❻ Examples of the word in use.
❼ Words that are connected with it.

Let's break down a dictionary's entry for the word **moral** in order to show these seven points in practice:

Moral ① (say *Morr*l) ②
(Latin *mores*, meaning 'customs') ③

1 (plural noun) ④ beliefs about right and wrong, standards of behaviour.
2 (noun) lesson taught by ⑤ a story, eg. 'The moral is: ⑥ all work and no play makes Jack a dull boy.'
3 (adjective) virtuous, concerning principles of right and wrong behaviour, having acceptable standards, eg. 'She is bound to keep her word, because she has high moral standards.'

moral support ⑦ (phrase) encouragement, eg. 'I shall need lots of moral support if I am going to win.'
morally (adverb)
morality (noun)

And here is how the word's entry would appear in another dictionary:

moral ('mɔrəl) *adj.* **1.** concerned with or relating to human behaviour, esp. the distinction between good and bad or right and wrong behaviour: *moral sense.* **2.** adhering to conventionally accepted standards of conduct. **3.** based on a sense of right and wrong according to conscience: *moral courage; moral law.* **4.** having psychological rather than tangible effects: *moral support.* **5.** having the effects but not the appearance of (victory or defeat): *a moral victory.* **6.** having a strong probability: *a moral certainty.* ~*n.* **7.** the lesson to be obtained from a fable or event. **8.** a concise truth; maxim. **9.** (*pl.*) principles of behaviour in accordance with standards of right and wrong. **10.** *Austral. sl.* a certainty: *a moral to win.* —'**morally** *adv.*

The entries in a dictionary are of course arranged alphabetically. If the first two letters of a word are the same, then the third decides the order:

crAm
crEak
crIme
crOckery
crUst

If the first three letters are the same, then the fourth letter decides:

briAr
briBe
briCk
briDe
briGht

And so on.

To help you find the page you want in a dictionary, it is usual to see one or two words printed at the top of the page to tell you the range of entries. If the two words are **crew** and **critical** and you are looking for **crib**, you know you are right because **crib** comes between the words:

crEw crIb criTical

---

crew   231   **critical**

crew[1] (kru:) *vb. Arch.* a past tense of **crow**[2].
crew cut *n.* a closely cropped haircut for men.
crewel ('kru:ıl) *n.* a loosely twisted worsted yarn, used in fancy work and embroidery. —'**crewelist** *n.* —'**crewel,work** *n.*
crew neck *n.* a plain round neckline in sweaters. —'**crew-,neck** *or* '**crew-,necked** *adj.*
crib (krıb) *n.* **1.** a child's bed with slatted wooden sides; cot. **2.** a cattle stall or pen. **3.** a fodder rack or manger. **4.** a small crude cottage or room. **5.** *N.Z.* a weekend cottage: term is South Island usage only. **6.** any small confined space. **7.** a representation of the manger in which the infant Jesus was laid at birth. **8.** *Inf.* a theft, esp. of

esp. with curling tongs. **4.** *U.S. inf.* to hinder. ~*n.* **5.** the act or result of folding or pressing together or into ridges. **6.** a tight wave or curl in the hair. —'**crimper** *n.* —'**crimpy** *adj.*
Crimplene ('krımpli:n) *n. Trademark.* a synthetic material similar to Terylene, characterized by its crease-resistance.
crimson ('krımzən) *n.* **1. a.** a deep or vivid red colour. **b.** (*as adj.*): *a crimson rose.* ~*vb.* **2.** to make or become crimson. **3.** (*intr.*) to blush. —'**crimsonness** *n.*
cringe (krındʒ) *vb.* (*intr.*) **1.** to shrink or flinch, esp. in fear or servility. **2.** to behave in a servile or timid way. ~*n.* **3.** the act of cringing. —'**cringer** *n.*

It is good practice to use a dictionary frequently; the more familiar you are with the way your dictionary works, the better:

- do check spelling when you have finished drafting a piece of writing
- look up the meanings of words you don't know

However, when you are reading a story and you come across a word whose meaning you don't know, try to guess – and carry on reading. The chances are your guess may well be right, because the surrounding words and what is happening in the story will probably give you an idea. You can always check later, and you won't have interrupted the flow of the story. If it is vital to understand the word, because you can't follow the action, then look it up, of course.

Some writers even explain what a word or phrase means. Here is an extract from *Black Beauty*, a book that has been popular for well over a century.

> I had to walk and trot and gallop before him; he seemed to like me, and said, 'When he has been broken in, he will do very well.' My master said he would break me in himself, as he should not like me to be frightened or hurt, and he lost no time about it, for the next day he began.

Everyone may not know what breaking in is, therefore I will describe it. It means to teach a horse to wear a saddle and bridle and to carry on his back a man, woman or child; to go just the way they wish and to go quietly. Besides this, he has to learn to wear a collar, a crupper, and a breeching, and to stand still whilst they are put on; then to have a cart or a chaise fixed behind him, so that he cannot walk or trot without dragging it after him: and he must go fast or slow, just as the driver wishes. He must never start at what he sees, nor speak to other horses, nor bite, nor kick, nor have any will of his own; but always do his master's will, even though he may be very tired or hungry; but the worst of all is, when his harness is once on, he may neither jump for joy nor lie down for weariness. So you see this breaking in is a great thing.

Did you know?

The word *salary* comes from the Latin *salarium* which, in turn, comes from *sal* – salt. The *salarium* was the *salt* ration given to soldiers in the Roman legions for their pay. If a man was lazy, he wasn't *worth his salt*.

Now test yourself

• Find out from an encyclopedia why salt was considered valuable.

USING A THESAURUS

A reference book to *treasure* is a *thesaurus*. Look up the word in a dictionary that tells you where words come from and see if you can find out why the book is *valuable*!

Do you ever have difficulty in getting just the right word? If you do, a thesaurus is a gold mine! It gives you lots of alternative words to use. Writing about a trip to the zoo? What sounds did the animals make? A thesaurus might give you a list like this:

bark, bellow, bleat, bray, buzz, cackle, chatter, croak, crow, growl, hiss, honk, hoot, howl, moo, neigh, quack, roar, screech, snort, snuffle, squawk, squeak, squeal.

How do you find the list of suitable words? You first need to know that a thesaurus is arranged in two sections:

❶ The lists, arranged under main headings and sub-divisions, each with a number.
❷ The index.

Though the index is second, that's the section for you to look at first. Let's take an example. You are writing a story in which a villain is running away from the scene of a crime. You feel that you have used 'run' too many times and you would like to use another word. In the index at the back of the thesaurus, you select 'run', the key word, and find:

run

chase n. 602	move fast vb. 274
continuance n.141	run away vb. 603
flow vb. 362	series n. 62
liquefy vb. 343	voyage vb. 261
manage vb. 695	

'Move fast' seems nearest in meaning to the one you want, so you look for section 274. You discover a great many words to choose from:

shift, travel, speed, pelt, flash, scud, drive, streak, nip, cut, tear, rip, rush, dash, fly, whizz, hurtle, zoom, bolt, scurry, dive, hare, dart, spurt, sprint.

Not all of them are ideal, but there are at least half a dozen that are suitable.

Now test yourself

Look at the piece below. The word 'run' is used too many times. By consulting a thesaurus, choose a different word to replace 'run' each time it appears. You may have to rework the phrase or sentence to make a sensible context in which your new word can appear. When you have chosen your new words, write out the story again.

The robber grabbed the bag of notes and made a run for the door. 'Quick, Fingers,' he said to his partner, 'run for it!'

The two villains burst out of the bank, into the street and began to run from the scene of the crime.

The cashier, working free the knots that bound his hands and legs, dashed to the office phone to ring for the police, but the line had been cut!

'Blast! I'll have to run to the police station. There's no time to waste!'

'Don't worry Sir,' said the Constable at the station. 'We'll get our best men onto it. We'll run the thieves to ground!'

R EADING POEMS

The novelist Leslie Thomas writes:

> Each morning she (the teacher) would bring one of us to the front of the class to read a passage from the Bible. She selected passages from each of the books starting at Genesis, and we read one a day.
> One November day, with the rain washing the school's small windows, Maggie called me out and gave me the open Bible to recite. I read it as we had always read it, gabblingly fast, the quicker the better, and get it over with. But only so far like that …
> Suddenly I knew what the words were; that put together they sang like a song. I stumbled, then started again. But more slowly:

For, lo, the winter is past,
The rain is over and gone;
The flowers appear on the earth;
The time of the singing of birds is come,
And the voice of the turtle is heard in our land;
The fig tree putteth forth her green figs,
And the vines with the tender grape
Give a good smell.

When I got to the piece about 'the rain is over and gone' they all howled because it was teeming outside. But I did not look up at them. The words of Solomon's song made me ache inside and I was afraid it might show. I gave the Bible back to Maggie and, although she did not know it, and never knew it, she had taught her first and only lesson at Narborough. I knew about words, and I went on seeking them, discovering them, and wondering and delighting in their shape and beauty. For me Maggie had made a miracle.

This magic of being 'caught' by a poem, when you feel a surge of excitement, may not have come to you as dramatically as it did to Leslie Thomas, but you may have experienced something like it.

For several thousand years or so, poetry has mattered a great deal. Before people could read or write, in fact, poetry was the means of conveying all manner of important things, because it was easy to remember and pass on to others. Even rules for being a successful farmer in England were turned into poetry by a man named Thomas Tusser. Navigational information and early medical knowledge also were put into poetry.

Strong rhythms used in work songs helped to keep those involved in hauling equipment like timber, anchors, and sails all working together.

The young English student at work

Find and read 'Rio Grande', 'Shenandoah' and 'Sally Brown', which are all slow-moving and were sung as sailors walked slowly round the capstan of the ship, pushing a spoke-like bar in front of them.

Though there has been an obvious decline in the need for poetry of this kind, people have turned to poetry as a way of expressing their feelings about things that matter: birth, harvest, growing up, love, illness, the seasons, battles, death and so on. Poetry helps people to understand the thoughts and feelings of themselves and others.

Poetry can have a powerful effect. It is not surprising that advertisers use poetic devices in their catchphrases and jingles, so that the words work on people's minds and linger there.

'Devices' mean such matters as alliteration, metaphors and similes, rhythm and rhyme, for example. (These are explained in the glossary at the back of this book.) Learning to identify and label these can be fun and can help you to understand, **but** when reading a poem, you mustn't make this your main purpose. You should try to enjoy the words and their sounds. Some poems will work their magic, some will make you say, 'That's right, that's just how I felt when ...', some will let you realize what other people have felt and experienced.

Most poems have to be read two or three times before you can do them justice. Reading poems is not like reading stories. And if you don't understand everything, don't worry. Some poems release their meaning slowly, and some may baffle you for many years. The secret is not to give up and not to worry when you get stuck on one or two lines.

Read the following poems – several of which may be familiar to you – preferably aloud in order to 'savour' the words. Feel the words as you pronounce them, not in a public-speaking, recitation voice, but with as normal a voice as the words will allow!

THE TYGER

Tyger! Tyger! burning bright
In the forests of the night,
What immortal hand or eye
Could frame thy fearful symmetry?

In what distant deeps or skies
Burnt the fire of thine eyes?
On what wings dare he aspire?
What the hand dare seize the fire?

And what shoulder, & what art,
Could twist the sinews of thy heart?
And when thy heart began to beat,
What dread hand? & what dread feet?

What the hammer? what the chain?
In what furnace was thy brain?
What the anvil? what dread grasp
Dare its deadly terrors clasp?

When the stars threw down their spears,
And water'd heaven with their tears,
Did he smile his work to see?
Did he who made the Lamb make thee?

Tyger! Tyger! burning bright
In the forests of the night,
What immortal hand or eye,
Dare frame thy fearful symmetry?

William Blake

Notice the mysterious and exciting power of the tiger. Have you seen that the poem is made up of question after question? This seems to help us understand the poet's wonder at the beast; he questions because he is impressed and amazed. The repetition of the first verse at the end of the poem makes the poem very satisfying. Is it a complete repetition? Did you spot that one of the words changes?

What would your instinct be if you saw a snake?
Here is D H Lawrence writing about an experience he had in Sicily:

SNAKE

A snake came to my water-trough
On a hot, hot day, and I in pyjamas for
the heat,
To drink there.

In the deep, strange-scented shade of the great dark
carob-tree
I came down the steps with my pitcher
And I must wait, must stand and wait, for there he
was
at the trough before me.

He reached down from a fissure in the earth-wall in
the gloom
And trailed his yellow-brown slackness soft-bellied
down, over the edge of the stone trough
And rested his throat upon the stone bottom,
And where the water had dripped from the tap, in a
small clearness,
He sipped with his straight mouth,
Softly drank through his straight gums, into his slack
long body,
Silently

Someone was before me at
my water-trough,
And I, like a second comer, waiting.

He lifted his head from his drinking, as cattle do,
And looked at me vaguely, as drinking cattle do,
And flickered his two-forked tongue from his lips, and
mused for a moment,
And stooped and drank a little more,
Being earth-brown, earth-golden from the burning
bowels of the earth
On the day of Sicilian July, with Etna smoking.

The voice of my education said to me
He must be killed,
For in Sicily the black, black snakes are innocent, the
gold venomous.

And voices in me said, If you were a man
You would take a stick and break him now, and finish
him off.

But I must confess how I liked him,
How glad I was he had come like a guest in quiet, to
drink at my water-trough
And depart peaceful, pacified, and thankless,
Into the burning bowels of this earth.

Was it cowardice, that I dared not kill him?
Was it perversity, that I longed to talk to him?
Was it humility, to feel so honoured?
I felt so honoured.

And yet those voices:
If you were not afraid, you would kill him!

And truly I was afraid, I was most afraid,
But even so, honoured still more
That he should seek my hospitality
from out the dark door of the secret earth.

He drank enough
And lifted his head, dreamily, as one who has drunken,
And flickered his tongue like a forked night on the air,
   so black,
Seeming to lick his lips,

And looked around like a god, unseeing, into the air,
And slowly turned his head,
And slowly, very slowly, as if thrice adream,
Proceeded to draw his slow length curving round
And climb again the broken bank of my wall-face.

And as he put his head into that dreadful hole,
And as he slowly drew up, snake-easing his shoulders,
   and entered farther,
A sort of horror, a sort of protest against his withdrawing
   into that horrid black hole,
Deliberately going into the blackness, and slowly drawing
   himself after,
Overcame me now his back was turned.

I looked round, I put down my pitcher,
I picked up a clumsy log
And threw it at the water-trough with a clatter.
I think it did not hit him,
But suddenly that part of him that was left behind convulsed
   in undignified haste,
Writhed like lightning, and was gone
Into the black hole, the earth-lipped fissure in the wall-front,
At which, in the intense still noon, I stared with fascination.

And immediately I regretted it.
I thought how paltry, how vulgar, what a mean act!
I despised myself and the voices of my accursed human
   education.
And I thought of the albatross,
And I wished he would come back my snake.

For he seemed to me again like a king,
Like a king in exile, uncrowned in the underworld,
Now due to be crowned again.
And so, I missed my chance with one of the lords
Of life.
And I have something to expiate;
A pettiness.

The poet captures the way the snake moves and behaves, with the long lines
imitating effectively the snake's lazy movement in the heat:

> 'He reached down from a fissure in the earth-wall in the gloom
> And trailed his yellow-brown slackness soft-bellied down,
>   over the edge of the stone trough'

The word 'Silently', stuck on its own at the end of the section in which these lines
appear, seems to make the reader feel the silence, because he or she pauses at the
end of the previous line and there is a gap after it, of course, before the next section.

The pace at which the poet wants the lines to be read varies from the long
slow-moving snake, with gentle sounds being used, to the more abrupt, and
contrasting:

'I looked round, I put down my pitcher,
I picked up a clumsy log
And threw it at the water-trough with a clatter.'

We feel his action is awkward and wrong simply in the way we have to read it. The k, d, t, p, cl sounds, which come thick and fast, make it difficult to read smoothly. Apart from the alliteration (when consonants are repeated), the poet has tried to imitate the sound of the log hitting the water-trough by the sounds of the very words he has used. Look and listen to the t sounds in 'threw it at the water-trough with a clatter' as you say the last line aloud. The word 'clatter' is onomatopoeic. (Look in the glossary if you do not know the meaning of this word.)

Look again at the poem. Can you find some words in the section beginning 'I think it did not hit him …' which help to convey the snake's action effectively?

The poem does more than describe a snake; it tells a lot about the poet, particularly about the way he feels he has behaved towards the snake. The last section lets the reader know he needs to make amends for his silly action.

The young English student at work

What do you think the poet means by 'I thought of the albatross'? To find out, read the poem 'The Rime of the Ancient Mariner' by Samuel Taylor Coleridge. Though it is close on two hundred years old, the poem is not generally difficult to follow and once you have read it, you will not forget it. You should be able to find the poem quite easily.

Turning to a very different poem, we can see that this poem relies heavily on rhythm and sound, in general, to help with the meaning.

"

NIGHT MAIL
I
This is the Night Mail crossing the Border,
Bringing the cheque and the postal order,

Letters for the rich, letters for the poor,
The shop at the corner, the girl next door.

Pulling up Beattock, a steady climb:
The gradient's against her, but she's on time.

Past cotton-grass and moorland boulder,
Shovelling white steam over her shoulder,

Snorting noisily, she passes
Silent miles of wind-bent grasses.

Birds turn their heads as she approaches,
Stare from bushes at her blank-faced coaches.

Sheep-dogs cannot turn her course;
They slumber on with paws across.

In the farm she passes no one wakes,
But a jug in a bedroom gently shakes.

II
Dawn freshens. Her climb is done.
Down towards Glasgow she descends,
Towards the steam tugs yelping down a glade of
    cranes,
Towards the fields of apparatus, the furnaces
Set on the dark plain like gigantic chessmen.
All Scotland waits for her:
In dark glens, beside pale-green lochs,
Men long for news.

III
Letters of thanks, letters from banks,
Letters of joy from girl to boy,
Receipted bills and invitations
To inspect new stock or to visit relations,
And applications for situations,
And timid lovers' declarations,
And gossip, gossip from all the nations,
News circumstantial, news financial,
Letters with holiday snaps to enlarge in,
Letters with faces scrawled on the margin,
Letters from uncles, cousins and aunts,
Letters to Scotland from the South of France,
Letters of condolence to Highlands and
    Lowlands,
Written on paper of every hue,
The pink, the violet, the white and the blue,
The chatty, the catty, the boring, the adoring,
The cold and official and the heart's outpouring,
Clever, stupid, short and long,
The typed and the printed and the spelt all wrong.

IV
Thousands are still asleep,
Dreaming of terrifying monsters
Or a friendly tea beside the band in Cranston's or
    Crawford's:
Asleep in granite Aberdeen,
They continue their dreams,
But shall wake soon and hope for letters,
And none will hear the postman's knock
Without a quickening of the heart.
For who can bear to feel himself forgotten?

W H Auden

Were there some parts of the poem you read at a different pace from others?
Which were they? Was there any particular reason? Do you think the poet set out
deliberately to vary the pace? There are four 'parts' to the poem. Think of the
train's journey. Which stages of the train's journey is each part describing?

Part I ....

Part II ....

Part III ....

Part IV ....

Just as *Snake* tells us something about people (in this instance the poet) as well
as snakes, so *Night Mail* doesn't just tell us about mail trains; the last three lines

'And none will hear the postman's knock
Without a quickening of the heart.
For who can bear to feel himself forgotten?'

express the simple wish to be remembered and to receive letters.

Not all poems have to be serious. Take this poem, for example:

FATHER SAYS
Father says
Never
let
me
see
you
doing
that
again
father says
tell you once
tell you a thousand times
come hell or high water
his finger drills my shoulder
never let me see you doing that again

My brother knows all his little sayings off by heart
so we practise them in bed at night.

Michael Rosen

BALLADS

As you watch *Top of the Pops* on television or listen to a CD, you are probably unaware that the singer, playing his guitar and singing of love and sorrow, is the modern version of a tradition going back over many centuries. The old ballads (the word itself being connected with singing and dancing) told simple stories of magic, adventure, love, murder, local and national history. The legends and stories of Robin Hood provided material for many.

We have no idea who wrote the old ballads; it remains a mystery! And strictly speaking, they weren't written down anyway. It would be better to say that they were composed, probably by a single author, and then altered and adapted as they were passed on from generation to generation by word of mouth. It was many, many years later that the ballads were written down.

So, how did they survive for so long? It's because they were **memorable**: first, because the stories were enjoyable and satisfied those who knew them; and secondly, because ballads have a strong rhythm – mainly due to their musical origins – and generally have the second and fourth lines rhyming.

Ballads use simple language and set the scene economically, with the minimum of description, telling the story dramatically through dialogue and action. Here is a little-known ballad – a simple love story:

THE ROYAL FISHERMAN

As I walked out one May morning,
   When May was all in bloom,
O there I spied a bold fisherman,
   Come fishing all alone.

I said to this bold fisherman,
   'How come you fishing here?'
'I'm fishing for your own sweet sake
   All down the river clear.'

He drove his boat towards the side,
   Which was his full intent,
Then he laid hold of her lily-white hand
   And down the stream they went.

Then he pulled off his morning gown
   And threw it over the sea,
And there she spied three robes of gold
   All hanging down his knee.

Then on her bended knee she fell:
   'Pray, sir, pardon me
For calling you a fisherman
   And a rover down the sea.'

'Rise up, rise up, my pretty fair maid,
   Don't mention that to me,
For not one word that you have spoke
   Has the least offended me.

'Then we'll go to my father's hall,
   And married we shall be,
And you shall have your fisherman
   To row you on the sea.'

Then they went to his father's house,
   And married now they be;
And now she's got her fisherman
   To row her down the sea.

Notice how the story unfolds. There aren't many details, though enough information is given for us to visualize the scene and feel the girl's shock at realizing that the fisherman is a prince.

Love of a rather different kind is the subject of a modern ballad by the poet B S Johnson:

SONG OF THE WAGONDRIVER

My first love was the ten-ton truck
they gave me when I started
and though she played the bitch with me
I grieved when we were parted.

Since then I've had a dozen more,
the wound was quick to heal
and now it's easier to say
I'm married to my wheel.

I've trunked it north, I've trunked it south,
on wagons good and bad,
but none were ever really like
the first I ever had.

The life is hard, the hours are long,
sometimes I cease to feel,
but I go on, for it seems to me
I'm married to my wheel.

Often I think of my home and kids,
out on the road at night,
and think of taking a local job
provided the money's right.

Two nights a week I see my wife,
and eat a decent meal,
but otherwise, for all my life,
I'm married to my wheel.

Now test yourself

Have a go at writing your own ballad. Look in today's newspaper and choose a news item that catches your attention – it can be funny or sad – and use it as your theme. Remember, the early ballad composers took their ideas from the news of their day.

Have you ever woken up at night to hear the wind and rain beating hard against the windows? This Ted Hughes poem begins by capturing that experience:

WIND

This house has been far out at sea all night,
The woods crashing through darkness, the booming hills,
Wind stampeding the fields under the windows
Floundering black astride and blinding wet

Till day rose. Then under an orange sky,
The hills had new places, and wind wielded
Blade-light, luminous black and emerald
Flexing like the lens of a mad eye.

At noon I scaled along the house-side as far as
The coal-house door. I dared once to look up:
Through the brunt wind that dented the balls of my eyes
The tent of the hills drummed and strained its guy-rope,

The fields quivering, the skyline a grimace,
At any second to bang and vanish with a flap:
The wind flung a magpie away, and a black
Back gull bent like an iron bar slowly. The house

Rang like some fine green goblet in the note
That any second would shatter it. Now deep
In chairs, in front of the great fire, we grip
Our hearts and cannot entertain book, thought,

Or each other. We watch the fire blazing,
And feel the roots of the house move, but sit on,
Seeing the window tremble to come in,
Hearing the stones cry out under the horizons.

Read again the first line of the poem. What does it make you feel? It so vividly makes the reader imagine the house as a ship out at sea. Now go through the rest of the poem, line by line, and put a pencil mark underneath any words you find expressive. Whilst you are doing this also notice how the poet shows the effect of the wind on the magpie and gull:

'The wind flung a magpie away, and a black
Back gull bent like an iron bar slowly.'

How does the movement of the two birds differ?

There now follow some poems for you to read. After each one write down in the space provided the effect the poem has on you. Then underline or highlight words, phrases, sounds or images which appeal to you. When you have read all the poems choose your favourite and explain why you prefer it over all the others.

HALF ASLEEP
Half asleep
And half awake
I drift like a boat
On an empty lake.
And the sounds in the house
And the street that I hear
Though far away sound very clear.
That's my sister Betty
Playing by the stairs
Shouting like teacher
At her teddy bears.
I can hear Mum chatting
To the woman next door
And the tumble drier
Vibrates through the floor.
That's Alan Simpson
Playing guitar
While his Dad keeps trying
To start their car.
Dave the mechanic
Who's out on strike

Keeps revving and tuning
His Yamaha bike.
From the open window
Across the street
On the August air
Drifts a reggae beat.
At four o'clock
With a whoop and a shout
The kids from St John's
Come tumbling out.
I can hear their voices
Hear what they say
And I play in my head
All the games that they play.

Gareth Owen

My comments about this poem are:

....

....

....

....

....

Now test yourself

Try writing a similar poem of your own about the sounds you hear sometimes while you are lying half asleep.

THE DIS-SATISFIED POEM

I'm a dissatisfied poem
    I really am
there's so many things
    I don't understand
like why I'm lying
    on this flat white page
when there's so much to do
    in the world outside
it makes my blood curl
    it makes me want to stay inside
and hide
    please turn me quick
before I cry
    they would hate it if I wet the pages.

Grace Nichols

My comments about this poem are:

....

....

....

....

....

This is an unusual poem, looking at the world from a poem's point of view. Did you write something along these lines in your comments box?

THE CHOOSING

We were first equal Mary and I
with the same coloured ribbons in mouse-coloured hair,
and with equal shyness
we curtseyed to the lady councillor
for copies of Collins' Children's Classics.
First equal, equally proud.

Best friends too Mary and I
a common bond in being cleverest (equal)
in our small school's small class.

I remember
the competition for top desk
or to read aloud the lesson
at school service.
And my terrible fear
of her superiority at sums.
I remember the housing scheme
Where we both stayed.
The same house, different homes,
where the choices were made.

I don't know exactly why they moved,
but anyway they went.
Something about a three-apartment
and a cheaper rent.
But from the top deck of the high school bus
I'd glimpse among the others on the corner
Mary's father, mufflered, contrasting strangely
with the elegant greyhounds by his side.
He didn't believe in high-school education,
especially for girls,
or in forking out for uniforms.

Ten years later on a Saturday–
I am coming home from the library–
sitting near me on the bus,
Mary

with a husband who is tall,
curly haired, has eyes
for no one else but Mary.
Her arms are round the full-shaped vase
that is her body.
Oh, you can see where the attraction lies
in Mary's life–
not that I envy her, really.

And I am coming from the library
with my arms full of books.
I think of the prizes that were ours for the taking
and wonder when the choices got made
we don't remember making.

Liz Lochhead

My comments about this poem are:

....

....

....

....

....

As happens frequently in poems, the essential idea of the poem occurs in the last few lines:

> 'and wonder when the choices got made
> we don't remember making.'

What are the choices Mary and the poet seem to have made without realizing?

TICH MILLER

Tich Miller wore glasses
with Elastoplast-pink frames
and had one foot three sizes larger than the other.

When they picked teams for outdoor games
she and I were always the last two
left standing by the wire-mesh fence.

We avoided one another's eyes,
stooping, perhaps, to re-tie a shoelace,
or affecting interest in the flight

of some unfortunate bird, and pretended
not to hear the urgent conference:
'Have Tubby!' 'No, no, have Tich!'

Usually they chose me, the lesser dud,
and she lolloped, unselected,
to the back of the other team.

At eleven we went to different schools.
In time I learned to get my own back,
sneering at hockey-players who couldn't
spell.

Tich died when she was twelve.

Wendy Cope

My comments about this poem are:

....

....

....

....

....

THAW
Over the land freckled with snow half-thawed
The speculating rooks at their nests cawed
And saw from elm-tops, delicate as flower of grass,
What we below could not see, Winter pass.

Edward Thomas

My comments about this poem are:

....

....

....

....

....

What sounds does the poet repeat in this short poem? Why do you think he uses these sounds? When the poet writes that the elm-tops are 'delicate as flower of grass', from whose point of view does he seem to be writing?

I LOVE ME MUDDER (MOTHER)
I love me mudder and me mudder love me
we come so far over de sea,
we heard dat de streets were paved with gold
sometime it hot sometime it cold
I love me mudder and me mudder love me
we try to live in harmony
you might know her as Valerie
but to me she is my mummy.

She shouts at me daddy so loud some time
she don't smoke weed she don't drink wine
she always do the best she can

My comments about this poem are:

....

....

....

....

....

she work damn hard down ina England,
she's always singing some kind of song
she have big muscles and she very very strong,
she likes pussy cats and she love cashew nuts
she don't bother with no if and buts.

I love me mudder and me mudder love me
we come so far over de sea
we heard dat de streets were paved with gold
sometime it hot sometime it cold,
I love her and she love me too
and dis is a love I know is true
my family unit extends to you
loving each other is de ting to do.

Benjamin Zephaniah

This poem celebrates the mother. What qualities does the poet see in her? What is the most important idea he has learnt from her? What does the poem gain by being written in Creole (a language that is a mixture of two other languages, one of which is European)?

My comments about this poem are:

....

....

....

....

....

CHILDHOOD

I used to think that grown-up people chose
To have stiff backs and wrinkles round
    their nose,
And veins like small fat snakes on either
    hand,
On purpose to be grand.
Till through the banisters I watched one
    day
My great-aunt Etty's friend who was going
    away,
And how her onyx beads had come
    unstrung.
I saw her grope to find them as they rolled;
And then I knew that she was helplessly
    old,
As I was helplessly young.

Frances Cornford

Does this simile (see the glossary on pages 195 to 197 if you're not sure what this word means) of 'small fat snakes' suggest to you anything more than the appearance of the veins? Anything unpleasant?

DEMOLITION

They have blown up the old bridge
connecting the coal works with the
coke works.
Useful and unimposing,
it was ever a chapel of small waters,
a graceful arch toothworked with
yellow bricks notched into red bricks,
reflecting there sudden bright winks
from the Browney – an oval
asymmetrical image
which must have delighted, as fisher-
children,
these shiftless but solid grey men
who follow so closely the toil of its demolition.

The digger's head drops and grates and swings up,
yellow fangs slavering rubble and purple brickdust;
but the watchers wear the same grave, equivocal
expression.
They might be grieving
(their fathers built it, or their fathers' fathers)
or they might be meaning
Boys won't be going to the mine no more.
Best do away with what's not needed.
That's Jock Munsey's lad in the cab there, surely.
Good job it's at home, not away on the telly.

Anne Stevenson

My comments about this poem are:

....

....

....

....

....

Do you think it is helpful to see the digger in terms of an animal?

MEN ON ALLOTMENTS
As mute as monks, tidy as bachelors,
They manicure their little plots of earth.
Pop music from the council house estate
Counterpoints with the Sunday-morning bells,
But neither siren voice has power for these
Drab solitary men who spend their time
Kneeling, or fetching water, soberly,
Or walking softly down a row of beans.

Like drill-sergeants, they measure their recruits.
The infant sprig receives the proper space
The manly fullgrown cauliflower will need.
And all must toe the line here; stem and leaf,
As well as root, obey the rule of string.
Domesticated tilth aligns itself
In sweet conformity; but head in air
Soars the unruly loveliness of beans.

They visit hidden places of the earth
When tenderly with fork and hand they grope
To lift potatoes, and the round, flushed globes
Tumble like pearls out of the moving soil.
They share strange intuitions, know how much
Patience and energy and sense of poise
It takes to be an onion; and they share
The subtle benediction of the beans.

They see the casual holiness that spreads
Along obedient furrows. Cabbages
Unfurl their veined and rounded fans in joy,
And buds of sprouts rejoice along their stalks.
The ferny tops of carrots, stout red stems
Of beetroot, zany sunflowers with blond hair
And bloodshot faces, shine like seraphim
Under the long flat fingers of the beans.

Ursula Fanthorpe

My comments about this poem are:

....

....

....

....

....

Does the poet admire the men who tend their allotments? Pick out any words that give evidence of her feelings towards them.

CLOWN

He was safe
behind the whitened face
and red nose of his trade,
vocation more certain
than doctor's or priest's
to cheer and heal.
Hidden away from himself
he could always make us laugh
turning troubles like jackets
inside out, wearing
our rents and patches.
Tripping up in trousers too long
he made us feel tall;
and when we watched him
cutting himself down,
missing the ball,
we knew we could cope.

What we never knew
was the tightrope he walked
when the laughter had died.
Nowhere to hide in the empty night,
no one to catch his fall.

Phoebe Hesketh

My comments about this poem are:

....

....

....

....

....

Why do you think the poet left a gap before the last section? Does it help us to understand the poem?

Now that you have read and commented on these poems, which one is your favourite and why?

My favourite poem is: ....

Because: ....

....

....

And supposing you had the opportunity to meet the poets who wrote these poems, what questions would you like to ask them? On a piece of paper jot down one or two questions for each poem.

If you have been wondering why so long has been spent looking at poems, it is because poetry matters, since it helps us to understand ourselves and others, and also because a good poem uses words carefully and accurately. By doing so, language is kept alive and in good health. If we get used to looking closely at words, what they say and imply, we are better equipped to withstand the persuasion of advertisers, politicians, journalists, and so on, some of whom try to manipulate the way we think and feel.

Did you know?

Dr Samuel Johnson published a very famous book in 1755: *A Dictionary of the English Language*. Having marked thousands and thousands of passages from his reading, he employed six clerks, working upstairs in his house in Gough Square, London, to copy the passages onto little slips of paper. It took eight years to prepare the dictionary.

All those who have compiled dictionaries in English since then, have been greatly indebted to him.

WATCHING AND READING PLAYS

During the course of your English work, you may watch plays on stage and on television, but you may also want to read them. As you read, remember that playwrights intend their plays to be staged rather than read, so try to stage the play in your head. You have to be your own director, grouping the actors, 'hearing' them speak their lines, and so on.

Just as you look at the blurb of a novel to gain some idea of what to expect from the world the novelist has created, so you should look for the playwright's clues. Look at the list of characters and see what information is given. Who is related to whom? Are we told about their age and profession? Are there any physical details? Then there will be the location, which could be vague or quite detailed. A quick browse in the drama section of a library will give some idea of how much information – or how little – playwrights choose to give. Compare the opening stage directions/description of J B Priestley's *An Inspector Calls*, for example, with *Hamlet*.

Here is a very short piece by Harold Pinter, entitled *Last to Go*:

> *A coffee stall, a BARMAN and an old NEWSPAPER SELLER. The BARMAN leans on his counter, the OLD MAN stands with tea.*
>
> *Silence.*
> MAN   You was a bit busier earlier.
> BARMAN Ah!
> MAN   Round about ten.
> BARMAN Ten, was it?
> MAN   About ten.
> *Pause.*
> I passed by here about then.
> BARMAN Oh yes?
> MAN   I noticed you were doing a bit of trade.
> *Pause.*
> BARMAN Yes, trade was very brisk here about ten.
> MAN   Yes, I noticed.
> *Pause.*

MAN	I sold my last one about ten. Yes. About nine forty-five.
BARMAN	Sold your last then, did you?
MAN	Yes, my last 'Evening News' it was. Went about twenty to ten.

Pause.

BARMAN	'Evening News', was it?
MAN	Yes.

Pause.

Sometimes it's the 'Star' is the last to go.

BARMAN	Ah!
MAN	Or the … whatsisname.
BARMAN	'Standard'.
MAN	Yes.

Pause.

All I had left tonight was the 'Evening News'.

Pause.

BARMAN	Then that went, did it?
MAN	Yes.

Pause.

Like a shot.

Pause.

BARMAN	You didn't have any left, eh?
MAN	No. Not after I sold that one.

Pause.

BARMAN	It was after that you must have come by here then, was it?
MAN	Yes, I come by here after that, see, after I packed up.
BARMAN	You didn't stop here though, did you?
MAN	When?
BARMAN	I mean, you didn't stop here and have a cup of tea then, did you?
MAN	What, about ten?
BARMAN	Yes.
MAN	No, I went up to Victoria.
BARMAN	No, I thought I didn't see you.
MAN	I had to go up to Victoria.

Pause.

BARMAN	Yes, trade was very brisk here about ten.

Pause.

MAN	I went to see if I could get hold of George.
BARMAN	Who?
MAN	George.

Pause.

BARMAN	George who?
MAN	George … whatsisname.
BARMAN	Oh!

Pause.

Did you get hold of him?

MAN	No. No, I couldn't get hold of him. I couldn't locate him.
BARMAN	He's not about much now, is he?

Pause.

MAN	When did you last see him then?
BARMAN	Oh, I haven't seen him for years.
MAN	No, nor me.

Pause.

BARMAN	Used to suffer very bad from arthritis.
MAN	Arthritis?
BARMAN	Yes.
MAN	He never suffered from arthritis.
BARMAN	Suffered very bad.

Pause.

MAN	Not when I knew him.

Pause.

BARMAN	I think he must have left the area.

Pause.

MAN	Yes, it was the 'Evening News' was the last to go tonight.
BARMAN	Not always the last though, is it, though?
MAN	No. Oh no. I mean sometimes it's the 'News'. Other times it's one of the others. No way of telling beforehand. Until you've got your last one left, of course. Then you can tell which one it's going to be.
BARMAN	Yes.

Pause.

MAN	Oh yes.

Pause.

I think he must have left the area.

Though it is very short, it shows the playwright's skill in creating dialogue that seems hauntingly real and familiar: the pauses as the two characters stumble through their conversation, the trivial details mentioned, and the way in which the subject of conversation changes and comes back.

Humour presents itself in the form of obvious statements: there is no way of telling which paper will be last, until there is only one left. But in spite of some humour, there remains an air of sadness. The characters cannot, or will not, reveal too much of themselves to each other.

With the help of a friend, make a cassette recording of *Last to Go*. You will need to have a few practice attempts first. One of the most difficult aspects will be the frequent pauses; they have to be just the right length. If you pause too long, it will fall apart.

Shakespeare

Read these lines aloud:

This done, he took the bride about the neck,
And kissed her lips with such a clamorous smack
That at the parting all the church did echo.

That sounds quite a kiss! Notice the **k** and **s** sounds as you read. Why were those sounds used? (Do you remember the word used for describing the imitation of sounds? Look back at the discussion following D H Lawrence's poem *Snake*.) Perhaps you are not familiar with the word 'clamorous', but you can probably guess its meaning. Some of the words that Shakespeare wrote have changed in meaning or have gone out of use – and he used many more than we do. But think of all the words we use now that he cannot have known about. He could not have used *word-processing software* on his *computer*, nor could he have gone to a *disco*.

Shakespeare wrote about people who share the same concerns and interests that we have in the twentieth century. In *The Merchant of Venice*, there is prejudice and intolerance. Marriage between two teenagers whose families are at loggerheads is the subject of *Romeo and Juliet*. Have you ever heard of a political leader being assassinated? *Julius Caesar* and *Macbeth* deal with just that situation. In *Othello*, a man is so obsessed with the belief – mistaken, in fact – that his wife has been unfaithful to him, he is driven to murder her. You only have to read the newspapers for a few weeks to decide whether or not that is irrelevant nowadays.

The basic situation in most of the plays is relatively easy to understand. John Mortimer's father bombarded him with Shakespeare from an early age:

'Is execution done on Cawdor?' This was my father's frequent greeting to me and I found it, at the age of six, a pretty tough question to answer. I needn't have worried; he didn't, of course, expect any reply … It's difficult for me to imagine a childhood without Shakespeare, or to feel anything but amazement at the suggestion that his work is remote or inaccessible to children. My father told me the stories and they seemed at least as exciting as Grimm's Fairy Tales and much more interesting. In fact, the comedies are miraculous fairy stories, just as the tragedies are compulsive thrillers, tales of murder, mystery and revenge. The plots are compulsive, the dramatic technique as sudden and surprising as that of any movie-maker.

Shakespeare knew what would grab our attention right at the beginning. *Romeo and Juliet* begins with two groups of servants spoiling for a fight, and talking in a rowdy manner; *Macbeth* begins with thunder, lightning, and witches; *Julius Caesar* begins with two officials trying to quell a rather jubilant mob; *A Midsummer Night's Dream* begins with the problem of a disobedient daughter – she is refusing to marry the man her father wants her to marry, because she is in love with somebody else.

Take a look at this scene [Act 3, scene 3] from *Julius Caesar*. Caesar has been killed and the mob is after those responsible for his death. Unfortunately, the mob finds someone who, although innocent, has the same name as one of the conspirators:

A STREET IN ROME
Enter CINNA the Poet, and after him the PLEBEIANS.

CINNA	I dreamt tonight that I did feast with Caesar,
	And things unluckily charge my fantasy; *[weigh on my mind]*
	I have no will to wander forth of doors,
	Yet something leads me forth.

The Plebeians surround him.

FIRST PLEBEIAN	What is your name?
SECOND PLEBEIAN	Whither are you going?
THIRD PLEBEIAN	Where do you dwell?
FOURTH PLEBEIAN	Are you a married man or a bachelor?
SECOND PLEBEIAN	Answer every man directly.
FIRST PLEBEIAN	Ay, and briefly.
FOURTH PLEBEIAN	Ay, and wisely.
THIRD PLEBEIAN	Ay, and truly, you were best.
CINNA	What is my name? Whither am I going? Where do I dwell? Am I a married man or a bachelor? Then to answer every man directly and briefly, wisely and truly; wisely I say, I am a bachelor.
SECOND PLEBEIAN	That's as much as to say they are fools that marry. You'll bear me a bang for that, I fear. Proceed, directly. *[I will hit you for saying that]*
CINNA	Directly, I am going to Caesar's funeral.
FIRST PLEBEIAN	As a friend or an enemy?
CINNA	As a friend.
SECOND PLEBEIAN	That matter is answered directly.
FOURTH PLEBEIAN	For your dwelling, briefly.
CINNA	Briefly, I dwell by the Capitol.
THIRD PLEBEIAN	Your name, sir, truly.
CINNA	Truly, my name is Cinna.
FIRST PLEBEIAN	Tear him to pieces! He's a conspirator.
CINNA	I am Cinna the poet, I am Cinna the poet.
FOURTH PLEBEIAN	Tear him for his bad verses, tear him for his bad verses!
CINNA	I am not Cinna the conspirator.
FOURTH PLEBEIAN	It is no matter, his name's Cinna; pluck his name out of his heart, and turn him going.
THIRD PLEBEIAN	Tear him, tear him!

They attack Cinna.
Come, brands, ho, firebrands! To Brutus', to Cassius'; burn all! Some to Decius' house, and some to Casca's; some to Ligarius'. Away, go!

Now test yourself

This scene is not central to the play; none of the major characters appears. So, why do you think Shakespeare included this scene?

You should be able to make a good guess even if you do not know the play.

Did you know?

Shakespeare made a will, in which he left various sums of money and property to his family and friends. But the most surprising, and well known, entry is:

'Item 1 gyve unto my wief my second best bed with the furniture'

But that doesn't mean she didn't get anything else, because by law she would have had a third share for life of her husband's estates and the right to live in their house!

G ETTING THE MESSAGE ACROSS

PRESENTING THE MESSAGE

Let's consider two boys of the same age, 14, living in South Africa:

The first is a white South African living in a comfortable, wealthy district. His bedroom is large: sleeping area, tastefully furnished with a high quality bed; study area (he has ambitions to be a lawyer) has a desk with modern high-tech lighting so that he doesn't strain his eyes, and ample, well-stocked bookshelves. There is a third area, dominated by a large settee with two or three scatter cushions, a huge window with a panoramic view over luxuriantly fertile valleys and hills. A remote-controlled hi-fi system, television and video fit neatly into a designer unit his grandmother gave him for his birthday.

He views, with some *horror*, the events that have been taking place in South Africa. White *supremacy* has been firmly fixed in his mind for as long as he can remember. He feels that the white population has been *betrayed* by *making concessions* to black *pressure groups*.

The second is a Zulu and is a close friend of one of Chief Buthelezi's relatives. He lives within a kraal, an enclosure of huts and cattle, that forms a circle, which means for him a feeling of unity and wholeness. The settlement's self-sufficient agricultural system has changed gradually over the years. The population are well fed and healthy; there is little waste. No one knows precisely when they settled in that particular place. He is proud of his Chief: appearances on television, meetings with foreign leaders, conferences. Political moves towards equality had been slow, but increasingly more fruitful.

He views, with some *hope*, the events that have been taking place in South Africa. White *domination* has been firmly fixed in his mind for as long as he can remember. He feels that the black population has been helped by *restoring rights* to black *political parties*.

These two views of the situation in South Africa have been used to highlight how differently a message can be presented. How we use and understand words is vital. Words are very important, and reveal our attitudes and feelings.

THE MEDIA

Here is a newspaper article that may well shock you; if it does, at least it will have started you thinking about the media. It was written in late 1990, a period of great tension in the Gulf, but before the Gulf War had actually begun.

THE FIRST CASUALTY OF WAR IS TRUTH

When nations go to war sense goes out of the window. Primitive emotions are released; violent, dangerous, murderous emotions. Remember the old army recruitment joke: 'Join the Army, travel the world, meet interesting people *and kill them!*'

When nations go to war the carnage can be unspeakable. No sane person could face it in their normal, everyday state of mind. Governments have to get cracking to change the normal, everyday state of mind of their people.

You can't go to war without popular support. Politicians have to psych themselves and the country up to send in the troops. The media psychs itself up to do its patriotic duty. And parents have to face the fact of their sons coming home in body bags.

Among all this confusion of blood and death and fury, truth is the first casualty. The propaganda machine gets into gear.

Every country's propaganda output will say roughly the same things:

1 We are going to win, and win quickly.
2 The enemy is led by an evil lunatic who is feared and distrusted by his suffering people.
3 The enemy forces are also evil lunatics capable of unspeakable atrocities even though they fear and distrust their evil lunatic leader.
4 Our army never makes mistakes.
5 Our army never commits atrocities.

The psychological objective is to 'satanize' the enemy. To make him non-human. To put him wholly in the wrong, to turn him into a savage even though he might be acting in a similar way to ourselves. In the *Commando* comics a German pilot shoots an unarmed parachutist: 'Murdering swine!' is the British pilot's response. But when the British pilot shoots an unarmed parachutist: 'That's for what you did to Tommy!'

Recent history has seen the emergence of the media as a powerful propagandist. During the first world war it was used to new extremes. Vivid stories were told about German cruelty: rape; mutilation and murder of babies, etc. Stereotypes of bloodlusting, barbaric Germans were built up. Terms like 'Evil Hun' were used. 'Defend your beloved country from the murdering hordes of evil foreigners!' the propaganda machine yelled.

When the war was over, people realized that they had swallowed a lot of tosh. And this had a serious effect.

During the 1930s, when reports started to filter back to Britain about Hitler's treatment of the Jews, Britain didn't particularly believe it.

They had been desensitized by the exaggerated claim of the previous propaganda. When evil did come into the world, we thought it was propaganda crying wolf.

During the present conflict in the Gulf we should remember:

1 The conflict will probably not be resolved quickly.
2 Saddam Hussein is probably not a lunatic feared and distrusted by his people.
3 The Iraqis have committed and will commit atrocities – all forces do in full-scale war.
4 The allies dropped two atom bombs on Japan in 1945 killing 180 000.

If there is a war in the Gulf then we must devoutly hope to win. But let's try and keep our heads while we do so.

The *media* is the term we give to television and films, radio, newspapers and magazines, advertisements. It is unwise to make general statements about the media, as there are good and bad films, stimulating and boring magazines, deceptive and helpful advertisements.

All branches of the media are involved in 'getting the message across', whether fact or opinion.

The media uses *images* (with the exception of radio, of course) and *words* to present what they have to say. Whether as a teenager, or later as an adult, we need to think carefully about what is presented to us.

When an estate agent is asked to put a property on the market, photographs, measurements and details are taken. To attract customers, the estate agent makes sure that the photographs, the description – and sometimes, a video film – show the property to the best advantage. The photographer will look at the property from various angles to show the most flattering views, missing out, if at all possible, the flapping and rather rusty corrugated iron roof under which you keep the coal. The writer of the advertisement will highlight any attractive features, including how near the shops are or what the reputation of the local school is, if felt desirable. Have a look at some property details, perhaps by peering into an estate agent's window, and see for yourself!

The key word to both images and words is **selection**.

Now test yourself

- Suppose the rest of your family is set upon moving home, but you don't want to. You are quite happy to stay exactly where you are. Take a sequence of photographs of various views of the house and write a description of the exterior and interior selecting items that you feel would **discourage** the prospective buyer. What an estate agent would call your 'cosy' bedroom might become a bedroom 'barely able to take a small bed'!

- Look at two or three photographs in a newspaper and try to work out for each one:
  - why a particular angle has been taken
  - whether a close up or distant shot was chosen.

Take a good look at this drawing which is based on a photograph that appeared in a newspaper advertisement. What feelings do you have towards each of the boys? Can you make a guess at the kind of personalities they have? Where is each one looking? Why?

Would it have altered your response if there had been two girls instead? A boy and a girl? (See the article *Selling us a Stereotype* on page 116.)

Can you suggest why a map has been placed on the wall? Would it have made a difference if there had been a computer work-station behind the boys? Do you think the picture was composed on purpose or is it just an ordinary classroom scene?

Now read the words that made up the rest of the advertisement:

It's easy for the teacher to ask the boy on the left, because he's always ready to answer.

SHOULD THE TEACHER ASK THE BOY ON THE RIGHT?

Keen pupils should always be encouraged, but the teacher has to remember that all pupils need to be involved. Why didn't the boy on the right put up his hand?

Was it because he was day-dreaming, so didn't hear the question properly? Perhaps the teacher asked the question in a way the boy didn't understand. Is he simply shy and doesn't like answering questions? There are a lot like that.

It could be that he knows the right answer, but is frightened in case he gets it wrong. (That can happen to a gifted child just as easily as it can to a slower one.)

Somehow the teacher will need to bolster his confidence. But how? The teacher can ask him a question he is certain to be able to answer – or offer him several possible answers, so that the boy is less likely to get it wrong.

A class is made up of individuals, each pupil having his or her own particular worries, difficulties and needs.

When you become a teacher, you have to learn to understand and be sensitive to the needs of every single one of those in front of you. Quick thinking to change the direction of a lesson, if the feedback from the class demands it. That's teaching!

Teaching the same material to a different group? No two lessons are the same; any teacher can tell you that.

And the satisfaction gained from seeing pupils grapple with, and then understand, what you present to them: there's nothing quite like it.

Make teaching your career; it brings out the best in people.

Do you now think differently about the boys?

It's worth remembering that not all advertisements are designed to sell a product. Ask an adult also to look at the advertisementon the right and pass a judgement on how effective he or she thinks it is.

Is this road-safety advertisement helped by the image of a person stepping outside the triangle, as if putting a foot into the road? Is there any need for the words or is the image sufficient on its own?

GIVE WAY TO PEDESTRIANS AT JUNCTIONS

Nearly 59,000 pedestrians were killed or injured in road accidents in 1988.

- Most accidents involving pedestrians happen at, or near, junctions.

- Look out for pedestrians at junctions, especially the elderly, children and the disabled. They take longer to cross the road and may have difficulty judging your speed and distance.

- WHEN TURNING AT A ROAD JUNCTION, *GIVE WAY* TO PEDESTRIANS WHO ARE CROSSING THE ROAD

LOOK OUT FOR PEDESTRIANS – THEY NEED TO CROSS ROADS

The young English student at work

Look at the advertisement below.

Some questions to ask yourself:

1. If you are shy, will the wearing of a certain brand of jeans help you?

2. Can't you be a teenager without one particular make of jeans?

3. How can the jeans be exclusive if they are on sale at *all* good fashion shops?

4. Designer jeans? Isn't every article of clothing designed in some way or another?

5. Can a particular brand of jeans make you popular?

Choose a television advertisement that appeals to you. Which fear does it play upon to make you want the product? Being the odd one out, ignored, unattractive? Are you told any facts or do you merely get an advertisement company's opinion? How does the visual scene help to promote the product?

The media need to judge carefully the people for whom the advertisement or broadcast is designed, the so-called *target audience*. Do you remember reading about *audience* on page 14?

If people didn't respond to advertisements, manufacturers wouldn't spend so much money on advertising.

Try to find out how much money a car manufacturer spends on advertising each year. Can you discover how much is for television advertising and how much for newspapers, magazines and hoardings? What percentage of the company's expenditure does it represent? A librarian might be able to point you in the right direction for finding this information.

Advertisements aren't a new idea. Over a hundred years ago, you could have opened your newspaper to find this:

Liver, Nerves, Stomach, and Lungs Restored without medicine
DU BARRY's
delicious health-restorer food
REVALENTA ARABICA,
cures speedily and without expense
as it saves **50 times** its cost
in other remedies,

indigestion, (dyspepsia) flatulency, phlegm, habitual constipation, all nervous, bilious, and liver complaints, dysentry, diarrhoea, acidity, palpitation, heartburn, haemorrhoids, headaches, hysteria, neuralgia, debility, despondency, cramps, spasms, nausea and sickness, sinking fits, coughs, asthma, bronchitis, consumption, also children's complaints, and is admirably adapted to rear and strengthen delicate infants.

Recommended by Drs Ure, Shorland, Harvey, Campbell, Ingram, and 50 000 other respectable persons whose health has been perfectly restored by it, after all other means had failed.

Satisfactory proofs of cure and references to respectable families, may be had gratis and free by post from Barry du Barry and Co., 77, Regent Street, London

---

Now test yourself

Have a go at writing your own advertisement. Imagine that you have thought up a wonderful new invention, drug or type of sweet. What is it? What are you going to call it? Who are you going to try and sell it to? Will your advert be explanatory with a description of the product, or will it use pictures and a catchy punchline?

Read this article, then look at advertisements in magazines, newspapers and on television to see whether the article is right.

SELLING US A STEREOTYPE

Advertising is part of our social fabric. Every day you are assaulted by thousands of messages. They are selling things. But beyond the pert packaging of the pitch there is a significant sub-theme. Ads show us how we live our lives.

The little girl asks 'Mummy, why are your hands so soft?' – because Daddy does the washing up? Oh, no. Perish the thought. Washing-up is for mummies.

Daddies come home in gleaming and purring company cars. They look exhausted, wipe the sweat (caused by working to earn money to feed the wife and kids) from their brows and say 'Cor, I've had a terrible day, love.' Then daddies ask what's for dinner.

Mummies go to the convection microwave set into the Poggenpohl fitted kitchen and produce the latest exotically-named variant on the frozen oven-ready meal, served with a smile.

But sexual stereotyping in advertising doesn't start here. Take toy advertising.

How many middle-class, play-acting daughters do you see ready to blow the neighbourhood away with the latest injection-moulded plastic laser guns?

And how often does Johnny take tea in the Wendy house at three o'clock?

And we very soon get told who takes the lead in social situations too. The latest ad for a certain beefburger is a pastiche of *Casablanca* with six-year-old small-screen symbols. Guess which of them is doing the chatting up? And guess who's like putty in his hands?

Later on when you're growing up and going out you've got to look beautiful. But in adland teenstyle, only physical features matter. Brains can wait – you can be as vacant as a disused toilet so long as you look good.

So we all know what our roles are in life – what a boy should be and what a girl should be. But why are we portrayed in this way?

Because advertising reflects life. Women *do* do most washing-up. More men have company cars than women. Boys *do* chat up girls rather than vice-versa.

Advertising has never created a trend in its life. It jumps on bandwagons with abandon.

The danger is that the stereotypes in ads will indoctrinate a generation and things won't change. But you can be sure that the admen (and women) will be there at the slightest sniff of a social shift. Just think of the avenging woman in the K-shoes commercial and bevy of business women in the Midland Bank, Gold Blend, Volkswagen …

What is your reaction to this article? Note it down in the space below.

My reaction to this article is: ....
....
....
....

Now test yourself

Get hold of several magazines and have a look through them. Count the number of advertisements that bear out what the article says. Is it always women who appear in adverts that have a cleaning or cooking theme? And men in advertisements for cars? Are there any adverts that don't rely on a stereotyped male/female role?

Do you ever watch television news? If you have access to a video recorder, record two news programmes, one from the BBC and the other from ITV. On a piece of paper list each news item covered in order, for both channels, and put the time spent on each alongside. Here is an example taken from an evening in January 1995:

Nine o'clock News – BBC1

1. Brief summary of first three items coming up.   15 secs.

2. Fiftieth anniversary of the liberation of the Auschwitz concentration camp by the Russian army.
                                                                                                              5 mins.

3. Footballer Eric Cantona banned for rest of season for attacking an abusive spectator.
                                                                                                   3 mins. 25 secs.

4. Man aged 21 sentenced to 25 years imprisonment (+ 9 life-sentences) for planting a bomb in a shop in the Shankhill Road in which 10 people died.   2 mins. 42 secs.

5. Blizzards in the north of England cause problems for traffic and hospitals.   3 mins. 34 secs.

6. Verdict of 'unlawful killing' announced following the Waco siege in America.   1 min. 49 secs.

7. Violent conflict in South Africa between police on strike and their non-striking colleagues.   2 mins.

8. Political storm about Europe. Cabinet split suggested and denied.   2 mins. 52 secs.

9. United Nations claim that UK breaches convention on rights for child offenders. 2 mins. 13 secs.

10. Cricket in Australia – fourth test. Mike Gatting gets a century.   30 secs.

11. Situation in Sierra Leone deteriorating. UK nationals advised to leave.   3 mins. 50 secs.

12. Brief reminder of the item about Auschwitz, 'the biggest crime in history'.   15 secs.

News at Ten – ITN

1. Brief summaries of four items coming up.   17 secs.

2. The liberation of Auschwitz.   2 mins. 53 secs.

3. Eric Cantona suspended.   3 mins. 17 secs.

4. Shankhill Road bomber gets jail sentence.   2 mins. 16 secs.

5. Introduction of drug tests in some prisons.   52 secs.

6. Waco disaster inquest.   1 min. 55 secs.

7. Brief summaries of three items coming after the break for advertisements.   30 secs.

8. Serious floods in Belgium, Holland, France, Germany.   2 mins. 5 secs.

9. Rugby Union and Rugby League officials meet after a hundred-year split between amateurs and professionals.   1 min. 28 secs.

10. Two Channel Tunnel trains break down at Folkestone. Cars and passengers take ferry.   18 secs.

11. Toddler found dead between parents who appear to have died from drugs.   15 secs.

12. Potato shortage through mild weather rotting stocks.   18 secs.

13. Accusations that President Clinton may have known about drug/gun-running when he was Governor of Arkansas.   4 mins. 2 secs.

14. Test match.   22 secs.

15. Closing headlines reminding of first three main items.   34 secs.

16. Final item about Australian tennis tournament hit by freak storm.   30 secs.

Have a look at your results. Is there any big or important difference in the news programmes you watched? Do you think the channels tried to keep to facts? Choose one item that appeared on both channels and compare them:

❶ How many seconds were spent in the studio?
❷ How many on location/interview/eyewitnesses?
❸ Did both channels try to be fair? Was an opposing view presented?

Look at some newspapers the following morning to see how their news items compare with television news. Which items have been included? What sense of priority have the items been given in terms of position in the paper and the amount of space allocated?

One of the most successful types of programme on television is the soap opera.

Are you addicted to one or more? Which one? ....

....

What do you think will happen in the next episode? ....

....

Why are these types of programme called soap operas?..

....

If you don't know, go away and find out!

The young English student at work

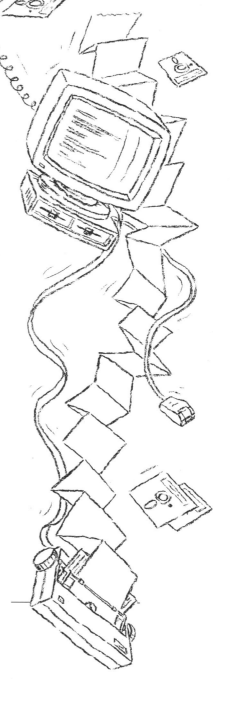

Just think: all the information in a filing cabinet drawer can be stored quite simply on a floppy disc! What's more, the information on a disc is more easily and quickly found (you don't have to rummage through lots of files) – and it doesn't waste lots of paper. If some of the information is out-of-date or of no use, it can be amended or discarded by pressing the relevant keys of the keyboard.

If you have access to a computer, why don't you store information on it? You could use it for keeping records of:

1. Video or audio cassettes and compact discs – titles, contents, duration, type (mystery, documentary, soap opera, group, etc).

2. Books – titles, authors, date when read, type (whodunnit, adventure, humour, etc).

3. Photographs – names of friends/family on them, where taken, date, type (portrait, social gathering, seaside, etc).

With the necessary data base software, you could have fun classifying the various categories, so that you could, for example, produce on the VDU all the books you have about your hobby or by a particular author, or all the tracks on your cassettes by one group.

Seize as many opportunities as possible to use a range of software, including multimedia. Using an encyclopedia on CD-Rom can often help you to find information quickly. But you must resist the temptation simply to print out a complete entry. Select only the relevant information and express it in your own words.

Compile a list of all your reading, even if you do not write lengthy pieces about each book you read.

Apart from writing the date, author and title, note down the type of book you have read – factual books about a hobby, novels, biography, poetry, for example. Try to read as wide a range as possible.

R EADING CHART

Use this page to log books you have read, and refer to the level descriptions to see which one best fits how you read various books and what you gained from each reading experience.

Date completed	Title and Author	Type

LEVEL DESCRIPTIONS: READING

At the start of Key Stage 3 the majority of pupils will have reached at least Level 4 in reading. By the end of Key Stage 3 most pupils should be within the range of Levels 4–7. Levels 5–6 are the target for 14-year-olds. Level 8 is the standard reached by very able pupils.

Use our checklist to assess the Level reached, by ticking the skills that have been mastered.

Level 4

☐ In responding to a range of texts, show understanding of significant ideas, themes, events and characters, beginning to use inference and deduction.
☐ Refer to the text when explaining views.
☐ Locate and use ideas and information.

Level 5

☐ Show understanding of a range of texts, selecting essential points and using inference and deduction where appropriate.
☐ In responses, identify key features, themes and characters, and select sentences, phrases and relevant information to support views.
☐ Retrieve and collate information from a range of sources.

Level 6

☐ In reading and discussing a range of texts, identify different layers of meaning and comment on their significance and effect.
☐ Give personal responses to literary texts, referring to aspects of language, structure and themes in justifying views.
☐ Summarize a range of information from different sources.

Level 7

☐ Show understanding of the ways in which meaning and information are conveyed in a range of texts.
☐ Articulate personal and critical responses to poems, plays and novels, showing awareness of their thematic, structural and linguistic features.
☐ Select and synthesize a range of information from a variety of sources.

Level 8

☐ Response is shown in the appreciation of and comment on a range of texts, and the ability to evaluate how authors achieve their effects through the use of linguistic, structural and presentational devices.
☐ Select and analyse information and ideas and comment on how these are conveyed in different texts.

Exceptional performance

☐ Confidently sustain responses to a demanding range of texts, developing ideas and referring in detail to aspects of language, structure and presentation.
☐ Make apt and careful comparison between texts, including consideration of audience, purpose and form.
☐ Identify and analyse argument, opinion and alternative interpretations, making cross-references where appropriate.

PROJECT: BOOKS AGAINST THE BOX!

The most important thing we've learned,
So far as children are concerned,
Is never, **never, never** let
Them near your television set –
Or better still, just don't install
The idiotic thing at all.
In almost every house we've been,
We've watched them gaping at the screen.
They loll and slop and lounge about,
And stare until their eyes pop out.
(Last week in someone's place we saw
A dozen eyeballs on the floor.)
They sit and stare and stare and sit
Until they're hypnotized by it,
Until they're absolutely drunk
With all that shocking ghastly junk.

Oh yes, we know it keeps them still,
They don't climb out the window sill,
They never fight or kick or punch,
They leave you free to cook the lunch
And wash the dishes in the sink –
But did you ever stop to think,
To wonder just exactly what
This does to your beloved tot?
IT ROTS THE SENSES IN THE HEAD!
IT KILLS IMAGINATION DEAD!
IT CLOGS AND CLUTTERS UP THE MIND!
IT MAKES A CHILD SO DULL AND BLIND
HE CAN NO LONGER UNDERSTAND
A FANTASY, A FAIRYLAND!
HIS BRAIN BECOMES AS SOFT AS CHEESE!
HIS POWERS OF THINKING RUST AND
FREEZE!
HE CANNOT THINK – HE ONLY SEES!

'All right!' you'll cry, 'All right' you'll say,
'But if we take the set away,
What shall we do to entertain
Our darling children! Please explain!'
We'll answer this by asking you,
'What used the darling ones to do?
How used they keep themselves contented
Before this monster was invented?'
Have you forgotten? Don't you know?
We'll say it very loud and slow:
THEY … USED … TO … READ! They'd
READ and READ,
And READ and READ, and then proceed
To READ some more. Great Scott!
Gadzooks!
One half their lives was reading books!
The nursery shelves held books galore!
Books cluttered up the nursery floor!
And in the bedroom, by the bed,
More books were waiting to be read!

Such wondrous, fine, fantastic tales
Of dragons, gypsies, queens, and whales
And treasure isles, and distant shores
Where smugglers rowed with muffled oars,
And pirates wearing purple pants,
And sailing ships and elephants,
And cannibals crouching round the pot,
Stirring away at something hot.
(It smells so good, what can it be?
Good gracious, it's Penelope.)
The younger ones had Beatrix Potter
With Mr Tod, the dirty rotter,
And Squirrel Nutkin, Pigling Bland,
And Mrs Tiggy-Winkle and –
Just How the Camel Got His Hump,
And How the Monkey Lost His Rump,
And Mr Toad, and bless my soul,
There Mr Rat and Mr Mole –
Oh books, what books they used to know,
Those children living long ago!
So please, oh please, we beg, we pray,
Go throw your TV set away,
And in its place you can install
A lovely bookshelf on the wall.
Then fill the shelves with lots of books,
Ignoring all the dirty looks,
The screams and yells, the bites and kicks,
And children hitting you with sticks –
Fear not, because we promise you
That, in about a week or two
Of having nothing else to do,
They'll now begin to feel the need
Of having something good to read.

And once they start – oh boy, oh boy!
You watch the slowly growing joy
That fills their hearts. They'll grow so keen
They'll wonder what they'd ever seen
In that ridiculous machine,
That nauseating, foul, unclean,
Repulsive television screen!
And later, each and every kid
Will love you more for what you did.

Roald Dahl *Charlie and the Chocolate Factory*

Do you agree with this?

Many young people have become 'hooked on books' by what Roald Dahl wrote, so if you haven't read any of his books, try some.

In another of his books Roald Dahl returns to the 'books against the box' debate:

> At the age of *four*, Matilda could read fast and well and she naturally began hankering after books. The only book in the whole of this enlightened household was something called *Easy Cooking* belonging to her mother, and when she had read this from cover to cover and had learned all the recipes by heart, she decided she wanted something more interesting.
>
> 'Daddy,' she said, 'do you think you could buy me a book?'
>
> 'A *book*?' he said. 'What d'you want a flaming book for?'
>
> 'To read, Daddy.'
>
> 'What's wrong with the telly, for heaven's sake? We've got a lovely telly with a twelve-inch screen and now you come asking for a book! You're getting spoiled, my girl!'

Matilda

Here is a letter which was published in *The Independent*;

> **Reading by example**
> Sir: Regarding the report concerning the decline in the reading ability of seven-year-olds, I raise two questions.
>
> One, how many seven to eight-year-olds read as a form of relaxation instead of/as well as watching television?
>
> Two, how many seven to eight-year-olds *see* their parents reading as a form of relaxation instead of/as well as watching television?
>
> Blame not the teachers, or the schools – children learn by example.
> Yours faithfully,

M Smith
Sheffield

And an article which appeared in a local newspaper:

> There was a time when children were regularly beaten as a matter of course in schools, but no child ever learned how to read from being beaten. They may have learned lots of other things about the world from that experience but never, never, never how to read.
>
> Just a little thought would make it plain that children can't be regimented and disciplined into learning to read. Reading has to be an activity that is found by the child to be interesting and enjoyable.
>
> Reading has also to be seen as something that is valuable and as something that is valued by others. The example of others is vital. A child who has not seen other people enjoying the experience of reading will not learn to read.

John White in *East Cambridgeshire Town Crier*

The most depressing thing about doorstepping, at election time for instance, is the glimpses you get of life behind the lace curtains. Behind every curtain in every street is a television set switched on. As door after door is opened, there is the screen flickering in the corner. It is as if nobody in the entire nation can think of anything else to do.

 The British Film Institute conference on television and the family offered some guidelines to parents:
– no extra television sets in children's bedrooms;
– no television after 9pm, even for an educational programme about the Amazon basin;
– no switching on at all unless for a specific programme;
– absolutely no buying of television-inspired toys.

Valerie Grove in *The Sunday Times*

 Finally, here is Michael Rosen, writing in *Radio Times*:

Picture the scene: it's two hours since the children opened their Christmas presents. One gizmo didn't work, another broke. Chocolate money has been ground into the carpet and one child is sitting sobbing and won't say why. Just when a bit of parenting is needed to stop a fight over the batteries (you forgot to buy enough), you've got to turn the spuds over. 'Ah, the video!' you think; 'a quiet half-hour in front of … what? They'll only argue about which one, because one of them's seen *Home Alone* four times and the other hates Mr Bean anyway…' Under these circumstances, there's only one activity that's going to keep the greatest number of people happiest for the longest time. Reading.

Project Action

1. During the course of the next week, write down at the end of each day:

–how many minutes you spent watching television or videos
–how many minutes you spent reading for pleasure
–(as far as you are able, or dare!) the same information for other members of the family

To make your job easier, work out a simple form to fill in before you start. Perhaps you could draw up a form like the one below.

Name		
	Minutes spent:	
Day of week	Watching TV + Videos	Reading for pleasure
MONDAY		
TUESDAY		
WEDNESDAY		
THURSDAY		
FRIDAY		
SATURDAY		
SUNDAY		

2. If you think you need to increase the amount of time spent reading, explain to other members of the family why, using the extract from *Charlie and the Chocolate Factory* to get some ideas. You can, of course, add your own ideas.
3. Television isn't going to disappear just so that people can read more. Write down a list of some arguments to support watching television. A useful starting point might be to list *types* of programmes – comedies, soap operas, documentaries, the news, sport, etc – and see what you can say about each type.
4. Compose a letter to a newspaper stating any conclusions you have come to, as a result of reading what Roald Dahl and others have said about books.

P ROJECT: LEARNING

You read on pages 58 to 60 a suggestion that, next century, schools would be replaced by mechanical, in-the-home teachers. In many ways you may have found it an attractive idea, though Margie in the story clearly thinks she has missed out.

JOIN THE NEPALI PUPILS

Moylama, Jhanka and Kumari are all 11 years old. At seven o'clock every morning, they set out for the ActionAid class where they are learning to read and write. It's not far because the class takes place in a field or, if it's cold or raining, in a barn in their village. They live in Nepal, a mountainous country where there are very few roads, so sometimes it takes a couple of hours for children to walk to the nearest school.

Moylama and Kumari have never been to an official school but they come to this Child Literacy Centre because it's so close to their homes and the class only lasts for two hours. Jhanka went to school when he was much younger, but he didn't like it much. 'At school you only did reading and writing, but here we learn all sorts of things, like how to make a latrine and how to keep our village tapstand clean.'

The book that the children study from is very different from the school textbooks. There are pictures of village life and in every lesson they learn how to read and write a new word. Today the word is 'family'.

'Do you think it's better to have a big family or a small family?' asks the teacher.

'I think if there are many people in a family they will be happier, because they can all do some work,' says Jhanka. 'If there are only a few people, it's a big problem. Then one person has to cut grass, fetch the water and wood all by himself. I have six brothers and three sisters and we all do some work, like cutting grass to feed the cattle.'

'But if there are lots of people in the house, they might fight,' Kumari suggests.

The teacher asks the class to look at today's picture and see if they can work out who's in the picture.

Today the class is learning a new letter, which the teacher asks the children to find in the day's word. Then he asks them to draw a circle round the letter every time they can see it on the page. After that the children practise writing the letter.

At the class, Moylama, Jhanka and Kumari practise reading all the words with the letter in them. Then they read a story about a family. The best part of the lesson is at the end when they do the puzzles and games.

The class finishes at 9 am and the children go back to their homes. Sukuman, another student at the literacy centre, explained what he would do for the rest of the day. 'I'll eat rice when I get home and do some more reading from this book. Then I'll go grass-cutting in the jungle with my friends. When I get back home I'll have a chapati to eat.

'Sometimes in the afternoon I do knitting – I knit sweaters from old wool for my little brothers and sisters. In the evening I do my homework for the class next day and play with my brothers and sisters.'

The ActionAid class only runs for six months, but some of the children have already decided to go to a government school afterwards. Sukuman says he wants to study more.

'... because then I won't be cheated and I will be able to write letters. And if I study a lot, I can become a master and go to the town. It's nice to see the lights in the town. I've been to the town three times with my dad.'

The best thing is that girls, like Kumari, are now coming to the class and school to learn to read and write. Parbati Gurung, a mother with three young daughters, said things had changed since she was young. 'People used to say "boys write letters not girls" and if we asked to go to school, they would say "you have to do work at home". But now girls are going to school and I will send my daughters when they are old enough. We sing a song round here that says "On one hand is the boy and on the other hand is the girl. Nothing is different, both are equal".

This attitude to education is very different from that which Margaret Higginson encountered as a teacher:

'Solly don't need to learn anything, Miss – 'e's got a barrer waitink for 'im!' This terse summary of the local attitude to education was one of the first things I heard when I became class teacher to 3D. My pupils' attitude to teachers was equally definite. They viewed them in a practical and sporting spirit, as wild colts presumably view the riders who try to break them in, as burdens to be bucked off. They felt their status depended on being the worst class in the school. ('Everybody says so, Miss!') And they cherished their status symbols – their non-uniform, their eye-shadow, their avoidance of physical exercise, their bubbles of bright pink chewing-gum.

They were, so to speak, permanently pleated against education. To teachers individually they could be affable, even sympathetic. They would offer kindly advice – 'You ought to bash us, Miss – you're too soft!' – but collectively they were as restless as a pan of milk incessantly coming to the boil, if not actually boiling over.

James Kirkup describes his classroom in the 1930s:

The classrooms were dull. They smelt of sand, disinfectant and chalky blackboard dusters. There was a sour chill in the cloakrooms. The walls of some of the classrooms were made of varnished partitions through which you could hear the class next door stodging through the alphabet or the Lord's Prayer or Thirty Days hath September. On the walls hung religious pictures, maps of the Empire, a large calendar and the alphabet. On the window-sills were bulb vases of dark green glass, and a saucer or two with carrot-tops growing in them … I learned to write, painfully gripping the thin ribbed shank of a new school pen by copying out dozens of times set phrases like 'Virtue is its own Reward'.

In spite of the dull classrooms, however, James Kirkup's early learning was not without excitement:

We had one wonderful 'art' lesson, in which I learned to mix colours. We were given an oblong piece of white cartridge paper and a piece of red pastel. We had to lay the colour on very heavily at one end of the oblong, then use it more and more sparingly until, when we got to the other end, the paper was more or less white. Then – oh, mystery! – we were given a piece of yellow pastel, and told to use it as we had used the red, but starting at the opposite end of the oblong. I shall never forget my amazed delight when I found myself creating a new colour – orange. My excitement increased when I found that red and blue made purple, and blue and yellow made green. Then we were all told about the spectrum, and about primary and secondary colours, and in the next art lesson I made a very smudgy spectrum.

One aspect of learning is homework. Inspectors from the Department of Education and Science declare that:

Properly designed homework can play a valuable part in a pupil's education. Certainly, over a school career, it can add a substantial amount of study time. It offers opportunities for work which is independent of the teacher; it can exploit materials and sources of information which are not accessible in the classroom; it allows pupils to complete work started in school or to practise skills learned in class; it permits the setting of tasks in accordance with the abilities of individual pupils; and it can help to strengthen the liaison between the home and the school.

Do you think Philip Callow, the writer of the next piece, would have agreed with this view?

My father tried to help me with my homework. He sat hunched over a textbook and I stood by the armchair looking over his shoulder, struggling to follow his reasoning. The hands of the clock rushed round and hardly anything would be done. There were awful pauses, with my father sitting motionless, breathing heavily. I tried to bluff by agreeing with him, to try to hurry him on to an answer, but he kept catching me out.

'It's no good if you don't understand it,' he told me. 'How are you going to learn it like that?'

It was useless telling him that if I did not have most of the problems done or something on paper to show, I should be caned for laziness. He wanted me to understand them, once and for all. He was patient and thorough. I knew I would never understand compound interest and problems with trains travelling at different speeds in opposite directions.

In despair I would stare at my mother. If she was worried, uncertain of what to do, she flew into irritation. 'Help the lad,' she cried at my father. 'Can't you help him?'

'That's what I'm doing!' he shouted back. 'Trying to get him to grasp it!'

'There isn't time for all that. What d'you have to be so long-winded for? Just do them, do them. Oh, I wish I could do sums!'

'How about tomorrow night? He'll be in a mess again, won't he? He'll be back again tomorrow night, you daft–'

'Rubbish!' my mother cried.

I stood with a set face. It was finished now. My father had pushed the textbooks off his knee and let the pencil drop. In the morning I should be caned.

Project Action

1. Make a list of the main advantages of being taught by a mechanical teacher. Would it be possible for *all* subjects to be taught by this means? Which aspects of your schooling could not be covered? What would you be unhappy about if you didn't go to school but learnt at home?

2. Reading about conditions for education in other countries can help to make us appreciate our own situations. Were there any details in the article on Nepal that surprised you? Compose a letter to one of the pupils mentioned, explaining what school life is like for you and drawing attention to the differences.

3. Try to write a dictionary definition of **education** without looking it up in a dictionary first.

4. During a conversation with family and friends, consider what makes a good teacher, a good school, and *above all* what makes a good learner?

5. Interview your grandparents to find out what they enjoyed and loathed about their education.

6. Design a fully equipped, modern classroom that could be used for teaching several subjects. How would you make it attractive without being distracting?

7. Think carefully about occasions on which you have been excited by learning something. Write about two of them.

8. What is your attitude to homework? Should parents help their children? What is your favourite type of homework? List your thoughts in your notebook.

9. Continue Philip Callow's story as you think it might have developed. What might he have said to his maths teacher the next day?

PROJECT: THE ROMANS INVADE

" The soldiers, unfamiliar with the ground and with their hands full, had to jump down from the ships, get a footing in the waves, and fight. The enemy, standing on dry land, threw spears and galloped their horses into the sea. This frightened our soldiers until the standard-bearer shouted, 'Jump down, comrades, unless you want to lose our Eagle.' He leapt from the boat and advanced towards the enemy. When they saw this, the soldiers jumped from the boat and followed him. Both sides fought hard. Caesar loaded small fast boats with troops to be sent to any point where his men were in trouble. Once the soldiers had got a foothold on the beach they charged the enemy and put them to flight. "

Julius Caesar *The Conquest of Gaul*

" Marcus asked his slave – once a freeman – why the people resent the coming of the Romans:

Marcus leaned back, his hands behind his neck, and looked up at his slave. 'Esca, why do all the Frontier tribes resent our coming so bitterly?' he asked on a sudden impulse.

'We have ways of our own,' said Esca. He squatted on one heel beside the bench.

'But these things that Rome had to give, are they not good things?' Marcus demanded. 'Justice, and order, and good roads; worth having surely?'

'These be all good things,' Esca agreed. 'But the price is too high.'

'The price? Freedom?'

'Yes – and other things than freedom.'

'What other things? Tell me Esca; I want to know. I want to understand.'

Esca thought for a while, staring straight before him. 'Look at the pattern embossed here on your dagger-sheath,' he said at last. 'It is beautiful, yes, but to me it is as meaningless as an unlit lamp.'

'The sheath was made by a British craftsman,' Marcus said stubbornly. 'I bought it at Anderida when I first landed.'

'By a British craftsman, yes, making a Roman pattern. One who has lived so long under the wings of Rome – he and his fathers before him – that he has forgotten the ways and the spirit of his own people.' He laid his shield down. 'You are the builders of stone walls, the makers of straight roads and justice and disciplined troops. We know that, we know it all too well. When we rise against you, we break against the discipline of your troops, as the sea breaks against a rock. And we do not understand. And when the time comes that we begin to understand your world, too often we lose the understanding of our own.'

For a while they were silent. Then Marcus said, 'When I came out from home, a year and a half ago, it all seemed so simple.' His eyes dropped. Between individual people, people like Esca, and Marcus, the distance narrowed so that you could reach across it, one to another, so that it ceased to matter. "

Rosemary Sutcliff *The Eagle of the Ninth*

ROMAN WALL BLUES

Over the heather the wet wind blows,
I've lice in my tunic and a cold in my nose.

The rain comes pattering out of the sky,
I'm a Wall soldier, I don't know why.

The mist creeps over the hard grey stone,
My girl's in Tungria; I sleep alone.

Aulus goes hanging around her place,
I don't like his manners, I don't like his face.

Piso's a Christian, he worships a fish;
There'd be no kissing if he had his wish.

She gave me a ring but I diced it away;
I want my girl and I want my pay.

When I'm a veteran with only one eye
I shall do nothing but look at the sky.

W H Auden

HIDDEN MINTING KIT MADE COUNTERFEIT ROMAN COINS

A cache of illicit Roman minting equipment used to make Britain's first loose change has been discovered in Buckinghamshire.

It is the first time a complete set of Roman minting equipment has been found anywhere. The equipment – coin dies, blank coins and metal in three Roman pots – was found by a man with a metal detector near Fenny Stratford, on the edge of what was once the Roman town of Magiovinium.

Archaeologists believe the operation was one of several thousand illicit coin-minting workshops which flourished between 270 and 285 AD. They produced millions of coins which served as Britain's first widely-used low denomination coinage. The fake coins were regarded by the population as real money – and for about 15 years the authorities turned a blind eye to their production. Indeed, the counterfeiters were performing a public service, there being a shortage of official coins.

In about AD 284 the government acted to halt the coin faking, and the Magiovinium counterfeiter would have had to hide the equipment. Penalties for counterfeiters were gruesome: freeborn Romano-Britons would have been sent into exile, but slaves risked being crucified or garrotted. The Magiovinium find consists of more than 800 items:

- two iron coin dies, the first iron examples of Roman date found in Britain
- 350 blank coins ready to be stamped by the dies
- 250 copper alloy pellets, ready for conversion into blank coins
- 250 tiny lengths of copper alloy rod (each around 3mm long) used to make the pellets
- three pots in which the materials were hidden.

The entire kit would have been enough to make 850 coins – each probably worth the equivalent of less than a modern 10p piece. The equipment is now on show at the Civic Offices in Milton Keynes.

The Independent

Project Action

1. Re-read the piece about Hadrian's Wall on page 72.

2. From all that you have read here, and anywhere else, about Roman Britain, do you think the Roman Invasion helped Britain in any way? List as many points as you can, with reasons, then arrange them in order of importance.

3. Read Rosemary Sutcliff's *The Eagle of the Ninth*, which is the tale of a young centurion's quest for his missing father – a quest from which there might well be no return. Chapter 5 describes Roman games. Particularly moving is the section beginning: 'Here was the real thing: a fight to the death. At first sight the two would seem to be unequally armed, for while one carried sword and buckler, the other ...'
Read on and find out. You should find a copy in a library or a bookshop.

4. In *Roman Wall Blues* the Roman soldier on duty in a place very different from his home keeps thinking about his girlfriend and a possible rival, Aulus. Write the letter he might have sent her.

5. In *The Eagle of the Ninth* after the conversation with his slave, Esca, Marcus decides to write an article for his legion's newspaper, setting down various views of the conquest of Britain. The editor is delighted but tells Marcus that there is only space for 250 words. Write the article Marcus might have written.

6. Imagine the Roman authorities coming across counterfeit coin-making equipment. Write a detective story of how they track down and pursue the gang they believe to have been operating the equipment.

CHAPTER 3

Writing

S KETCH PAD IN WORDS

Got any hobbies? If you have, you will probably agree that you cannot start many for less than £1. But an exciting and worthwhile hobby is yours for the price of some paper and a pencil. And you could probably find those indoors quite easily without having to go to a shop to buy them!

If you like drawing, you wouldn't think twice about sketching a pair of trainers, a milk bottle, or the cat on the settee. Why not start a 'sketch pad in words'? Look about you and note down snippets of description or of things that have happened. You may never use some of the bits you write down, but you cannot be sure. The famous sculptor, Henry Moore, wrote:

> 'I still do drawings in notebooks, usually in the evening as I sit by the fire after a day's work in the studio. But they are not drawings which I envisage being framed afterwards or exhibited, they are either sketchbook tryouts of possible ideas for sculpture or just scribbles in which I hope that some new idea might come.'

Try the same – only in words!

The young English student at work

- Start your sketch pad in words – today!
You may find it developing into a diary or a journal where you can put down your ideas, dreams and nightmares, hopes and fears, fragments of conversation, thoughts about what you see around you. Let the seeds germinate!

Here is a short piece by a young person, having visited an office at the end of the afternoon:

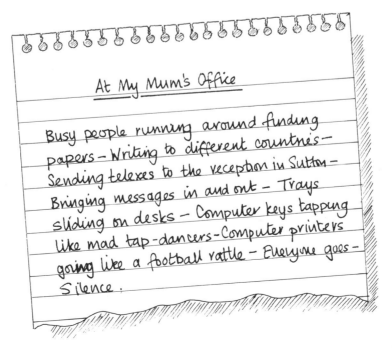

At My Mum's Office

Busy people running around finding papers – Writing to different countries – Sending telexes to the reception in Sutton – Bringing messages in and out – Trays sliding on desks – Computer keys tapping like mad tap-dancers – Computer printers going like a football rattle – Everyone goes – Silence.

Delve into your early childhood. How far back can you remember? To when you were five? Or perhaps earlier? Do you actually remember or is it that you heard others talk so often that you seem to remember?

Grace Nichols, a poet from Guyana, shows how important her childhood was for her:

Whenever I remember the country village along the Guyana coast, where I spent my small-girl days, I can't help seeing water, water everywhere. Brown silky water when it rained heavily. Fish swimming into people's yards and children catching them in old baskets. One of the best memories I have of myself is standing up to my calves in the sunlit water, watching the shapes of fish go by and every now and then cupping my own hands underneath and feeling slippery fish slip through my fingers. My favourite fish was the sunfish. It was a little longer than some of the other fishes, with a fine grey scale on top and a reddish orange glow of a belly below.

My childhood life in that country village plays a big part in my poetry because a lot of poems are about creatures and back-home happenings. Just as how your own imagination might be stirred by thoughts of winter for example – of crunching through thick powdery snow, tobogganning, making a snowman, maybe curling up in front of fires with a hot drink – so my own imagination is stirred by my childhood. I was awakened by tropical things.

And here is a very different childhood memory from Eric Newby, a travel writer who seems to see life and energy in any experience:

Behind the Mason's Arms, the pub which stood next door to the cottage, there was a yard surrounded by various dilapidated outbuildings and a piece of ground overgrown with grass and nettles which concealed various interesting pieces of rusted, outmoded machinery, the most important of which was an old motor car smelling of decaying rubber and dirty engine oil. The stuffing of what was left of its buttoned leather upholstery was a home for a large family of mice. This yard was to be the scene of some of the more memorable games I played with my best friend, Peter Hutchings, whose mother kept a grocery, confectionery and hardware shop on the corner opposite Mr Hayman, the butcher's.

There in the inn yard, in the long summer evenings, we used to sit in the old motor car, either myself or Peter at the wheel, taking it in turn, the driver making BRRR-ing noises, the one sitting next to him in the front making honking noises – the horn had long ceased to be – as we roared round imaginary corners, narrowly missing imaginary vehicles coming in the opposite direction, driving through an imaginary world to an imaginary road, a pair of armchair travellers.

When we got tired of driving our car we ourselves used to become motor cars, tearing up and down the street outside making BRRR-ing noises of varying intensity as we changed gear, disturbing the elderly ladies.

FROM BRAINSTORMING TO FINAL PRESENTATION

BRAINSTORMING

What is a brainstorm? Does it sound painful, with an image of exploding heads?

A good starting-point whenever you write something is to take a piece of paper and scribble down as many words and ideas as you can think of. This is called brainstorming. You will probably find that one idea will spark off another. Write quickly as the ideas come, to get them down, not worrying about neat handwriting.

Let's take the example of a piece of writing you want to do, having read this poem:

LITTLE THINGS
After she's gone away to camp, in the early
evening I clear my girl's breakfast dishes
from the rosewood table, and find a small
crystallized pool of maple syrup, the
grains standing there, round, in the night. I
rub it with my fingertip
as if I could read it, this raised dot of
amber sugar, and this time
when I think of my father, I wonder why
I think of my father, of the beautiful blood-red
glass in his hand, or his black hair gleaming like a
broken-open coal. I think I learned to
love the little things about him.

So when I fix on this tiny image of resin
or sweep together with the heel of my hand a
pile of my son's sunburn peels like
insect wings, where I peeled his back the night before camp,

I am doing something I learned early to do, I am
paying attention to small beauties,
whatever I have – as if it were our duty to
find things to love, to bind ourselves to this world.

Sharon Olds

Try writing a poem about:

– little things that appeal to you;
– the breakfast table after everyone has left it, perhaps later in the day when you return, having had to leave before clearing up;
– or an imaginary letter written by the mother in the poem to her daughter or son, the evening they left;
– or your memories of an occasion when your brother or sister went away – perhaps on a school holiday or camp – and you missed their idiosyncracies. (Look up this last word, if you don't know what it means. It comes from two Greek words: *idios* – own, personal and *sygkresia* – mixture. That's not very far from the derivation of *idiot*!)

Suppose you decide to pick the second of the poem suggestions – returning to the breakfast table after a speedy departure. You might put something like this:

```
- cereal packets - bright colours
- cornflakes, crumbs stuck on rims of bowls
- bit of lumpy porridge left in sister's bowl
- drop of marmalade - run down outside of jar - dried on
- sunflower oil, margarine
- tea leaves at bottom of cups
- toaster - smell of slightly burnt crumbs - sliced loaf
  alongside, polythene wrapper half turned over
- no enthusiasm for clearing up - everything dried on - crumbs all hard
- ought to have got up earlier - could have cleared up before leaving
```

What is the next step? You have to organize your notes by putting them into some order. Will you begin with your thoughts as you come into the kitchen and remember you haven't cleared away? Is the faint smell of toast and tea the first hint reminding you? Or will you make it appear as if your eyes have scanned the kitchen from one side to the other? Perhaps you could look upon the scene as if you were a fly or a wasp hovering over the table.

Let's now move to another example of brainstorming. Imagine your thoughts turning towards whether going to a boarding school has advantages or disadvantages. You may have been asked to write down your views for a project at school, or you may just feel like putting the case one way or the other, because you hear that your friend is going to be a boarder:

FOR BOARDING	AGAINST BOARDING
— useful to learn independence — get used to lots of others — have to leave home eventually anyway — at home during holidays and possibly weekends — better relationship with teachers — get to know them more	— easy to be lonely and rejected — know your family less well — all right if you were clever or good at sport — easy to feel a failure if you're not — have to hide your feelings, so making you less sensitive later — no one really close to turn to when in trouble

ORGANIZING NOTES

In organizing your planning notes, after your brainstorming, whether you are to write a poem or a newspaper article, short story or playscript, you need to know:

❶ WHY you are writing
Is it to *persuade*? Are you wanting to *inform*? Or to *entertain*? Or to *find out what you think*, for as someone once said: 'How do I know what I think until I see what I have written?' Writing helps to *clarify* our thoughts and feelings. It also helps to *fix* them, so that we remember them.

❷ WHO your audience is
Do you remember the section on audience in Chapter 1, page 14?) When you make notes or write a diary entry, you are your own audience, so you can use slang, abbreviations, or your own secret code! When you write for someone else, you will need to bear your audience clearly in mind. The words you choose and the style in which you write will need to be suitable for the person or people who will be reading what you write.

Well, I've found his diary – but I haven't a clue what he's saying...

Sometimes your audience is known to you – a teacher, a friend, your class, a relative and so on. But sometimes it won't be possible to know. When a journalist writes in a newspaper, a physicist writes an encyclopedia article, or a novelist writes a novel, the audience is wide and is not known personally. If you look back over the many examples of writing in Chapter 2 and think about the audience in each case, you will get the 'feel' of what is needed.

THE FIRST DRAFT

Now is the time to do a first draft. In starting to write, you need to juggle three things:

① What you want to say – the CONTENT
② Why you want to say it – the PURPOSE
③ To whom you are writing – the AUDIENCE

Write quickly, following your plan, until you feel you have finished.

REFINING YOUR DRAFT

Once you have a draft in front of you, you can begin the exciting task of improving and refining. It can be very satisfying turning your effort into a piece you can be proud of. There are a number of steps you can take:

❶ **The beginning**
Is your title or headline likely to gain someone's interest?

Your opening sentence needs to be interesting and possibly intriguing. You could begin with a question or a quotation, an unexpected remark or a comment that seems as if it has nothing to do with the title.

Now test yourself

- Look back at some of the pieces in the last chapter – the stories and articles – and see whether you find the beginnings effective.

- Choose one particular piece and write a few lines saying how the beginning captured your interest.

❷ **Paragraphs**
Paragraphs, by breaking up the page into useful and manageable chunks, help the reader to sort out the various stages in the story. They indicate that a new point is being made or that there is a change in situation.

Each paragraph should have a sense of unity, of its being about one topic. In fact, you can often find a sentence that sums up what a paragraph is about, and this is called the topic sentence. Read this first paragraph of an article called *The Thrill of the Circus*:

> The lights dim, the band strikes up a fanfare, and the ring, 13 metres in diameter, is suddenly ablaze with spotlights. The ringmaster in dazzling red coat announces the grand procession: first, the elephants lumber across the centre of the ring, followed by the flying-trapeze artistes in costumes sparkling with sequins. Around the perimeter of the ring clowns are engaging the audience in conversation – or at least, trying to – one clown sporting in his lapel a large flower which shoots a jet of water into the face of another clown who comes to sniff the 'fragrant' bloom. The circus has started.

Notice how all the ideas – about the light, the band, spotlights, ringmaster, and so on – lead up to the final sentence: the circus has started. It is the topic of the paragraph.

Here is the rest of the article. You will see that each paragraph looks at a different aspect of the circus:

> The circus provides entertainment for the family, both young and old. And as the entertainment is visual, no language barrier prevents enjoyment and the big circuses can employ artistes from several countries.

The world of ancient Greece, Rome, and Egypt had circuses with acrobats, tumblers, and jugglers similar to those of today, but the violent and bloody scenes involving wild animals and gladiators are a far cry from the modern circus.

Philip Astley, a sergeant-major in the dragoons, is really the father of the modern circus in Europe, Russia and America. It is he who, in front of audiences in London in the second half of the 18th century, performed astonishing feats on horseback. His fame spread and he gradually added acrobats, clowns, and a tightrope walker to the proceedings. So flourishing did his shows become that he was invited to perform with his company in front of Marie-Antoinette and the Court of France. Hughes, one of Astley's company and later a rival, took a group to Russia where Catherine the Great had an arena specially made for him in the Royal Palace. And it was one of Hughes' *proteges*, Bill Ricketts, who founded a circus in America.

Tricks on horseback, similar to those of Astley, still provide an important part of the modern circus. Horses are carefully chosen for their colour, shape, and grace of movement, so that they are pleasing to the eye. With horses, and indeed with all the many types of animals that are found in circuses, it is their intelligence and skill that amazes us, not only of animals like horses, dogs, and chimpanzees, but also of the ferocious and potentially lethal lions, tigers, and bears. But then is it really so surprising? In order to survive in their natural habitat, the animals need to use their intelligence and skill.

All circus acts, whether with or without animals, require careful practice to reach the perfection necessary to perform in public. Acrobats straining their muscles or contorting their bodies to achieve what, to most of us, appears impossible with such ease and agility, have dedicated themselves to their acts. We do not know how many times they have failed while practising. Turning a somersault having been launched from a spring-board and landing on top of a human pyramid three people high is not learnt overnight. Nor indeed is juggling with several hoops, balls or plates.

The drum-roll that announced the flying trapeze heightens the audience's tension; no one can witness the breathtaking leaps through space without feeling some measure of fear for the participants. The trapeze, which requires split-second timing and nerve, as well as skill, was invented by a Frenchman, Leotard, after whom the one-piece costume known as the leotard is named. He saw ventilator cords hanging from the roof of his father's swimming pool and experimented, tying bars of wood to the cords. Failure, of course, meant getting wet!

After the excitement and fear of the flying trapeze, it is the clown who brings us safely back to earth, literally, by making us laugh. Not only does he relieve the tension, but he fills the gaps between acts, so that the ring-hands can clear away equipment used in previous acts and prepare for the next. But this is not to belittle the clowns, for they have important and skilful acts of their own. Clowns have a long history and are popular with audiences. Distinguished very often by their baggy, colourful clothes, big boots and their grotesque make-up, they reveal a mixture of craftiness and stupidity at the same time; for the clown who is clever enough to deliver a custard pie accurately to someone's face usually ends up being drenched by a bucket of whitewash himself!

Paragraphs don't have to be of any particular length. As you can see from *The Thrill of the Circus*, the second and third paragraphs are fairly short in comparison with the others.

When you are handwriting a piece (as opposed to typing or word-processing), each paragraph begins on a new line and the first word is a couple of centimetres to the right of the margin. This is called indenting. Modern printing style very often doesn't bother with indenting the first word, but to make it easier leaves a blank line between paragraphs. This is called double-spacing.

❸ The ending
Be honest, have you ever written a page and felt, when you have reached the bottom of the page, that you've written enough? A piece of writing that just stops abruptly isn't very satisfying to read. Think of the intended audience and ask yourself whether the ending is suitable.

Now test yourself

Go back and re-read through the stories and articles you have encountered in this book so far. Then, in the spaces below, write down which of the stories and which of the articles you think ends most effectively. Why do you think this?

Story: ....

Because: ....

....

Article: ....

Because: ....

....

REDRAFTING

Most pieces of writing benefit from being left for a time before you look back to see whether improvements are possible. The novelist Graham Greene talked, in a radio interview, about revising his work and leaving it overnight:

> 'When I'm at work on a book, I read over and correct what I've done during the day, after dinner, last thing before going to bed. I believe that the subconscious picks up. There may sometimes be a snag – when I'm not sure quite how to go on. But when I come to work in the morning, it goes. I'm a great believer in the subconscious.'

Don't be frightened of taking a pencil and crossing through parts of your piece of writing that aren't really necessary or that are confused. Get someone else to read it and comment about it. Make changes until you are satisfied.

Look up words in a thesaurus to see if you could use words that are more interesting or precise. Have you been adventurous with the words you have used?

Make sure that the word you want to use has the right implications. Some words have a similar *literal* meaning, but imply very different ideas. I might regard myself as **self-confident** and regard you as **pig-headed** or **arrogant**. Is there any difference? You might be **tolerant**, he might be **uncaring**.

Read it aloud and see whether it sounds right.

PROOF-READING

When you have made all the alterations you think are necessary, re-read through your piece and check the accuracy of spelling and punctuation. This is called proof-reading. You may be surprised that this hasn't been mentioned earlier, but it's not that spelling and punctuation are unimportant. They are important, but they must be less important than the content.

See what you think of this. It begins a fascinating, disturbing, but very moving story called *Flowers for Algernon* by Daniel Keyes:

> Dr Strauss says I shoud rite down what I think and remembir and evrey thing that happins to me from now on. I dont no why but he says its importint so they will see if they can use me. I hope they use me becaus Miss Kinnian says maybe they can make me smart. I want to be smart. My name is Charlir Gordon I werk in Donners bakery where Mr Donner gives me 11 dollars a week and bred and cake if I want. I am 32 yeres old and next munth is my birthday. I tolld dr Strauss and perfesser Nemur I cant rite good but he says it dint matter he says I shud rite just like I talk and like I rite compushishens in Miss Kinnians class at the beekim collidge center for retarded adults where I go to lern 3 times a week on my time off. Dr Strauss says to rite a lot evrything I think and evrything that happins to me but I cant think anymor becaus I have nothing to rite so I will close for today… yrs truly Charlie Gordon.

Is it difficult to understand? And what are your feelings and thoughts about Charlie?

PRESENTATION

When you are fully satisfied that your final draft is perfect in every way, you will want to present it as attractively as possible, whether handwritten, typed or word-processed.

Good, legible handwriting is an asset both in school and in later life. If your handwriting is slovenly and difficult to read, now is the time to do something about it. There are various styles of handwriting, but they all have several points in common:

- they are legible
- the letters are even (a e o r, for example, are all the same height)
- if the letters slant at all, at least they slant the same way. This is especially important with those letters that project below the line.

Apart from taking care with handwriting, you should try to make the overall appearance of a page attractive. Leave a clear margin all round, training your eye to avoid a line ending in a jumbled group of letters crammed together.

Set the margins of a typewriter or word processor so that there is an even margin either side and at the top and bottom.

Use stencils and transfer letters for headlines if you wish. Experiment with capital letters, bold type, underlining, centring, thin border lines, and so on. Explore the possibilities of using a desk-top publishing package, if your school has one. There are now so many opportunities to present work to its best advantage – and it's worth it, if you have spent some time and effort on drafting, redrafting and proof-reading.

Did you know?

When you can't seem to concentrate because your thoughts have gone *haywire*, your thoughts are like the wire used to keep the hay in bales. The wire, strong and springy, seemed to have a life of its own and was difficult to control – just like your thoughts!

IDEAS FOR WRITING

THIS IS MY LIFE!

Begin your autobiography! You can try to remember odd episodes and outings, family celebrations, your first day at school, the time when you realized you knew how to read. The list is endless.

Have your parents kept a newspaper of the day you were born? It is possible to buy back numbers of certain newspapers. See if you can get hold of a copy, so that you can find out what was going on in the world, what the weather was like, and what programmes were on television and radio.

The young English student at work

Question parents, grandparents, relatives and friends to find out what they can remember of your early years. Are there any amusing incidents they can remember? And do they have any visual reminders like photographs or film of you on holiday or at home?

All kinds of experiences can be included. You may have read this episode from *Kes* by Barry Hines – it's very popular – but if you haven't, it's worth seeing how important the event was, even though a character in the book, Anderson, begins by saying:

'I don't know owt, Sir.'
  'Anything at all Anderson, anything that's happened to you, or that you've seen which sticks in your mind.'
  'I can't think of owt, Sir.'
  'What about when you were little? Everybody remembers something about when they were little. It doesn't have to be fantastic, just something that you've remembered.'
  Anderson began to smile and looked up.
  'There's summat. It's nowt though.'
  'It must be if you remember it.'
  'It's daft really.'
  'Well tell us then, and let's all have a laugh.'
  'Well it was once when I was a kid. I was at Junior school, I think, or somewhere like that, and went down to Fowlers Pond, me and this other kid. Reggie Clay they called him, he didn't come to this school; he flitted and went away somewhere. Anyway, it was Spring, tadpole time, and it's swarming with tadpoles down there in Spring. Edges of t'pond were all black with 'em, and me and this other kid started to catch 'em. It was easy, all you did, you just put your hands together and scooped a handful of water up and you'd got a handful of tadpoles. Anyway we were mucking about with 'em, picking 'em up and chucking 'em back and things, and we were on about taking some home, but we'd no jam

jars. So this kid, Reggie, says "Take thi wellingtons off and put some in there, they'll be all right 'til tha gets home." So I took 'em off and we put some water in 'em and then we started to put taddies in 'em. We kept ladling 'em in and I says to this kid, "Let's have a competition, thee have one welli' and I'll have t'other, and we'll see who can get most in!" So he started to fill one welli' and I started to fill t'other. We must have been at it hours, and they got thicker and thicker, until at t'end there was no water left in 'em, they were just jam packed wi'taddies.

'You ought to have seen 'em, all black and shiny, right up t'top. When we'd finished we kept dipping our fingers into 'em and whipping 'em up at each other, all shouting and excited like. Then this kid says to me, "I bet tha daredn't put one on." And I says, "I bet tha daren't." So we said we'd put one on each. We wouldn't though, we kept reckoning to, then running away, so we tossed up and him who lost had to do it first. And I lost, oh, and you'd to take your socks off an' all. So I took my socks off, and I kept looking at this welli' full of taddies, and this kid kept saying, "Go on then, tha frightened, tha frightened." I was an' all. Anyway I shut my eyes and started to put my foot in. Oooo. It was just like putting your feet into live jelly. They were frozen. And when my foot went down, they all came over t'top of my wellington, and when I got my foot to t'bottom, I could feel 'em all squashing about between my toes.

'Anyway I'd done it, and I says to this kid, "Thee put thine on now." But he wouldn't, he was dead scared, so I put it on instead. I'd got used to it then, it was all right after a bit; it sent your legs all excited and tingling like. When I'd got 'em both on I started to walk up to this kid, waving my arms and making spook noises; and as I walked they all came squelching over t'tops again and ran down t'sides. This kid looked frightened to death, he kept looking down at my wellies so I tried to run at him. He just screamed out and ran home roaring.

'It was a funny feeling though when he'd gone; all quiet, with nobody there, and up to t'knees in tadpoles.'

Silence. The class up to t'knees in tadpoles.

Now test yourself

Do you remember a time when you took up a challenge? Write a story about it.

Did you know?

Both *cosmetics* and *cosmos* (the universe, the world) come from the same Greek word, meaning *order, tidy arrangement*.
What is a *cosmonaut*? The Greek *nautes* means a *sailor*, from which we get the word … ?

Perhaps there was a time you got lost, when you were in a big store and you wandered off in another direction from the family, or when you started to explore. Here is Eric Newby again. It's from the same chapter as the extract on pages 136 to 137:

"I continued to follow the stream, racing twigs down it, until it vanished into a sort of tunnel from which proceeded a delightful roaring sound. At the other end it emerged beyond a wicket gate to flow more placidly under a bridge and in these calmer waters I spent some time stirring up the bottom with my stick and frightening some water beetles, the air about me filled with the droning of innumerable insects.

From this point it ran to join the main stream in the middle of the valley and here the path turned away from it to the left beyond a five-barred gate which, because I could not open it unaided, I squeezed underneath, to find myself in a beautiful and what seemed to me immense green meadow, hemmed in by hedgerows and huge trees and filled with buttercups, while high about it to the right were the hanging woods we had seen the previous morning from the car, the open down about them alive with gorse.

At the far end of this field the now augmented stream was spanned by a small wooden footbridge with a white painted handrail. When I eventually reached the stream, in spite of all these distractions and making a number of more or less unsuccessful attempts to spear on the end of my stick some of the older, harder sorts of cow flop in which the field abounded, and launched them into the air, the water tasted even funnier than it had done in the village outside Mrs Hutchings' shop and I stung myself on the nettles getting down to it.

Beyond the bridge the path continued uphill, dappled with sunlight under the trees, and here the air struck chill after the heat of the meadow. Then it dipped and suddenly I found myself out in the sun on the edge of an immense shingle beach which had some boats hauled out on it, and in my ears there was the roar of the sea as with every wave it displaced and replaced millions upon millions of pebbles. To the left it stretched to where a cluster of ivy-coated white pinnacles rising above a landslip marked the last chalk cliffs in southern England; to the right the brilliant red cliffs around Sidmouth; and beyond it, out to sea, on what was a near horizon, for there was already a haze of heat out in Lyme Bay. I could see the slightly blurred outlines of what Harry Hansford, the local fisherman who lived opposite the blacksmith's shop, would soon teach me to identify as a Brixham trawler, ghosting along under full sail.

There was a sound of feet slithering on the pebbles behind me. It was Kathy, panting slightly, as she had been running. 'Whatever did you do that for, Eric, you naughty little boy, without telling me?' She said. 'Your mum's ever so worried, and your dad, too. He'll be ever so cross if he finds out where you've been. You'd better keep quiet when you get back. I'll say I found you in the field.'

Together, hand in hand, we went back up the hill towards the village where the church bells were now beginning to announce the early service."

The young English student at work

Keep a loose-leaf folder so that you can add bits and pieces to your autobiography as you come across them while keeping it in chronological order.

POETIC IDEAS!

Sometimes, the notes you make might more easily become a poem. The poet, William Wordsworth, and his sister, Dorothy, saw lots of daffodils when they were out for a walk near their home in the Lake District. Wordsworth wrote a poem, his sister wrote in her diary.

This is what Wordsworth's sister wrote:

> When we were in the woods beyond Gowbarrow Park we saw a few daffodils close to the waterside. We fancied that the lake had floated the seeds ashore, and that the little colony had so sprung up. But as we went along there were more and yet more; and at last, under the bough of the trees, we saw that there was a long belt of them along the shore, about the breadth of a country turnpike road. I never saw daffodils so beautiful. They grew among the mossy stones about and about them; some rested their heads upon those stones as on a pillow for weariness; and the rest tossed and reeled and danced, and seemed as if they verily laughed with the wind, that blew upon them over the lake; they looked so gay, ever glancing, ever changing. This wind blew directly over the lake to them. There was here and there a little knot, and a few stragglers a few yards higher up; but they were so few as not to disturb the simplicity, unity, and life of that one busy highway.

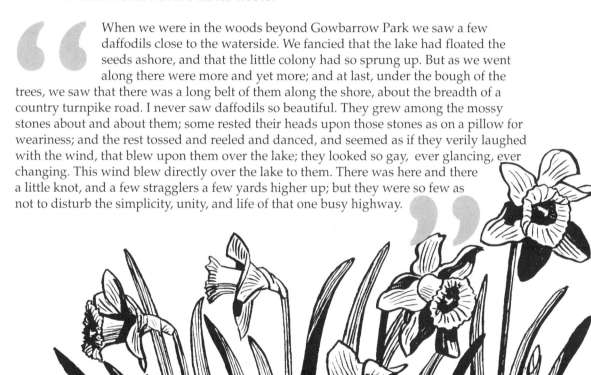

And this is what Wordsworth wrote:

> I wandered lonely as a cloud
> That floats on high o'er vales and hills,
> When all at once I saw a crowd,
> A host, of golden daffodils;
> Beside the lake, beneath the trees,
> Fluttering and dancing in the breeze.
>
> Continuous as the stars that shine
> And twinkle on the milky way,
> They stretched in never-ending line
> Along the margin of the bay:
> Ten thousand saw I at a glance,
> Tossing their heads in sprightly dance.
>
> The waves beside them danced; but they
> Out-did the sparkling waves in glee:
> A poet could not but be gay,
> In such a jocund company;
> I gazed – and gazed – but little thought
> What wealth the show to me had brought:
>
> For oft, when on my couch I lie
> In vacant or in pensive mood,
> They flash upon that inward eye
> Which is the bliss of solitude;
> And then my heart with pleasure fills,
> And dances with the daffodils.

If you found this rather difficult, don't worry, you will understand the next poems which might also spark off ideas for similar poems in you. They are all written by young people:

THE BEAR

His sullen shaggy-rimmed eyes followed my every move,
Slowly gyrating they seemed to mimic the movements of his massive head.
Similarly his body rolled unceasingly
From within.
As though each part possessed its own motion
And could think
And move for itself alone.
He had come forward in a lumbering, heavy spurt;
Like a beer barrel rolling down a plank.
The tremendous volume of his blood-red mouth
Yawned
So casually
But with so much menace.
And still the eye held yours.
So that you had to stay.
And then it turned.
Away.
So slowly.
Back
With that same motion
Back
To the bun-strewn
And honey-smelling back of its cage.

Frederick Brown

MAC

They call him Mac and make fun of him,
He is too afraid to fight back.

Mac! Mac! they yell at him and he leaves
His seat and goes to them
They tease him and in the end they
Tease him so much that he strikes
With his fists but misses them.

They try to make him mad again.
Mac! Mac! you can't catch us Mac!
He comes to them again and
Catches a boy whom he brings
Hurling to the ground.

When he gets up he goes for him
Again.
Mac! Mac! let go of me Mac.
The boy wears a tattered coat and
His unbrushed hair is blown in the Wind.

John Williams

Did you know?

Sandwiches have nothing to do with sand, though when you are trying to have a picnic at the seaside you might think so! John Montagu, the 4th Earl of Sandwich, was so hooked on gambling that instead of leaving the gambling table to take a meal, he had some bread, together with a filling of some sort, brought in to him.

MEMORIES

I remember my first enemy.
The pert, provoking child they said was my
cousin.
I remember despising her straight limp hair,
The green glowering eyes,
And her slight, lively body.
And that she despised my fluffy brown curls,
Pink complexion,
And plumpness.
They made us learn to dance together.
She was clumsy,
Her mouth pouted when she danced
But she said I was too fat to dance.
I wasn't.
They made us walk to school together.
She didn't even know her tables.
She couldn't knit.
I could knit when I was five,
But she laughed at me.
At home they made us play together:
She prodded me with bony fingers,
She pushed me down the stairs.
And when I saw her laughing
I screamed, until she cried.
I remember how I hated my cousin.

Rosalind Levi

BONFIRE

A bright slim figure leaps up the fireplace,
And slips down again,
A flicker of a friend does the same,
Up goes another, and down,
Lashing shafts of light in the room.
Up jumps another and another,
Who can jump the highest?
Children dressed in red and yellow
Leaping up.

Clare Tawney

GETTING HOME

Getting home after a weary day at school
I find it easier to write.
What use to be a hatred of mine
is now
one of my best hobbies,
Poetry,
I love writing poetry
It gives me a relaxed feeling
inside of myself …

Neil Hoggan

A POEM ABOUT A STATUE
He stands there still, cold and grey,
His arms held in one position
By cold, grey stone,
His cloak carved out of solid rock,
His face sad and forlorn
Standing in sadness,
For being a captive clapped in stone.

I look at him and wonder
How his limbs must ache
Standing in the same position
For all the centuries he has endured,
Through tornado and storm,
Siege and war.

Andrew Mudd

LIBRARY CHECKING
Sad,
To see the dust from a great book never
opened,
To breathe in its knowingness
With no desire to know.

Strange
To think that whoever wrote those thousand
pages
Sat up all night by lamplight
At his passionate livelihood.

'No,
No one reads him now; he is out of fashion.
But once the printers printed him:
He was popular once,' they say.

Blue
Of the binding is faded into a musty grey,
And the gold-stamped arabesque letters,
Unreadable, are dumb.

Nothing
But the catalogue, in its neat impersonal
order,
Remembers the obsolete volume
And passes on to the next.

Harriet Levine

Remember that poems do not have to rhyme and do not have to follow a particular pattern. It's just that many people enjoy having to fit their words into such a scheme.

A simple form of writing poetry that you may have come across already is *haiku*, a traditional Japanese verse-form which uses just three lines. There must be five syllables in the first line, seven in the second, and five in the third.

Usually when reading *haiku* poetry, there are two images or ideas which our imagination links together; the poet offers us clues and we do the rest.

In the light of this, let us consider a *haiku* poem:

> At every doorway,
> From the mud on the wooden clogs,
> Spring begins anew.

We picture the mud-covered clogs left at the door. This is the first idea. The second idea refers to the arrival of spring. And the connection? Even the mud, not generally thought to be attractive, is a sign for rejoicing, since it means that the ground, frozen hard during the winter, has softened with the warmer weather; in short, the mud is a sign of the welcome spring.

Here are some other *haiku*:

> A sunny spring day,
> People are doing nothing
> In the small village.

> On the temple bell
> Something rests in quiet sleep.
> Look, a butterfly!

> Oh thin little frog
> Don't lose the fight. Issa
> Is right here to help.

> A brilliant full moon!
> On the matting of my floor
> Shadows of pine fall.

Now test yourself

- Write down the unwritten connection between the two 'ideas' in each of the four haiku above.

- Have a go at writing in haiku form. You need 2 ideas and only 17 syllables!

INTERESTS AND HOBBIES

Do you have an interesting or unusual hobby to write about? Here is a journalist writing – not too seriously – about collecting things:

COLLECTOR'S COLUMN

From an early age we are pushed into the habit of collecting. You are engaged in some interesting and satisfying pursuit like picking the stuffing out of a cushion or peeling off bits of wallpaper or kicking the table leg, when the parents make that dreaded pronouncement: 'What that child needs is a hobby'.

'Thank you very much, but I already have a hobby,' you reply. 'I like to pick stuffing out of cushions. I also spend many happy hours peeling off little bits of wallpaper and I am noted as an enthusiastic kicker of table legs.'

'You must collect something,' the parents announce.

They are not impressed when you show them your collection of wallpaper slivers and your neatly-arranged heap of cushion stuffing. Their idea is that once you have collected something you will spend many happy and silent hours gloating over your collection, leaving them in peace to get on with their lives. Nearly all parents suffer from this delusion.

So it all begins. I was urged to set up a 'museum'. This consisted of a box which contained a lot of cotton wool, a flint axe head (or something shaped rather like an axe head) and an old lightbulb (probably 15th century).

Stamp albums are usually the next stage in the collector's education. There is a powerful snobbery about childhood stamp collecting. The innocent starts enthusiastically collecting the pretty ones – particularly the large glossy Hungarian stamps with their attractive pictures of exotic birds and butterflies.

The first disappointment comes when you discover from the catalogue that these are worth one penny each. Meanwhile fellow collectors at school are sneering. They specialize in the esoteric – Sierra Leone or Guatemala.

Realizing that specializing was part of the etiquette of stamp collecting and discovering that nice pictures of birds and butterflies were almost worthless in this hard world, I soon came to the conclusion that my own specialization would be The Most Boring Stamps in the World. They were usually pale sage green or washed-out orange in colour.

The collection of Most Boring Stamps in the World was so successful that I became utterly bored by it and abandoned it. Still, I learned some important lessons about collecting. First, you have to specialize; second, you have to be obsessional; third, in collecting, the things that look most dull are probably the most valuable.

Then there is the other childhood collector's item: miniature bottles. Usually you find that your parents will oblige by drinking the exotic liquors contained in these bottles so that you are not tempted to consume them yourself. So now you have your collection; a dozen or so small bottles that used to contain something delicious in very small amounts. The sensible person would trade them all in for a large bottle of brandy. The thought simply does not occur to the average collector.

So, now we have established that collectors are mad. Why is it, then, that more and more people are going in for collecting? A great deal of it must be blamed on what is known as the 'Antiques Roadshow' syndrome. We imagine ourselves seated coyly opposite the expert as he admires our collection of 450 aspirin bottles, some of which date back to as early as 1953. 'These are very collectable,' he says. 'The Japanese can't get enough of them.' You put on your unwordly money-never-entered-my-head expression as he says 'Have you had them insured? Would it surprise you to learn that they were worth something in the region of £800 000?'

Occasionally, in adult life, I pause in the middle of picking the stuffing out of cushions, peeling bits of wallpaper off the wall and kicking the table leg and I decide to make my fortune by collecting some item that will dramatically appreciate in value.

The problem is choosing what to collect. Impressionist paintings perhaps? No, somebody has probably thought of that already. Chippendale furniture? Been done. Traction engines? No room in the garden shed – full of mouldering stamp collections, rotting foreign dolls and dusty old miniature bottles.

I kick the table leg some more as I ponder on the problem. The trouble is that collecting mania has reached such a pitch that there is hardly anything left to collect. You try to think of something obscure and you soon discover that it is the basis of some hugely thriving trade.

Beer mats advertising defunct breweries are much sought-after; old copies of Beano and Dandy are treasured; Dinky toys are locked in the safes of millionaires in California; cartels of hard-eyed dealers have got the whole ginger beer bottle-top business sewn up. Every time a rock star decides to have a clear-out the auction houses hold their breath.

You decide to go for engravings of 16th century Icelandic torture instruments and then you read all about them in one of those collecting columns in a magazine or newspaper. Those people who write these columns cannot keep a secret. You decide to be the world's leading collector of free shower-caps from hotel bathrooms and the next thing you see is one of those collecting columns saying 'Shower Caps Are All the Rage'.

These columns tell you what you should have started collecting seven years ago. Or else they tell you that the old Sacha Distel LP you put in the jumble sale the week before last is now being hunted by avid and feverish collectors across three continents.

You sidle up to a friend and ask him where you might be able to lay your hands on a decent early Sainsbury's carrier bag and he says 'Sotheby's next Thursday. You could probably pick one up for as little as £22 000.'

At last I have decided what I am going to collect. It is something that no one else has thought of. In about three years' time the 'Antique Roadshow' will be agog when I place my board before the assembled experts. It will be the definitive collection of newspaper and magazine columns on collecting. Don't breathe a word to a soul.

Winston Churchill found that painting was a relaxing hobby. After experimenting one Sunday with a paint-box belonging to his children, he bought a complete set of oil paints the next morning.

Having bought the colours, an easel, and a canvas, the next step was **to begin**. But what a step to take! The palette gleamed with beads of colour; fair and white rose the canvas; the empty brush hung poised. My hand seemed arrested. But after all the sky on this occasion was unquestionably blue, and a pale blue at that. There could be no doubt that the blue paint mixed with white should be put on top of the canvas. One really does not need to have an artist's training to see that. It is a starting-point open to all. So very gingerly I mixed a little blue paint on the palette with a very small brush, and then with infinite precaution made a mark about as big as a bean upon the affronted snow-white shield. It was a challenge, a deliberate challenge; but so subdued, so halting, that it deserved no response. At that moment the loud approaching sound of a motor-car was heard in the drive. From it there stepped swiftly and lightly none other than the gifted wife of Sir John Lavery. 'Painting! But what are you hesitating about? Let me have the brush – the big one.' Splash into the turpentine, wallop into the blue and white, frantic flourish on the palette – clean no longer – and then several large, fierce strokes and slashes of blue on the absolutely cowering canvas. Anyone could see that it could not hit back. The canvas grinned in helplessness before me. The spell was broken. I seized the largest brush and fell upon my victim with berserk fury. I have never felt any awe of a canvas since.

Perhaps, instead of inspiring you to write about your hobby, these extracts will make you begin collecting odd items and (or) painting!

Writing Stories

The novelist, Anita Desai, caught sight of a 'decrepit' old foreigner wandering around the back streets of Bombay, collecting scraps for his cats. Though he looked poor he was in fact sufficiently wealthy to own racehorses. Later, she wrote a novel stimulated by her knowledge of the old man.

Choosing a character can be a good first step in writing a story. Perhaps you regularly see someone from the bus, someone who is completely unknown to you. Or there may have been someone you met briefly on holiday. Choosing a character from a novel and inventing a new chapter or episode might offer another possibility.

Conversation, overheard in a shop or in the street, could start you thinking. Write down in a notebook any snippets of conversation you overhear and see what you can do with them. They could be used as a beginning or come well into the story. For example, you might overhear and write down snippets like:

Ask yourself questions about your snippets. In the example above, why is it so important to 'make sure you get that'? Why might Colin be jealous? And so on. They might give ideas for plots and storylines.

The young English student at work

Look at the illustrations below. Choosing one of them, make up a short story using the character or situation as a central theme.

P LAYSCRIPT

Do you remember reading the extract from *Five Green Bottles* in Chapter 1? Turn back to page 8 and have a look at it again. In writing a playscript, you will see that:

- the **scene** is described at the beginning
- the **names** of the characters are printed on the left-hand side in capital letters
- the characters tell the **story** through what they **say** and do
- there are no speech marks
- **stage directions** tell the actors how to say their lines, how to react, and what actions to perform. They are printed in italics and placed within brackets.

Here is the first short scene from *Lalita's Way* by Soraya Jintah:

SCENE ONE

Music. The kitchen lights up, revealing lalita, *a seventeen-year-old girl dressed in a shalwar kammeez, rolling chapatis on the wooden bench. Her mother, a woman in her late thirties wearing a saree, is seen cooking the chapatis, behind* LALITA. *On the wall hangs a picture of Krishna with a garland hung round it.*

MRS PARMER Your father and I were talking to the Chauhans last Sunday at the wedding.
LALITA Oh, really.
MRS PARMER Do you know their son's working in a bank and he's still single?
LALITA So?
MRS PARMER The Chauhans are the same casts as we are. I must say the boy is very
    handsome. His name is Rajesh. I know you will approve of him.
LALITA **What?** (*Shocked to hear this.*) If you're trying to arrange a marriage for me, then don't
    bother. I don't intend to get married yet, especially to someone I don't even know.
MRS PARMER Oh, you'll get to know him soon. He's coming to see you tomorrow.
LALITA You arranged for him to see me without even consulting me first?
MRS PARMER That's right. So tomorrow I want you to tie your hair back and wear a saree.
    (LALITA *stares at her mother amazed.*) Well, turn the chapati over or it will burn.

Soraya Jintah began it as a short play for an English assignment at school. 'At that time my parents were in the process of arranging a marriage for me. I decided to write some of my experiences into this play.' Her play was extended and was performed at the Royal Court in London. The play can be read in its entirety in *First Lines*, published by Hodder and Stoughton. There are three other plays by young people in the book, too.

Now test yourself

Is there any situation that you feel strongly about and which you could turn into a playscript? A conflict with a brother or sister, parents, teacher? Think back to when you last had a disagreement with someone and perhaps find a starting-point there.

LETTERS

FORMAL LETTERS

At some stage we all have to write formal letters: letters to suggest to the local council how improvements can be made to a sports ground, to apply for a job, to request information, to complain, and so on.

The secret in writing formal letters is quite simple: be clear, be brief, be polite. A rude or muddled request will be put to one side. And when it comes to applying for a job or for a work experience placement, the applicant's letter is at first the only thing an employer knows about him or her.

Presentation is especially important, so remember the advice given earlier in this unit.

Important points when writing formal letters

❶ The **address** is in full.
❷ The **date** is given underneath the address.
❸ The address of the **person you are writing to** is given on the left-hand side.
❹ If you **begin** 'Dear Sir or Madam' or 'Dear Sirs', the usual form of addressing a company, then the **ending** is 'Yours faithfully' (capital 'Y', small 'f'). If you **begin** with a named person, then the **ending** is 'Yours sincerely' (capital 'Y', small 's').

On the next page are reprinted the Headteacher's letter and the letter from Alpha Electronics that have appeared elsewhere in this book. These are good examples of how to set out formal letters.

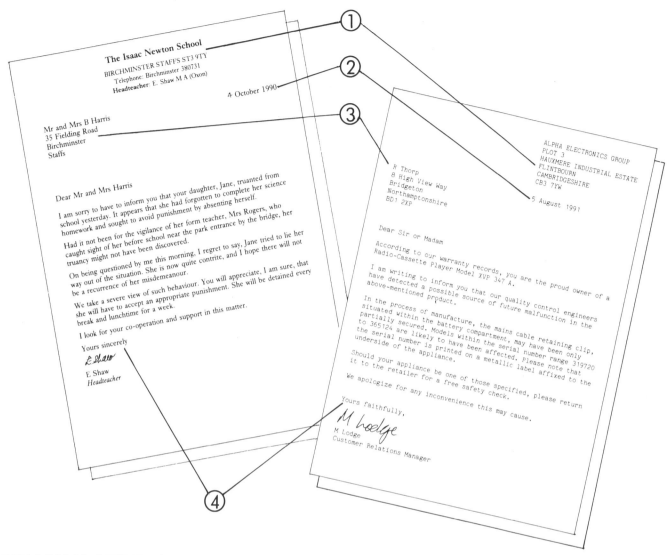

PERSONAL LETTERS

Personal letters may be thought of as a one-sided conversation, in tone. Nevertheless, though it will probably have the ring of speech about it, to write properly, you will need to give the letter some shape and to think carefully about the content.

When family or friends are separated from each other, a good letter can make all the difference. In writing to friends give plenty of news of what you have been seeing or doing, the places you have visited, the people you have met, and any amusing incidents that have occurred. You should also show an interest in the affairs of the person to whom you are writing.

Important points when writing personal letters

❶ The **address** is in full.
❷ The **date** is given underneath the address.
❸ You **begin** 'Dear Mr/Ms/Mrs/Miss/Uncle/Anna' (etc) and the **ending** is 'Yours sincerely' (capital 'Y', small 's') or

'With kind regards',
'Love from',
'Yours',

Note the comma in each case.
On the next page is an example of a personal letter. This should show you how to set out your own letters.

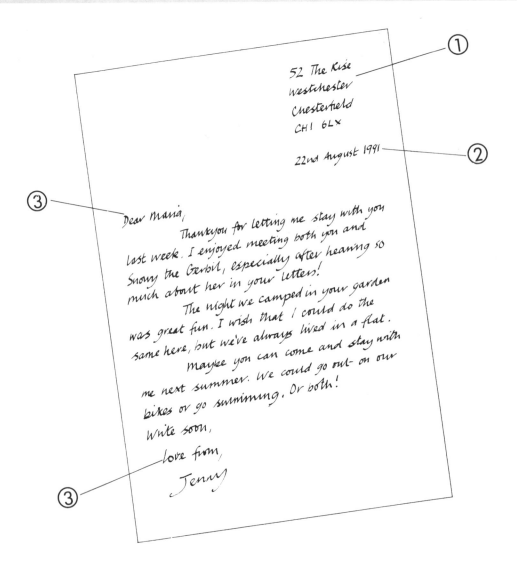

The best way to practise letter writing is to do it, so write a letter today. Is there someone you know who would welcome a letter from you? Don't forget those lines from *Night Mail*:

> 'And none will hear the postman's knock
> Without a quickening of the heart.
> For who can bear to feel himself forgotten?'

S PELLING

You **can** improve your spelling!

If you have been told you are bad at spelling, do not despair; *be positive* and adopt some of the methods recommended here.

❶ Rather than trying to memorize a long list of 'difficult' words, it is better to make your own list of words you want to remember.

❷ Write down words you misspell. Learn each word by:
  – looking at it carefully
  – saying it aloud, concentrating syllable by syllable
  – covering it up with a piece of paper or your hand, trying to say it without looking
  – writing it down – without looking at your original.

③ Learn groups of words with the same combination of letters:

science
conscience
conscientious
conscious

④ Learn how words are built up:

dis + appoint + ment = disappointment

in + complete + ly = incompletely

real + ly = really

It is helpful here to learn the two words: **prefix** and **suffix**. A prefix is a letter or group of letters that go in front of a word, like *dis* in disappointment; a suffix is a letter or group of letters that come after a word, like *ment* in disappointment. Many dictionaries have lists of prefixes and suffixes. It's a good idea to have a look from time to time, trying to remember some of them.

Now test yourself

Find out what the prefix **anti** does to a word. Try thinking about what an antiseptic does. And what is someone who is antisocial?

⑤ Learn where words have come from. Some of the *Did you know*? sections in this book will have proved useful to you.

Did you know?

The Latin word *pes, pedis* meant a *foot*, so we have the word *ped*al and *ped*estrian.
By looking up the prefix *centum*, you will be able to work out how many feet a centipede has.

Some useful tips:

① When using **dis** or **mis** or **un**, be careful not to alter the spelling of the main word:

dis + appear = disappear
dis + satisfy = dissatisfy
dis + approve = disapprove
dis + obedient = disobedient
dis + solve = dissolve
mis + trust = mistrust
mis + spent = misspent
un + natural = unnatural
un + necessary = unnecessary

When **all** is used as a prefix, it loses the final **l**:

almighty
almost
although
always
already

Note: All right is spelt as two words, though there doesn't seem to be a good reason for this.

② **-ful**: when 'full' is added to a word, it loses an **l**:

beauty	beauti**ful**
fright	fright**ful**
faith	faith**ful**
grace	grace**ful**
pity	piti**ful**

③ **-ly**: be careful not to change the word to which you add **-ly**:

immediate	immediate**ly**
real	real**ly**
complete	complete**ly**
final	final**ly**
sincere	sincere**ly**
extreme	extreme**ly**
careful	careful**ly**
beautiful	beautiful**ly**

④ **-ed**, **-ing**: if these suffixes follow a single consonant, the consonant doubles if the syllable is stressed. That may sound complicated, but it's not difficult in practice:

fit	fi**tt**ed
refer	refe**rr**ing
occur	occu**rr**ed
slim	sli**mm**ing
begin	begi**nn**ing

If the last syllable is not stressed, no doubling of the consonant is necessary:

benefit	benefited
focus	focusing

⑤ Verbs ending in a silent **e** (like **make**, **argue**, **hope**) omit the **e** when **-ing** is added:
make making   file filing
argue arguing   queue queuing
hope hoping

Note these two verbs in which the **e** is retained to avoid confusion:

dye	dyeing
singe	singeing

What confusion would occur if these two verbs followed the normal pattern?

⑥ **-ce** or **se**? Nouns take **c**, verbs **s**:
– I advise you to follow my advice. [Pronunciation helps here.]
– If you come to the hockey practice and practise hard, you might get a place in the team.
– You must license your car. You can easily buy a licence at the post office.

⑦ **i** before **e**,
except after **c**,
<u>when the sound is **ee**:</u>

bel**ie**ve	rece**i**ve
f**ie**ld	dece**i**t
retr**ie**ve	ce**i**ling
s**ie**ge	rece**i**pt
ach**ie**ve	

Exceptions:
seize   protein
weird

When the sound isn't **ee**, you simply have to learn each word:
foreign   height   society
reign   weight   heir
species

① Plurals of nouns ending in a **y** generally change the **y** into an **i** and add **es**:

fly	fl**ies**
lily	lil**ies**
factory	factor**ies**
territory	territor**ies**
lady	lad**ies**
possibility	possibilit**ies**

But if the letter before the **y** is a vowel, the plural is regular:

delay del**ays** convoy conv**oys**
valley vall**eys** guy g**uys**
chimney chimn**eys**

P ARTS OF SPEECH

Noun, pronoun, adjective, verb, adverb, preposition, conjunction and **interjection** are the eight parts of speech and every word in the language is one or other of these. At times you may find it helpful to be able to identify which part of speech a word is.

Nouns

A noun – a word which comes from the Latin **nomen** meaning 'a name' – is the word we give to a *thing*. There are four types of nouns: common, abstract, collective, proper.

A **common** noun is a thing you can see and touch: *tree, pen, needle*.

An **abstract** noun cannot be 'sensed' with our senses. It refers to qualities, states of mind, ideas, and attitudes: *happiness, anger, sorrow, truth*.

A **collective** noun is a single word meaning a collection of things: *crowd, herd, queue*.

A **proper** noun is an individual name: *Rachel, Sam, London, Buckingham Palace*.

Pronouns

Pronouns are words that replace nouns (like *she, him* and *it*) and are useful in cutting down repetition.

Take this example:

'Lisa hit the ball into Mr Wood's garden by mistake. When Lisa went to Mr Wood and asked for the ball back, Mr Wood told Lisa that Lisa must not hit the ball into Mr Wood's garden again.'

Using pronouns you would change the second sentence to:

'When **she** went to **him** and asked for **it** back, **he** told **her** that **she** must not hit **it** into **his** garden again.'

Adjectives

An **adjective** tells us what a noun is like: *beautiful* tree, *new* pen, *sharp* needle. Adjectives do not have to be placed before the noun. If you write:

'I think that tree is **beautiful**'

beautiful still remains an adjective.

Verbs

Verbs are the words that make nouns and pronouns work. If we take the example used on page 161 and miss out the verbs, the sentence falls apart:

'Lisa… the ball into Mr Wood's garden by mistake. When she … to him and … for it back, he … her that she … not … it into … garden again.'

Try substituting different verbs for the gaps.

Verbs can be of two types: **main** verbs, like eat, run, go, or they can be **auxiliary**. An auxiliary verb helps a main verb. Here are some examples:

I **could** arrive early at school.
You **should** do your homework.
She **had** written the story.
They **might** play tennis.

So what are the verbs helped by the auxiliary verbs?

Adverbs

Adjectives help to tell you more about a noun; adverbs tell you more about a verb.
    The wretched man **cheerfully** trod on my new scarf when it blew **suddenly** off my neck into the road, as I was riding my bike **hurriedly** to school.
    Adverbs tell you **how** the man trod on my scarf, **how** the scarf blew off my neck, **how** I was riding.
    What similarity do you notice in the three adverbs in the sentence? If you are not sure, think back to what a suffix is. Though some adverbs do not follow this pattern, the vast majority do.

Now test yourself

Pick out quickly any adverbs in the sentence you are reading carefully at this moment.

Prepositions

The Latin prefix *pre* means *before*. (What a good way to remember what a prefix is!) A preposition is positioned in front of a noun to make the meaning clear.

Take some flour **from** the cupboard, mix a beaten egg **with** the flour, and pour milk **into** the mixture. Place a frying-pan **on** the cooker. Heat some margarine or oil and pour **in** the mixture when hot. You should get a tasty pancake, if you're lucky!

Now test yourself

- Describe and write down how you would direct a stranger to your local post office.

- Then read through it and underline all the prepositions you have used.

Conjunctions

Conjunctions join words or groups of words together; you *and* I; it's been a hard day at school, *but* it's your turn to do the vacuuming.
Other conjunctions are words like **as, because, since, unless**.

Interjections

Words in this category (like **hello** and **oh**) are more often found in speech than in writing.

WORD GAMES

Play games with words. Here are some suggestions:

1. Can you make HATE into LOVE by changing just one letter at a time? Each change must make a proper word, too. Here is the way to get the BIRD into the NEST to show you the idea:

   BIRD
   BI**N**D
   B**E**ND
   BEN**T**
   BE**S**T
   NEST
   Others you might try are HEAD to FOOT, HOME to AWAY.

2. Play Scrabble.

3. Make up acrostics by printing a word like this:

   W
   O
   R
   D

and then, by using each letter as the start of a word, make up a sentence:

   Will
   Oliver
   Reach
   Dover?

4. Do 'wordsearch' puzzles (the ones you find in magazines and books) and devise some of your own.

⑤ Make up lists of words using the letters contained in a longer word, like:

SATISFIED

fed	ties	sad	
sat	die	deaf	
diet	safe	side	
fast	sit	fits	and so on

⑥ Solve anagrams and make up some for your friends. Have you learnt anything about:

LLSNIEPG

CADELIT

CTEACN

in this book?

P UNCTUATION

When you write, it is punctuation that helps you to make the meaning clear. Read your work aloud, to see how your voice pauses or falls. If it pauses, but does not fall, as it should do in this sentence, then you need to put a **comma** in each case. When the voice pauses and falls, put a **full stop**. Full stops indicate that a thought has come to an end. Your voice is your best judge, so trust it!

Apart from indicating natural pauses in sentences, **commas** are used for separating items in lists:

I bought a computer game, several comics, a pen and a watch.

– or for pushing a word or phrase into a sentence:

I was thinking, you know, that I had done enough work.

Semi-colons (;) sometimes separate two sentences that you want to show as being close together:

She came hurtling round the corner; the accident wasn't a surprise.

– or for separating a list in which each item has several words:

There are a number of things I want you to do before you go to the camp: tidy your bedroom and make your bed; go and say 'goodbye' properly to your grandmother; bring all your dirty washing and put it in the basket; and apologize to your brother for the way you spoke to him this morning.

Colons (:) are useful before listing various points. Quite a few have been used in this unit.

Question marks (?) indicate how to ask a direct question:
How long were you staying there?

Exclamation marks (!) are used when you are being dramatic! (But you need to use them sparingly or they lose their effect.)

Speech punctuation (' ' in this book, but often also used as " ") is for making direct speech – the exact words spoken – clear for the reader to understand. This is an extract from *Boy* by Roald Dahl.

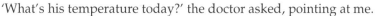

'What's his temperature today?' the doctor asked, pointing at me.

'Just over a hundred, doctor,' the Matron told him.

'He's been up here long enough,' the doctor said. 'Send him back to school tomorrow.' Then he turned to Ellis. 'Take off your pyjama trousers,' he said.

Ellis removed his pyjama trousers. The doctor bent forward and looked at the boil.

'Hmmmmm,' he said. 'That's a nasty one, isn't it? We're going to have to do something about that, aren't we, Ellis?'

'What are you going to do?' Ellis asked, trembling.

'Nothing for you to worry about,' the doctor said. 'Just lie back and take no notice of me.'

Notice from this piece how speech is punctuated:

- the exact words spoken are placed within speech marks
- the punctuation at the end of the spoken sentence goes inside the speech marks
- each change of speaker is shown by a new paragraph

Apostrophes (') are used for two purposes:

① to indicate letters that have been missed out:

I'll try to get this finished as soon as possible. (**I shall**)

He'd lose in any case. (**He would**)

It doesn't seem to matter one way or the other. (**does not**)

② to indicate possession:

Mind the doctor's scalpel, Ellis! (The scalpel of the doctor)

Roald Dahl's book is very funny. (The book of Roald Dahl)

Note: **Singular** noun + apostrophe + s

Pollution is caused by cars' exhausts. (The exhausts of the cars)

These are the girls' lockers. (The lockers of the girls)

Note: **Plural** noun + apostrophe

Women's clothes are on sale today. (The clothes of women)

I went to see the children's teachers at the school. (The teachers of the children)

Note: Plural noun **not ending in s** + apostrophe + s

WRITING CHART

Make a list of the writing you do, indicating whether it is autobiography, a personal letter, a short story, etc. A day or two after a piece of writing, make a few notes about how successful you think it was and which areas of your writing need more attention. Look at the description of the various levels that follow and see which best fits how you did.

Date	Title	Type

L EVEL DESCRIPTIONS: WRITING

At the start of Key Stage 3 the majority of pupils will have reached at least Level 4 in writing. By the end of Key stage 3 most pupils should be within the range of Levels 4–7. Levels 5–6 are the target for 14-year-olds. Level 8 is the standard reached by very able pupils.

Use our checklist to assess the Level reached, by ticking the skills that have been mastered.

Level 4

☐ Writing in a range of forms is lively and thoughtful.
☐ Ideas are often sustained and developed in interesting ways and organized appropriately for the purpose and the reader.
☐ Vocabulary choices are often adventurous and words are used for effect.
☐ Begin to use grammatically complex sentences, extending meaning.
☐ Spelling, including that of polysyllabic words that conform to regular patterns, is generally accurate.
☐ Full stops, capital letters and question marks are used correctly, and the beginning of use of punctuation within the sentence.
☐ Handwriting style is fluent, joined and legible.

Level 5

☐ Writing is varied and interesting, conveying meaning clearly in a range of forms for different readers, using a more formal style where appropriate.
☐ Vocabulary choices are imaginative and words are used precisely.
☐ Simple and complex sentences are organized into paragraphs.
☐ Words with complex regular patterns are usually spelt correctly.
☐ A range of punctuation, including commas, apostrophes and inverted commas, is usually used accurately.
☐ Handwriting is joined, clear and fluent and, where appropriate, is adapted to a range of tasks.

Level 6

☐ Writing often engages and sustains the reader's interest, showing some adaptation of style and register to different forms, including using an impersonal style where appropriate.
☐ Use of a range of sentence structures and varied vocabulary to create effects.
☐ Spelling is generally accurate, including that of irregular words.
☐ Handwriting is neat and legible.
☐ A range of punctuation is usually used correctly to clarify meaning, and ideas are organized into paragraphs.

Level 7

☐ Writing is confident and shows appropriate choices of style in a range of forms.
☐ In narrative writing, characters and settings are developed and, in non-fiction, ideas are organized and coherent.

☐ Grammatical features and vocabulary are accurately and effectively used.
☐ Spelling is correct, including that of complex irregular words.
☐ Work is legible and attractively presented.
☐ Paragraphing and correct punctuation are used to make the sequence of events or ideas coherent and clear to the reader.

Level 8

☐ Writing shows the selection of specific features or expressions to convey particular effects and to interest the reader.
☐ Narrative writing shows control of characters, events and settings, and shows variety in structure.
☐ Non-fiction writing is coherent and gives clear points of view.
☐ The use of vocabulary and grammar enables fine distinctions to be made or emphasis achieved.
☐ Writing shows a clear grasp of the use of punctuation and paragraphing.

Exceptional performance

☐ Writing has shape and impact and shows control of a range of styles maintaining the interest of the reader throughout.
☐ Narratives use structure as well as vocabulary for a range of imaginative effects, and non-fiction is coherent, reasoned and persuasive.
☐ A variety of grammatical constructions and punctuation is used accurately and appropriately and with sensitivity.
☐ Paragraphs are well constructed and linked in order to clarify the organization of the writing as a whole.

PROJECT: WRITE YOUR OWN STORY IN THE STYLE OF ROALD DAHL!

Roald Dahl, one of the most popular writers for young people, created some horrible and memorable adults. Here are a handful for you to read about:

MISS TRUNCHBULL

Miss Trunchbull, the Headmistress, was a gigantic holy terror, a fierce tyrannical monster who frightened the life out of the pupils and teachers alike. There was an aura of menace about her even at a distance, and when she came up close you could almost feel the dangerous heat radiating from her as from a red-hot rod of metal. When she marched – Miss Trunchbull never walked, she always marched like a storm-trooper with long strides and arms aswinging – when she marched along a corridor you could actually hear her snorting as she went, and if a group of children happened to be in her path, she ploughed right on through them like a tank, with small people bouncing off her to left and right.

She was above all a most formidable female. She had once been a famous athlete, and even now the muscles were still clearly in evidence. You could see them in the bull-neck, in the big shoulders, in the thick arms, in the sinewy wrists and in the powerful legs. Looking at her, you got the feeling that this was someone who could bend iron bars and tear telephone directories in half. Her face, I'm afraid, was neither a thing of beauty nor a joy for ever. She had an obstinate chin, a cruel mouth and small arrogant eyes. And as for the clothes … they were, to say the least, extremely odd. She always had on a brown cotton smock which was pinched in front with an enormous silver buckle. The massive thighs which emerged from out of the smock were encased in a pair of extraordinary breeches, bottle-green in colour and made of coarse twill. These breeches reached to just below the knees and from there on down she sported green stockings with turn-up tops, which displayed her calf muscles to perfection. On her feet she wore flat-heeled brown brogues with leather flaps.

Matilda

THE BFG

The Giant had truly enormous ears. Each one was as big as the wheel of a truck and he seemed to be able to move them inwards and outwards from his head as he wished.

'I is hungry!' the Giant boomed. He grinned, showing massive square teeth. The teeth were very white and very square and they sat in his mouth like huge slices of white bread.

'P … please don't eat me,' Sophie stammered.

The Giant let out a bellow of laughter. 'Just because I is a Giant, you think I is a man-gobbling cannybull!' he shouted. 'You is about right! Giants is all cannybully and murderful! And they *does* gobble up human beans!'

The BFG

MR TWIT

Mr Twit was one of these very hairy-faced men. The whole of his face except for his forehead, his eyes and his nose, was covered with thick hair. The stuff even sprouted in revolting tufts out of his nostrils and ear-holes.

Mr Twit felt that his hairiness made him look terrifically wise and grand. But in truth he was neither of these things. Mr Twit was a twit. He was born a twit. And now at the age of sixty he was a bigger twit than ever.

The hair on Mr Twit's face didn't grow smooth and matted as it does on most hairy-faced men. It grew in spikes that stuck out straight like the bristles of a nailbrush.

And how often did Mr Twit wash this bristly nailbrush of his?

The answer is NEVER, not even on Sundays.

He hadn't washed it for years.

The Twits

MRS TWIT

Mrs Twit was no better than her husband.

She did not, of course, have a hairy face. It was a pity she didn't because that at any rate would have hidden some of her fearful ugliness.

Take a look at her.

Have you ever seen a woman with an uglier face than that? I doubt it.

But the funny thing is that Mrs Twit wasn't born ugly. She'd had quite a nice face when she was young. The ugliness had grown upon her year by year as she got older.

Why would that happen? I'll tell you why.

If a person has ugly thoughts, it begins to show on the face. And when that person has ugly thoughts every day, every week, every year, the face gets uglier and uglier until it gets so ugly you can hardly bear to look at it.

A person who has good thoughts cannot ever be ugly. You can have a wonky nose and a crooked mouth and a double chin and stick-out teeth, but if you have good thoughts they will shine out of your face like sunbeams and you will always look lovely.

Nothing shone out of Mrs Twit's face.

In her right hand she carried a walking-stick. She used to tell people this was because she had warts growing on the sole of her left foot and walking was painful. But the real reason she carried a stick was so that she could hit things with it, things like dogs and cats and small children.

And there was the glass eye. Mrs Twit had a glass eye that was always looking the other way.

The Twits

GRANDMA

Most grandmothers are lovely, kind, helpful old ladies, but not this one. She spent all day and every day sitting in her chair by the window, and she was always complaining, grousing, grouching, grumbling, griping about something or other. Never once, even on her best days, had she smiled at George and said, 'Well, how are you this morning, George?' or 'Why don't you and I have a game of Snakes and Ladders?' or 'How was school today?' She didn't seem to care about other people, only about herself. She was a miserable old grouch.

George's Marvellous Medicine

MR VICTOR HAZELL

Mr Victor Hazell was a brewer of beer and he owned a huge brewery. He was rich beyond words, and his property stretched for miles along either side of the valley. All the land around us belonged to him, everything on both sides of the road, everything except the small patch of ground on which our filling station stood. That patch belonged to my father. It was our little island in the middle of the vast ocean of Mr Hazell's estate.

Mr Victor Hazell was a roaring snob and he tried desperately to get in with what he believed were the right kind of people. He hunted with the hounds and gave shooting parties and wore fancy waistcoats. Every weekday he drove his enormous silver Rolls-Royce past our filling station on his way to the brewery. As he flashed by we would sometimes catch a glimpse of the great glistening beery face above the wheel, pink as a ham, all soft and inflamed from drinking too much beer.

Danny, The Champion of the World

Project Action

An unforgettable bunch of characters! Now is your chance to put them into a story of your own.

1. Choose the location(s) for your story:
  - at school
  - in a supermarket
  - your house
  - a café
  - any other(s)? Note them down below:

  ....

  ....

2. Which character arrives first? Why has he or she come? How do the other characters get drawn into the story?

3. 'Brainstorm' the outline of a possible story.

4. Write a first draft, using whatever thoughts you have had so far.
(i) Do you now feel you need to change to another location, or can you keep to the same one?
(ii) Think of a possible ending. Can you bring in a last-minute twist that will surprise your reader?

5. Complete your first draft.

6. Look at your opening paragraph. Does it grab the reader? If not, try improving it. Are you in a better position to write a good beginning now that you know the ending?

7. Read your draft aloud to a friend or member of the family.

8. Any changes/further improvements to be made? Any dull parts?

9. Write, type, word-process, or record on cassette your finished story.

P ROJECT: THE WILD WEST

> I tried to go to sleep, but the jolting made me bite my tongue, and I soon began to ache all over. When the straw settled down, I had a hard bed. Cautiously I slipped from under the buffalo hide, got up on my knees and peered over the side of the wagon. There seemed to be nothing to see; no fences, no creeks or trees, no hills or fields. If there was a road, I could not make it out in the faint starlight. There was nothing but land: not a country at all, but the material out of which countries are made. No, there was nothing but land – slightly undulating, I knew, because often our wheels ground against the brake as we went down into a hollow and lurched up again on the other side. I had the feeling that the world was left behind, that we had got over the edge of it. I had never before looked up at the sky when there was not a familiar mountain ridge against it. But this was the complete dome of heaven, all there was of it. The wagon jolted on, carrying me I knew not whither. I don't think I was homesick. If we never arrived anywhere, it did not matter.

Willa Cather *My Antonia*

Jim Burden, the narrator of the novel from which this is taken, describes his arrival in Nebraska, USA, where he is to spend some years living with his grandparents. In those pioneering days a century or so ago, life was difficult, not least because of the weather: burning summers, freezing cold winters in which 'the whole country is stripped bare and grey as sheet-iron.' The pioneers learned to make something out of nothing; as Jim says, it wasn't a country at all, 'but the material out of which countries are made.'

In an article about a visit to where Willa Cather lived, William Howarth, writing in *National Geographic*, explains:

> Surveyors divided this country into a vast gridiron of square-mile sections. To find their section, settlers made crude odometers (the usual US and Canadian name for mileometer) – measure a wagon wheel, tie a rag to the rim, count the revolutions in each mile. They also improvised shelters: in a treeless land, blocks of sod were the best building material. The Cathers' first house in Nebraska sat on a barren slope encircled by 'nothing but rough, shaggy, red grass.'

Not all the areas of the Wild West, though, were treeless. Laura Ingalls Wilder, who was born just a few years before Willa Cather, listens to her father telling of his return through snowy woods:

> There were still six miles to walk, and I came along as fast as I could. The night grew darker and darker, and I wished for my gun, because I knew that some of the bears had come out of their winter dens. I had seen their tracks when I went to town in the morning.
>
> Bears are hungry and cross at this time of year; you know they have been sleeping in their dens all winter long with nothing to eat, and that makes them thin and angry when they wake up. I did not want to meet one.
>
> I hurried along as quick as I could in the dark. By and by the stars gave a little light. It was still black as pitch where the woods were thick, but in the open places I could see, dimly. I could see the snowy road ahead a little way, and I could see the dark woods standing all round me. I was glad when I came into an open place where the stars gave me this faint light.
>
> All the time I was watching, as well as I could, for bears. I was listening for the sounds they make when they go carelessly through the bushes.
>
> Then I came again into an open place, and there, right in the middle of the road, I saw a big, black bear.
>
> He was standing up on his hind legs, looking at me. I could see his eyes shine. I could see his pig-snout. I could even see one of his claws, in the starlight.
>
> My scalp prickled, and my hair stood straight up. I stopped in my tracks, and stood still. The bear did not move. There he stood, looking at me.

I knew it would do no good to try to go around him. He would follow me into the dark woods, where he could see better than I could. I did not want to fight a winter-starved bear in the dark. Oh, how I wished for my gun!

I had to pass that bear, to get home. I thought that if I could scare him, he might get out of the road and let me go. So I took a deep breath, and suddenly I shouted with all my might and ran at him, waving my arms.

He didn't move.

I did not run very far towards him, I tell you! I stopped and looked at him, and he stood looking at me. Then I shouted again. There he stood. I kept on shouting and waving my arms, but he did not budge.

Well, it would do me no good to run away. There were other bears in the woods. I might meet one any time. I might as well deal with this one as with another. Besides, I was coming home to Ma and you girls. I would never get here, if I ran away from everything in the woods that scared me.

So at last I looked around, and I got a good big club, a solid, heavy branch that had been broken from a tree by the weight of snow in the winter.

I lifted it up in my hands, and I ran straight at that bear. I swung my club as hard as I could and brought it down, bang! on his head.

And there he still stood, for he was nothing but a big, black, burned stump!

I had passed it on my way to town that morning. It wasn't a bear at all. I only thought it was a bear, because I had been thinking all the time about bears and being afraid I'd meet one. There I had been yelling, and dancing, and waving my arms, all by myself in the Big Woods, trying to scare a stump!

Little House in the Big Woods

The pioneers, in opening up the West, were pushing the Indians out of the land they had occupied for a long time. In 1830 The Indian Removal Bill authorized the removal of Indians from areas to the west of the Mississippi and confirmed the settlers' right to dispossess the Indians of their land wherever they were found. The Indians, outnumbered and out-gunned, were swept aside, slaughtered or pressed back. It was thought that by killing off the herds of buffalo, on which the Indians depended for food and clothing, there would be a quick victory. Here, an Indian brave remembers:

My name is Tokalulata or, in your language, Red Fox. I was a young brave when my uncle defeated General Custer in a great battle (in 1876) to protect our sacred places.

Almost everything I knew then passed away, leaving the world empty. The blood of 20 million buffalo has been spilled onto the plains. The wild horse has been enslaved; the vast forests have been cut down; the eagle has been shot from the sky; the rivers, lakes and streams have been polluted and the atmosphere poisoned, and the Indian is a prisoner of the civilization that has overwhelmed him.

I have achieved peace by accepting the fate of my people. I have acted in the movies and in Wild West shows, yet I have never forgotten my happy, free childhood when I lived in a tepee and heard the coyotes calling under the stars … when the night winds, the sun and everything in our world reflected the wisdom of the Great Spirit.

I remember seeing my mother bending over an open fire roasting buffalo meat and my father returning at night with an antelope on his shoulder. I shall never forget when my grandfather taught me to make a bow and arrow, and a fish hook from the rib of a field mouse.

Our tepee was made from buffalo hides and I slept on a bearskin mat with a frame of willow boughs woven into a bed by my mother. The tepee was held up by poles that came to a peak at the top. At bedtime, my mother would tell me stories about her childhood, when the tribes still hunted the buffalo on foot and the few white men who came among them were welcomed as friends.

No people had a deeper love of family than the Sioux. They never punished their children by beating them. I once heard an old Indian say, 'We love our children and beat our horses; the white man loves his horses and beats his children.' That's a big difference!

From my mother I learned the folklore of ancient times. She told me about the birds and animals that lived on the plains and in the forests, why the Great Creator gave wings to the birds, the fawn its spots, the goat, elk, buffalo and antelope their horns, the wolf its strong claws and teeth, and the rabbit its speed. We were told that the Great Spirit looked after everything in nature. We never knelt in prayer, but were taught to look up to the sky, and we used to dance and sing in praise of the buffalo and the eagle. The sun was the smile of the Great Spirit. Without that smile, the Indian knew no one could exist, for the sun is the power of all things.

We do not have a written language, so old people had to pass on all knowledge to the next generation. They taught the chants and rituals of the dances and ceremonies and also the sign language, through which the many tribes with different spoken languages could communicate and hold councils with as much understanding as is achieved among the nations of the world today. In the same way, our bright face paint that you call war paint says many things: it can show happiness, sorrow, peace, which tribe you belong to, where you live. When a girl painted her forehead red and braided her hair in a certain way, it was the symbol of marriage, just as a ring is for the white people.

Discovery

Project Action

1. By looking at encyclopedias and other reference books, read about:
   - Daniel Boone (1734–1820)
   - Thomas Jefferson (1743–1826). What did he send William Clark and Meriwether Lewis to do?
   - William 'Buffalo Bill' Cody (1846–1917)
   - Annie Oakley
   - Calamity Jane
   - The Oregon Trail
   - Salt Lake City
   - The American Civil War
   - The Gold Rush

2. Can you remember an occasion on which the darkness played tricks on you, but which had a happy ending, as it did for Mr Wilder? Record it on cassette or write it down.

3. If you were living in an isolated region far from neighbours, what would you miss most? And what would you like about it?

4. Read *The Long Winter* by Laura Ingalls Wilder.

5. Most films about cowboys and Indians take a rather one-sided view of life in the Wild West. Having read Tokalulata's account of Sioux Indian life, how has your attitude changed? Note down your thoughts.

PROJECT: JOURNEY INTO SPACE

Make Believe

When I wake up in the morning
Not all is what it seems
I drift through a world of make believe
Between my real life and my dreams.

Strange adventures from the Space book
That I read the night before
Crowd in upon my drowsiness
Through imagination's door.

Between sleeping and waking
The alarm clock's jangling cry
Becomes the roaring fire-tailed rocket
That hurls me through the sky.

My bed's a silver space craft
Which I pilot all alone
Whisp'ring through endless stratospheres
Towards planets still unknown.

Outside through the mists of morning
The spinning lights of cars
In my make-believe space voyage
Become eternities of stars.

Is that my mother calling something
That my dreams can't understand?
Or can it be crackling instructions
From far off Mission Command?

If I make believe my ceiling
Is space through which I fly,
If I make believe my bedroom
Is my capsule flying high,
If I make believe the light bulb
Is the moon fast drawing nigh,
If I make believe my counterpane
Is its cratered surface dry,
Then that's what it is,
That's what it is for me
That's what it is, that's what it is
That's what it is for me.

Gareth Owen

SPACE SHOT

Out of the furnace
The great fish rose
Its silver tail on fire
But with a slowness
Like something sorry
To be rid of earth.
The boiling mountains
Of snow white cloud
Searched for a space to go into
And the ground thundered
With a roar
That set tea cups
Rattling in a kitchen
Twenty miles away.
Across the blue it arched
Milk bottle white
But shimmering in the haze.
And the watchers by the fence
Held tinted glass against their eyes
And wondered at what man could do
To make so large a thing
To fly so far and free.
While the unknown Universe waited;
For waiting
Was what it had always been good at.

Gareth Owen

THE GIFT

Tomorrow would be Christmas and even while the three of them rode to the rocket port, the mother and father were worried. It was the boy's first flight into space, his very first time in a rocket, and they wanted everything to be perfect. So when, at the customs table, they were forced to leave behind the gift which exceeded the weight limit by no more than a few ounces and the little tree with the lovely white candles, they felt themselves deprived of the season and their love.

The boy was waiting for them in the Terminal room. Walking towards him, after their unsuccessful clash with the Interplanetary officials, the mother and father whispered to each other.

'What shall we do?'

'Nothing, nothing. What *can* we do?'

'Silly rules!'

'And he so wanted the tree!'

The siren gave a great howl and people pressed forward into the Mars rocket. The mother and father walked at the very last, their small pale son between them, silent.

'I'll think of something,' said the father.

'What…?' asked the boy.

And the rocket took off and they were flung headlong into dark space. The rocket moved and left fire behind and left Earth behind on which the date was December 24th, 2052, heading out into a place where there was no time at all, no month, no year, no hour. They slept away the rest of the first 'day'. Near midnight, by their Earth-time New York watches, the boy awoke and said, 'I want to go to look out the porthole.'

There was only one port, a 'window' of immensely thick glass, of some size, up on the next deck.

'Not quite yet,' said the father. 'I'll take you later.'

'I want to see where we are and where we're going.'

'I want you to wait, for a reason,' said the father.

He had been lying awake, turning this way and that, thinking of the abandoned gift, the problem of the season, the lost tree and the white candles. And at last, sitting up, no more than five minutes ago, he believed he had found a plan. He need only carry it out and this journey would be fine and joyous indeed.

'Son,' he said, 'in exactly one half-hour it will be Christmas.'

'Oh,' said the mother, dismayed that he had mentioned it. Somehow she had rather hoped the boy would forget.

The boy's face grew feverish and his lips trembled. 'I know, I know. Will I get a present, will I? Will I have a tree? You promised–'

'Yes, yes, all that, and more,' said the father.

The mother started. 'But–'

'I mean it,' said the father. 'I really mean it. All and more, much more. Excuse me now. I'll be back.'

He left them for about twenty minutes. When he came back he was smiling. 'Almost time.'

'Can I hold your watch?' asked the boy, and the watch was handed over and he held it ticking in his fingers as the rest of the hour drifted by in fire and silence and unfelt motion.

'It's Christmas *now*! Christmas! Where's my present?'

'Here we go,' said the father, and took his boy by the shoulder and led him from the room, down the hall, up a rampway, his wife following.

'I don't understand,' she kept saying.

'You will. Here we are,' said the father.

They had stopped at the closed door of a large cabin. The father tapped three times and then twice, in a code. The door opened and the light in the cabin went out and there was a whisper of voices.

'Go on in, son,' said the father.

'It's dark.'

'I'll hold your hand. Come on, mama.'

They stepped into the room and the door shut, and the room was very dark indeed. And before them loomed a great glass eye, the porthole, a window four feet high and six feet wide, from which they could look out into space.

The boy gasped.

Behind him, the father and mother gasped with him, and then in the dark room some people began to sing.

'Merry Christmas, son,' said the father.

And the voices in the room sang the old, the familiar carols, and the boy moved forward slowly until his face was pressed against the cool glass of the port. And he stood there for a long time, just looking and looking out into space and the deep night at the burning and the burning of ten billion billion white and lovely candles ….

Ray Bradbury *The Day It Rained Forever*

COLONIZING THE MOON

There is no question of turning the Moon into a kind of second Earth. The main problem is the lack of atmosphere. Unfortunately, the Moon is an airless world and there is not the slightest chance of providing it with a breathable atmosphere; the low escape velocity means that it is incapable of retaining a dense atmosphere similar to that of the Earth. Lack of atmosphere means a total lack of water and it now seems that – contrary to earlier expectation – it will not be practicable to extract water from the lunar rocks for the simple reason that there is none to extract. Neither is there any hope of finding underground supplies of ice. Colonists of the future will have to take everything with them and it will be a long time before a lunar station can hope to become self-supporting.

Science and the Universe

RETIRED

He was tired of his voyages,
the shuttles from planet to planet
from star to star.

In the late evening
he would sway in his rocking chair
and watch the moon through the trees.

'I was there once,' he thought
'I stood on that globe.
Now it is like a football
shining in space.'

And he could hardly believe it
that in his helmet
and in his bulky space suit
he'd stirred that far dust.

Iain Crichton Smith

Project Action

1. Do you ever have dreams of rocketing into space? What excitement do you think you would get from space travel? And what would you miss most about living on Earth if you were on a three-month scientific mission?
Write three diary entries:

   – the day of blast-off
   – half way through your mission
   – the day before returning to Earth

2. Write a science fiction story beginning with one of these:

a) In flicking the switch, I had taken charge of the craft; ground control could no longer direct operations.

b) It was difficult to realise that the dust I scooped up with my gloved fingers was not earth, at least not the earth of Earth.

c) Could the movement on the horizon be creatures or was it simply my imagination?

d) I was glad the first stage was over, but the most hazardous lay in front of me.

a) In flicking the switch, I had taken charge of the craft; ground control could no longer direct operations.

b) It was difficult to realize that the dust I scooped up with my gloved fingers was not earth, at least not the earth of Earth.

c) Could the movement on the horizon be creatures or was it simply my imagination?

d) I was glad the first stage was over, but the most hazardous lay in front of me.

3. By looking at reference books, find out:
–why 4 October 1957 is regarded as the beginning of Space Age
–why Yuri Gagarin became famous
–why July 1969 was important in the history of space travel

4. Read some science fiction stories by Isaac Asimov, Ray Bradbury, John Christopher, or Arthur C Clarke.

5. How much money do you think is spent on space programmes each year? Find out! Do you think that the money would be better spent on combating world poverty and disease? Write down reasons *for* and *against*.

ROJECT: THE WORLD AROUND US

TURNING OVER A NEW LEAF

Scientists in Dublin have found that the answer to monitoring urban pollution may be blowing in the wind. Leaves, they claim, produce pollution-responsive yeast colonies that show just how smog-bound a city is.

The pink yeast spores react far more sensitively to the levels of carbon dioxide and sulphur dioxide, two major pollutants, than any available piece of high-tech.

If an area has a low pollution count, then the yeast colonies on a leaf will thrive; if the count is high, the yeast yield is low. Tests in eight European cities managed to produce a grid pattern of the most affected suburbs.

It is so easy, your school could do it.

First, you divide your town into kilometre squares and then collect some leaves from the different areas (sycamore or any broad-leaved tree are best).

Cut a 1.2 centimetre disc from each leaf and fix them, with a blob of petroleum jelly, upside down to the inside of a sterile Petri dish lid. Put a solid yeast growing medium in the dish and replace the lid.

After four days incubation at room temperature remove the leaves and count the number of pink yeast colonies.

If your area is one of the most affected … move.

The Indy

DESTRUCTIVE MAN

Of all the creatures alive on earth, man is the most destructive. As Mark Twain expressed it, 'Man is the only animal that can blush or needs to'. For millions of years man has been destroying his environment by activities usually attributed to his intelligence. What is meant, of course, is that man's superior intellectual ability, his power to reason, has enabled him to seek and find ways of exploiting his environment that have never been discovered by other animals. This intelligence has largely protected him from the adverse effects of this exploitation.

Here is the introduction to a leaflet issued by the World Wide Fund for Nature:

WHAT ON EARTH CAN I DO?

WWF is working in Britain and in every continent to save endangered species and habitats. Our greatest global assets are being destroyed by mankind.

Logging is destroying the rainforest, pollution from fossil fuel use is contributing to the greenhouse effect and the world's animals and forests are under threat. That is why we at WWF are appealing to people everywhere to become conservationists in their daily lives.

What On Earth Can I Do? is your WWF guide to help the environment. The pressure on our planet has now become so great that a vital and urgent rethink into how we behave is now a necessity, not an option. Correct yesterday's mistakes today for a better tomorrow.

Wherever you are, whatever you are doing, you can all help the environment. **Today** we can **all** take responsibility for our planet.

BOY FORCES CHANGE IN TUNNEL BILL

Lobbying by a London schoolboy has forced a late change to the Channel Tunnel Bill and saved a wildlife haunt.

Lester Holloway, aged 16, gained the support of two MPs after bulldozers started tearing up heathland next to Wormwood Scrubs playing field, which is part of a mile-long haven for wildlife in central London.

The area is owned by British Rail and was earmarked as the site of a depot for Channel Tunnel trains.

But now the Channel Tunnel Bill has been changed at the committee stage and no work can begin on the land without consulting Hammersmith council and the London Wildlife Trust.

Lester, a keen birdwatcher who is a pupil at Burlington Danes School, Shepherds Bush, said: 'The law allowed bulldozers to flatten part of the best wasteland in London, north of Little Scrubs, this month. It is high time politicians changed their ways.

'When I heard that Scrubs Wood was threatened, I compiled a detailed report on its wildlife. I sent it to everyone I could think of who might help me save the woods.'

He lobbied the support of Mr Clive Soley, the MP for Hammersmith, who also involved the Fulham MP, Mr Nick Raynsford.

Mr Raynsford praised Lester yesterday. He said: 'This is wonderful. It has put a stop to any premature work by British Rail. All credit to him for his hard work and good sense.'

But Lester has not finished yet. He said: 'I want to apply for the area to be fully protected as a nature reserve.

'I'm going to lobby the House of Lords – especially members of the Royal Society for the Protection of Birds.'

Project Action

1. Talk to a science teacher at your school to see whether you can carry out the experiment described in the first item.

2. Lester Holloway discovered an area in which wildlife had set up home in central London. He used his initiative and energy to fight against the destruction of the area. Take a careful look at the area in which you live, noting particularly any plots of land that don't seem to be looked after. If there is a suitable plot, begin a survey of the wildlife and its habitat, possibly with a friend's help.

You will have to look in reference books to identify trees, shrubs, flowers, insects, etc, making lists of what you discover. Try to visit the area at regular intervals in order to note any changes.

If you are not sure who owns the land write a letter to your Local Council and ask. You could find the council's address by looking in the telephone directory or by asking at the post office.

By visiting the Local Council, you will be able to find out if any building projects have been submitted for permission. And, if a supermarket is planned for 'your' site, you know what to do…! Follow Lester's example.

3. How wasteful are you and your family? Consider what you throw away. How much paper do you waste? Do you save bottles for putting in bottle banks? Do you look out for recycled or biodegradeable products and packaging when you are out shopping? Or pump action sprays rather than aerosols? Talk to the members of your family about their views on the environment and, if they are not already, persuade them to become more environment friendly.

4. If a member of your family isn't particularly bothered about the environment, design and produce a poster (picture and words) that you can stick up in a prominent place!

5. Read magazines about conservation and the natural world, like *BBC Wildlife*. You should be able to find copies in a local or school library.

6. Write a short story beginning:

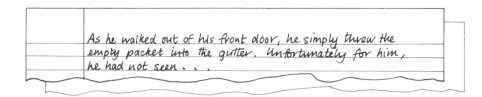

As he walked out of his front door, he simply threw the empty packet into the gutter. Unfortunately for him, he had not seen . . .

7. Find out about an endangered species, gather information, then write a poem including as many descriptive details as you can: what the animal looks like, its habitat, its way of moving, and so on.

CHAPTER 4
*P*ractice National Test questions

These are examples of the kind of questions you will meet in your Key Stage 3 National Test papers for English. Practising these example questions will help you to prepare for your test.

PAPER 1

Section A

Read the following story and answer questions 1 and 2.

HIS FIRST FLIGHT

The young seagull was alone on his ledge. His two brothers and his sister had flown away the day before. He had been afraid to fly with them. Somehow when he had taken a little run forward to the brink of the ledge and attempted to flap his wings he became afraid. The great expanse of sea stretched down beneath, and it was such a long way down – miles down.

He felt certain that his wings would never support him, so he bent his head and ran away back to the little hole under the ledge where he slept at night. Even when each of his brothers and his little sister, whose wings were far shorter than his own, ran to the brink, flapped their wings and flew away he failed to muster up courage to take that plunge which appeared to him so desperate. His father and mother had come around calling to him shrilly, upbraiding him, threatening to let him starve on his ledge unless he flew away. But for the life of him he could not move …

The sun was now ascending the sky, blazing warmly on his ledge that faced the south. He felt the heat because he had not eaten since the previous night-fall. Then he had found a dried piece of mackerel's tail at the far end of his ledge. He had searched every inch, rooting among the rough, dirt-caked straw nest where he and his brothers and sister had been hatched. He even gnawed at the dried pieces of spotted eggshell. It was like eating part of himself. He had then trotted back and forth from one end of the ledge to the other, his grey body the colour of the cliff, his long grey legs stepping daintily, trying to find some means of reaching his parents without having to fly. But on each side of him the ledge ended in a sheer fall of precipice, with the sea beneath. And between him and his parents there was a deep, wide chasm. Surely he could reach them without flying if he could move northwards along the cliff face? But then on what could he walk? There was no ledge, and he was not a fly. And above him he could see nothing. The precipice was sheer, and the top of it was perhaps farther away than the sea beneath him.

He stepped slowly out to the brink of the ledge, and, standing on one leg with the other leg hidden under his wing, he closed one eye, then the other, and pretended to be falling asleep. Still they took no notice of him. He saw his two brothers and his sister lying on the plateau dozing, with their heads sunk into their necks. His father was preening his feathers on his white back. Only his mother was looking at him. She was standing on a little high hump on the plateau, her white breast thrust forward. Now and again she tore at a piece of fish that lay at her feet, and then scraped each side of her beak on the rock. The sight of the food maddened him. How he loved to tear food that way, scraping his beak now and then to whet it! He uttered a low cackle. His mother cackled too, and looked over to him.

'Ga, ga, ga,' he cried, begging her to bring him over some food. 'Gaw-ool-ah,' she screamed back derisively. But he kept calling plaintively, and after a minute or so he uttered a joyful scream. His mother had picked up a piece of fish and was flying across to him with it. He leaned out eagerly, tapping the rock with his feet, trying to get nearer to her as she flew across. But when she was just opposite to him, abreast of the ledge, she halted, her legs hanging limp, her wings motionless, the piece of fish in her beak almost within reach of his beak. He waited for a moment in surprise, wondering why she did not come nearer, and then, maddened by hunger, he dived at the fish. With a loud scream he fell outwards and downwards into space. His mother had swooped outwards. As he passed beneath her he heard the swish of her wings. Then a monstrous terror seized him and his heart stood still. He could hear nothing. But it only lasted a moment. The next moment he felt his wings spread outwards. The wind rushed against his breast feathers, then under his stomach and against his wings. He could feel the tips of his wings cutting through the air. He was not falling headlong now. He was soaring gradually downwards and outwards. He uttered a joyous scream and flapped them again. He soared higher. He raised his breast and banked against the wind. 'Ga, ga, ga. Ga, ga, ga. Gaw-ool-ah.' His mother swooped past him, her wings making a loud noise. He answered her with another scream. Then his father flew over him screaming. Then he saw his two brothers and his sister flying around him curveting and banking and soaring and diving…

He was near the sea now, flying straight over it, facing straight out over the ocean. He saw a vast green sea beneath him, with little ridges moving over it, and he turned his beak sideways and crowed amusedly. His parents and his brothers and sister had landed on the green floor in front of him. They were beckoning to him, calling shrilly. He dropped his legs to stand on the green sea. His legs sank into it. He screamed with fright and attempted to rise again, flapping his wings. But he was tired and weak with hunger and he could not rise, exhausted with the strange exercise. His feet sank into the green sea, and then his belly touched and he sank no farther. He was floating on it. And around him his family were screaming, praising him, and their beaks were offering scraps of dogfish.

He had made his first flight.

Short Stories, Liam O'Flaherty

Answer **both** questions 1 and 2.

1. Describe in your own words the seagull's thoughts and feelings leading up to his first flight. You should find several ideas in most of the paragraphs.
2. What tactics do the gull's mother and father use in order to make him take his first flight?

Section B

Read the following extract and then answer questions 3 and 4.

FIRST DAY AT SCHOOL

I lived in West Helena a long time before I returned to school and took up regular study. My mother luckily secured a job in a white doctor's office at the unheard-of wages of five dollars per week and at once she announced that her 'sons were going to school again'. I was happy. But I was still shy and half paralyzed when in the presence of a crowd, and my first day at the new school made me the laughing stock of the classroom. I was sent to the blackboard to write my name and address; I knew my name and address, knew how to write it, knew how to spell it; but standing at the blackboard with the eyes of the many girls and boys looking at my back made me freeze inside and I was unable to write a single letter.

'Write your name,' the teacher called to me.

I lifted the white chalk to the blackboard and, as I was about to write, my mind went blank, empty; I could not remember my name, not even the first letter. Somebody giggled and I stiffened.

'Just forget us and write your name and address,' the teacher coaxed.

An impulse to write would flash through me, but my hand would refuse to move. The children began to twitter and I flushed hotly.

'Don't you know your name?' the teacher asked.

I looked at her and could not answer. The teacher rose and walked to my side, smiling to me to give me confidence. She placed her hand tenderly on my shoulder. 'What's your name?' she asked.

'Richard,' I whispered.

'Richard what?'

'Richard Wright.'

'Spell it.'

I spelled my name in a wild rush of letters, trying desperately to redeem my paralyzing shyness.

'Spell it slowly so I can hear it,' she directed me.

I did.

'Now, can you write?'

'Yes, ma'am.'

'Then write it.'

Again I turned to the blackboard and lifted my hand to write, then I was blank and void within. I tried frantically to collect my senses, but I could remember nothing. A sense of the girls and boys behind filled me to the exclusion of everything. I realised how utterly I was failing and I grew weak and leaned my hot forehead against the cool blackboard. The room burst into a loud and prolonged laugh and my muscles froze.

'You may go to your seat,' the teacher said.

I sat and cursed myself. Why did I always appear so dumb when I was called upon to perform something in a crowd? I knew how to write as well as any pupil in the classroom, and no doubt I could read better than any of them, and I could talk fluently and expressively when I was sure of myself. Then why did strange faces make me freeze? I sat with my ears and neck burning, hearing the pupils whisper about me, hating myself, hating them; I sat still as stone and a storm of emotion surged through me.

Richard Wright

Answer **both** questions 3 and 4.

3. By thinking carefully about what she says and does, write down your response to the teacher in this extract. Include anything you feel she failed to do that might have helped Richard during his ordeal.

4. How does the writer convey the extent of Richard's fears? Look at the words and phrases he uses.

Section C

5. Choose **ONE** of the following:

EITHER

(a) Write about a time when nerves or fear held you back when you faced a difficulty.

OR

(b) Continue the story in Section B. You could start with later that day or the next morning.

OR

(c) Imagine that you have been asked to write an article for a young person's magazine giving advice about the first day at secondary school. Write the article.

PAPER 2: SHAKESPEARE PLAY

PRACTISING FOR THE TEST

Select a scene from the play your teacher has chosen to study for the Key Stage 3 test, then answer the following, which you will be able to apply to any play by Shakespeare:

1. You have been asked to direct the scene. Write a set of instructions for each major character in the scene, setting out in detail how he or she must play the part.

   For each character, think of such matters as: the thoughts and feelings throughout the scene; the attitude towards the other characters; the variation of speed in speaking the lines.

2. (i)   In what ways is the scene important for the audience?
   (ii)   What do we learn about each of the major characters that we did not know before, if anything?
   (iii) How does the scene fit into the play? What has happened in the previous scene? How does it relate to this scene? And what does it lead into?
   (iv) What is the most vital piece of information given, in terms of the plot?

3. What makes the scene effective on the stage? Is there tension? Humour?

EXTENSION PAPER

If you have been reaching high levels in your work at school, you may be entered for the Extension Paper. You will have two or more texts to read, at least one of which will have been written before the twentieth century. You have to analyse and respond to the passages as well as comparing them. In addition, there will be an opportunity to produce a short piece of writing, which will be judged on its quality not its length.

Read the extracts. Then answer the questions which follow.

Extract A

Maggie Tulliver, having had her dark straight hair shortened by her brother Tom, is afraid to show herself. Tom persuades her to come down to dinner, at which there are some uncles and an unpleasant aunt. Kezia is the girl who helps Mrs Tulliver in the house.

Tom turned again at the door and said, 'But you'd better come, you know. There's the dessert – nuts, you know, and cowslip wine.'

Maggie's tears had ceased, and she looked reflective as Tom left her. His good-nature had taken off the keenest edge of her suffering, and nuts with cowslip wine began to assert their influence.

Slowly she rose from amongst her scattered locks, and slowly she made her way downstairs. Then she stood leaning with one shoulder against the frame of the dining-room door, peeping in when it was ajar. She saw Tom and Lucy with an empty chair between them, and there were custards on a side-table. It was too much. She slipped in and went towards the empty chair. But she had no sooner sat down than she repented, and wished herself back again.

Mrs Tulliver gave a little scream as she saw her, and felt such a 'turn' that she dropped the large gravy-spoon into the dish with the most serious results to the table-cloth. For Kezia had not betrayed the reason for Maggie's refusal to come down, not liking to give her mistress a shock in the moment of carving; and Mrs Tulliver thought there was nothing worse in question than a fit of perverseness, which was inflicting its own punishment by depriving Maggie of half her dinner.

Mrs Tulliver's scream made all eyes turn towards the same point as her own, and Maggie's cheeks and ears began to burn, while uncle Glegg, a kind-looking, white-haired old gentleman, said,

'Hey-day! what little gell's this? Why, I don't know her. Is it some little gell you've picked up on the road, Kezia?'

'Why, she's gone and cut her hair herself,' said Mr Tulliver in an undertone to Mr Deane, laughing with much enjoyment. 'Did you ever know such a little hussy as it is?'

'Why, little miss, you've made yourself look very funny,' said uncle Pullet, and perhaps he never in his life made an observation which was felt to be so lacerating.

'Fie, for shame!' said aunt Glegg, in her loudest, severest tone of reproof. 'Little gells as cut their own hair should be whipped and fed on bread and water – not come in and sit down with their aunts and uncles.'

'Ay,' said uncle Glegg, meaning to give a playful turn to this denunciation; 'she must be sent to jail, I think, and they'll cut the rest of her hair off there, and make it all even.'

'It's very bad luck, sister,' said aunt Pullet, in a pitying tone.

'She's a naughty child as'll break her mother's heart,' said Mrs Tulliver, with tears in her eyes.

Maggie seemed to be listening to a chorus of reproach and derision. Her first flush came from anger which gave her a power of defiance, and Tom thought she was braving it out, supported by the appearance of the pudding and the custard. Under this impression, he whispered, 'O my, Maggie, I told you you'd catch it.' He meant to be friendly, but Maggie felt that Tom was rejoicing in her disgrace. Her feeble power of defiance left her in an instant, her heart swelled, and she ran to her father, hid her face on his shoulder, and burst out into loud sobbing.

'Come, come, my wench,' said her father soothingly, putting his arm round her, 'never mind, you was right to cut it off if it plagued you. Give over crying; father'll take your part.'

Delicious words of tenderness! Maggie never forgot any of these moments when her father 'took her part'; she kept them in her heart, and thought of them long years after, when everyone else said that her father had done very badly by his children.

'How your husband does spoil that child, Bessy!' said Mrs Glegg, in a loud 'aside' to Mrs Tulliver. 'It'll be the ruin of her, if you don't take care. *My* father never brought his children up so, else we should ha' been a different sort o' family to what we are.'

Mrs Tulliver took no notice of her sister's remarks, but threw back her cap-strings and dispensed the pudding in mute resignation.

The Mill on the Floss
George Eliot

Extract B

Though they are sisters, Constance and Sophia Baines seem to be very different from each other. Sophia has offended her mother, first by refusing to take some castor-oil, now by going out…

Sophia came insolently downstairs to join her mother and sister. And nothing happened. The dinner was silently eaten, and Sophia rose abruptly to go.

'Sophia!'

'Yes, mother.'

'Constance, stay where you are,' said Mrs Baines suddenly to Constance, who had meant to flee. Constance was therefore destined to be present at the happening, doubtless in order to emphasize its importance and seriousness.

'Sophia,' Mrs Baines resumed to her younger daughter in an ominous voice. 'No, please shut the door. There is no reason why everybody in the house should hear. Come right into the room – right in! That's it. Now, what were you doing out in the town this morning?'

Sophia was fidgeting nervously with the edge of her little black apron, and worrying a seam of the carpet with her toes. She bent her head towards her left shoulder, at first smiling vaguely. She said nothing, but every limb, every glance, every curve, was speaking. Mrs Baines sat firmly in her own rocking-chair, full of the sensation that she had Sophia, as it were, writhing on the end of a skewer. Constance was braced into a moveless anguish.

'I will have an answer,' pursued Mrs Baines. 'What were you doing out in the town this morning?'

'I just went out,' answered Sophia at length, still with eyes downcast, and in a rather simpering tone.

'Why did you go out? You said nothing to me about going out. I heard Constance ask you if you were coming with us to the market, and you said, very rudely, that you weren't.'

'I didn't say it rudely,' Sophia objected.

'Yes, you did. And I'll thank you not to answer back.'

'I didn't mean to say it rudely, did I Constance?' Sophia's head turned sharply to her sister. Constance knew not where to look.

'Don't answer back,' Mrs Baines repeated sternly. 'And don't try to drag Constance into this, for I won't have it.'

'Oh, of course, Constance is always right!' observed Sophia, with an irony whose unparalleled impudence shook Mrs Baines to her massive foundations.

'Do you want me to have to smack you, child?'

Her temper flashed out and you could see ringlets vibrating under the provocation of Sophia's sauciness. Then Sophia's lower lip began to fall and to bulge outwards, and all the muscles of her face seemed to slacken.

'You are a very naughty girl,' said Mrs Baines, with restraint. ('I've got her,' said Mrs Baines to herself. 'I may just as well keep my temper.')

And a sob broke out of Sophia. She was behaving like a little child. She bore no trace of the young maiden sedately crossing the Square without leave and without an escort.

('I knew she was going to cry,' said Mrs Baines, breathing relief.)

'I'm waiting,' said Mrs Baines aloud.

A second sob. Mrs Baines manufactured patience to meet the demand.

'You tell me not to answer back, and then you say you're waiting,' Sophia blubbered thickly.

'What's that you say? How can I tell what you say if you talk like that?' (But Mrs Baines failed to hear out of discretion, which is better than valour.)

'It's of no consequence,' Sophia blurted forth in a sob. She was weeping now, and tears ricocheting off her lovely crimson cheeks on to the carpet; her whole body was trembling.

'Don't be a great baby,' Mrs Baines enjoined, with a touch of rough persuasiveness in her voice.

'It's you who make me cry,' said Sophia, bitterly. 'You make me cry and then you call me a great baby!' And sobs ran through her frame like waves one after another. She spoke so indistinctly that her mother now really had some difficulty in catching her words.

'Sophia,' said Mrs Baines, with god-like calm, 'it is not I who make you cry. It is your guilty conscience makes you cry. I have merely asked you a question, and I intend to have an answer.'

'I've told you.' Here Sophia checked the sobs with an immense effort.

'What have you told me?'

'I just went out.'

'I will have no trifling,' said Mrs Baines. 'What did you go out for, and without telling me? If you had told me afterwards, when I came in, of your own accord, it might have been different. But no, not a word! It is I who have to ask! Now, quick! I can't wait any longer.'

('I gave way over the castor-oil, my girl,' Mrs Baines said in her own breast. 'But not again! Not again!')

'I don't know,' Sophia murmured.

'What do you mean – you don't know?'

The sobbing recommenced tempestuously. 'I mean I don't know. I just went out.' Her voice rose; it was noisy, but scarcely articulate. 'What if I did go out?'

'Sophia, I am not going to be talked to like this. If you think because you're leaving school you can do exactly as you like –'

'Do I want to leave school?' yelled Sophia, stamping. In a moment a hurricane of emotion overwhelmed her, as though that stamping of the foot had released the demons of the storm. Her face was transfigured by uncontrollable passion. 'You all want to make me miserable!' she shrieked with terrible violence. 'And now I can't even go out! You are a horrid, cruel woman, and I hate you! And you can do what you like! Put me in prison if you like! I know you'd be glad if I was dead!'

She dashed from the room, banging the door with a shock that made the house rattle. It was a startling experience for Mrs Baines. Mrs Baines, why did you saddle yourself with a witness? Why did you so positively say that you intended to have an answer?

'Really,' she stammered, pulling her dignity about her shoulders like a garment that the wind has snatched off. 'I never dreamed that poor girl had such a dreadful temper! What a pity it is, for her own sake!' It was the best she could do.

Constance, who could not bear to witness her mother's humiliation, vanished very quietly from the room. She got half-way upstairs to the second floor, and then, hearing the loud, rapid, painful, regular intake of sobbing breaths, she hesitated and crept down again.

This was Mrs Baines' first costly experience of the child thankless for having been brought into the world. It robbed her of her profound, absolute belief in herself. She had thought she knew everything in her house and could do everything there. And lo! She had suddenly stumbled against an unsuspected personality at large in her house, a sort of hard marble affair that informed her by means of bumps that if she did not want to be hurt she must keep out of the way.

The Old Wives' Tale
Arnold Bennett

Answer both questions.

1. Each extract describes an incident in which there is a conflict between a mother and her daughter.

Compare the ways in which the writers tell their stories.

You may wish to include comments on:

- the ways in which the writers show the behaviour and attitudes of the adults;
- how Tom and Constance are used by the writers;
- the writers' choices of language.

2. Choose **ONE** of the following.

EITHER

(a) Write about someone who, like Maggie and Sophia, has offended a parent. Build up the tension and feelings of the character in your writing.

OR

(b) Is family conflict a necessary part of growing up?

A NSWERING THE TEST QUESTIONS

Reading the instructions

Each test that you take may have different instructions. Always make sure that you read very carefully what you are asked to do. Notice, for example, that you have to answer **both** questions on *His First Flight* and **both** questions on *First Day at School*, but when you come to question 5, you have a choice of three alternatives and you have to answer **only one of them**. Students so often neglect to read this 'EITHER … OR … OR …' type of instruction and attempt all three. Only the first will be given a mark.

Reading the passages

Always read the passages very carefully two or three times before you start to write your answers. It will not be time wasted and could save you from making silly errors.

Reading the question

It is just as important to read each question carefully.

- The first question asks you to **describe in your own words** – that does not mean copying out words and phrases from the extract; you need to use different words and phrases. In question 1, you need to write: 'The seagull has been frightened to fly away with his brothers and sister …' Avoid using the word 'afraid' which, incidentally, appears twice in the first paragraph.

- 'Leading <u>up to</u> his first flight' means that you cannot include details from the final paragraph because he is already flying by then.

- Look at each sentence to see if there are ideas hidden away or implied that are not immediately obvious. If you read the last sentence of the first paragraph ('The great expanse … miles down.'), you notice that his fear is linked with the height of his ledge above the sea so far below. It expresses his thoughts and feelings, but seems on the surface to be a simple description.

Planning the answer

In preparing to answer the questions, underline or make a note of details you will want to include. Put the details in a sensible order, checking that you are answering exactly what you have been asked and no more. There is no point in padding out your answer simply to fill page after page.

Suggested answer plans

Paper 1

1 Apart from the comments made above, you could have included: his belief that his wings were inadequate for keeping him airborne; he lacked courage for what seemed a rash and serious move; he seemed rooted to the spot; he attempted to think of an alternative way to reach his parents; he tried to attract attention by seeming unconcerned, pretending to be asleep; he was enraged by the sight of food; he felt elation at the sight of his mother flying towards him with a piece of fish; he waited in expectation, which frustrated him and caused him to swoop outwards.

2 You could have included: they called to him shrilly; they reproached him; they threatened to let him starve; the perched out of reach; they ignored him; his

mother taunted him by tearing at some fish, whetting his appetite; she treated him derisively, with disdain; she lured him out until he was clear of the ledge before he realised it.

3 Make sure you give your response to the teacher's words and actions. You could have included: appeared initially helpful – 'coaxed', 'smiling at me to give me confidence', 'placed her hand tenderly on my shoulder'; became cooler towards him – 'she directed me', 'You may go to your seat'; fails to check class's attitude and response when they burst out laughing.

4 The writer builds up our understanding by using precise and strong words and phrases, like: 'half paralyzed', 'laughing stock', 'freeze inside', 'my mind went blank, empty', 'I stiffened', 'my hand would refuse to move', 'I flushed hotly', 'trying desperately to redeem my paralyzing shyness', 'I was blank and void within', 'utterly I was failing and I grew weak', 'ears and neck burning', 'a storm of emotion surged through me'.

5 This question gives you scope to use your imagination. Whichever topic chosen, you will need to give structure and shape to your writing.

(a) In writing on the first topic, you need to describe a particular occasion, stressing the fear that you felt – your answer to question 4 will have given you an idea of how to communicate tension to the reader. Give sufficient background for the reader to understand the situation.

(b) Continuing the story calls for putting yourself into Richard's position. You will need to describe his thoughts and feelings, showing his relations with the other boys and girls, as well as with the teacher. You would also need to take into account the information contained in the opening paragraph. Changing the setting and circumstances of the original would bring your marks down.

(c) In planning to write a magazine article, you will need to jot down several topics that you feel would be helpful for new pupils to know. Think back to your first day at secondary school. What would you like to have known? What tips would have helped? How can you begin your article so that it attracts attention, making the reader want to find out more?

Shakespeare

You need to show that you have understood the play and can respond to it as a play. Select details to support the comments you make; short, apt quotations will impress those reading your answer. Though you will be concentrating on one scene of the play, make sure that you refer to other parts of the play if they are relevant to your answer. You may be asked to 'be' one of the characters. Put yourself in the character's shoes. How do you think and feel about what has gone before? How do you think and feel now? Who is on stage with you at this moment? What is your relationship with him/her/them?

Extension Paper

1 You will be making a comparison between texts. Take the areas that have been offered to you for guidance and look for similarities and differences. You will need to explain opinions and insights, illustrating them with short, relevant references from the passages. In the two passages given here, note for example: the use of dialogue to show people's reactions (extreme comments like 'Little gells as cut their own hair should be whipped and fed on bread and water' and 'she must be sent to jail'); the use of bracketed quotations in Extract B as a way of showing Mrs Baines' thoughts ('I gave way over the castor-oil, my

girl,' Mrs Bains said in her own breast. 'But not again! Not again!'); how Tom and Constance are brought in to play a part in heightening the tension; the precision of the words and phrases used, the variation in sentence length and structure, the use of dialect, and so on.

2 (a) Make sure that you pay full attention to the comment about building up the tension and feelings of the character. The description will need to create the atmosphere, using apt and precise vocabulary. Capturing the reader's interest must be a priority.

(b) Argue your points logically and precisely. Your paragraphing should reflect the organization of your thoughts.

GLOSSARY

Accent	A particular way of *pronouncing* words.
Adjective	A class of words describing or adding to nouns, to make their meaning more precise eg. The *young* girl bought an *interesting* book.
Adverb	A class of words adding to the meaning of a verb, adjective or other adverb, by telling how, why, when, or where an action takes place eg. The boy walked *slowly* to his home *today*.
Alliteration	Using the same consonant sound at the beginning of two or more words in the same sentence to gain an effect. It may be found frequently in poetry and advertising eg. With *b*eaded *b*ubbles winking at the *b*rim.
Apostrophe	Punctuation mark (') to show **(i)** where a letter or letters have been missed out eg. I'll get him for that! or **(ii)** possession eg. Karen's pen is broken.
Assonance	A similarity between sounds, especially vowel sounds. Listen to the *u* sounds (not just the letter *u*) as you read this line aloud: A shielded sc*u*tcheon bl*u*sh'd with bl*oo*d of queens and kings.
Audience	The name given to the person or people to whom you are writing or speaking.
Autobiography	The story of your own life.
Ballad	A simple narrative poem.
Brainstorming	Getting lots of ideas about a topic.
Colon	Punctuation mark (:) often used before a list eg. At the stationer's I bought: refills for my pen, a ruler, transfer letters and a notebook.
Comma	Punctuation mark (,) used between words or groups of words to show a short pause.
Conjunction	A word which joins a word or phrase with another word or phrase eg. Robert *and* Louise are students. Robert studied conscientiously, *but* Louise lacked interest. *Although* Louise wanted to do well, she did not study conscientiously. (Note, in the third example here, that the conjunction need not come between the words or phrases it joins.)
Dialect	The name given to the words used in a particular group or in a particular part of the country.
Drafting	Each stage of a piece of writing. We may make several attempts at a piece of writing before we are satisfied that it is right.

Exclamation mark	Punctuation mark (!) used to show emphasis. Got that!
Figure of speech	An expression, such as a metaphor or simile, in which words are not used in their usual sense.
Full stop	Punctuation mark (.) to show the end of a sentence or to show an abbreviation eg. Dr Johnson b. (short for 'born') 1709 d. (short for 'died') 1784.
Haiku	Japanese verse form in three lines of five, seven and five syllables.
Location	The setting(s) for a story, play, or poem.
Media	The name given to newspapers, television, radio and advertisements collectively.
Metaphor	A word applied to another object for comparison, as if they are literally the same eg. My brother's a lion when he gets fighting. (He isn't *literally* a lion, of course!)
Narrative	The way the events that happen in a story are put together.
Noun	A noun names a person (*girl, James*), a thing (*table, car*), or a quality (*beauty, comfort*).
Onomatopoeia	The use of words whose sound imitates an actual noise eg. Hiss, bang.
Paragraph	A group of sentences placed together because they have a common idea.
Parts of speech	The grouping of words (into nouns, verbs, adjectives, etc) according to the ways they are used in a sentence.
Playscript	The way a story is laid out so that it can easily be read by people acting it out.
Plot	The sequence of events that make up a story.
Preposition	A word that indicates the relation of a noun or pronoun to another word, suggesting position, manner, etc eg. The books are *on* the table, the ball went *through* the window.
Pronoun	A word which substitutes for a noun in order to avoid repetition eg. *I* am writing *it* down for *you* to read.
Proof-reading	Checking a piece of writing by reading carefully through it to see that there are no errors.
Question mark	Punctuation mark (?) used when asking a question or expressing a doubt eg. The ball just slipped out of your fingers?
Rhyme	The repetition of identical sounds, particularly at the end of lines of verse eg. She hurried at his words beset with *fears*, For there were sleeping dragons all *around*, At glaring watch, perhaps, with ready *spears* – Down the wide stairs a darkling way they *found*.

Rhythm

The regular pattern of strong and weak beats in verse
eg. The *sea* is *calm* to*night*.

Semi-colon

Punctuation mark (;) used to separate two sentences which you want to show as being very close in meaning.

Simile

The comparison between two things that are not really alike
eg. My love is like a red, red rose
The comparison works because a red rose is thought of as being beautiful, delicate, denoting love, etc; we don't think of the prickles and the greenfly!
A simile is introduced by the words *as* or *like*.

Slang

The informal language of certain groups, for example, young people at school. It is often disliked by those outside the group.

Speech punctuation

Punctuation marks (' ' or " ") used to make clear what someone actually says.

Standard English

A form of English which is understood by all English speakers and which you are taught in school.

Thesaurus

A book that groups words of similar meaning together.

Verb

A class of words that express actions or states
eg. The student *dawdled* to his lessons.
I *am* a student.

I NDEX

A

accents 24–5
adjectives 162
adverbs 162
advertisements 12, 113–17
alliteration, poetry 96
alphabetical order 88–9
Anglo-Saxons 20, 29–30
apostrophes 165
Asimov, Isaac 58–60
Auden, W H
   Night Mail 96–8
   Roman Wall Blues 133, 134
audience 14–15, 139
autobiography 62–8, 136–7, 144–7

B

ballads 98–100
Beaufort wind scale 87
Bennett, Arnold 188–9
Bignall, Philippa 33–4
Blake, William, *The Tyger* 93
Bradbury, Ray 176–7
brainstorming 137–9
Brontë, Bramwell 79
Brown, Frederick, *The Bear* 148

C

Caesar, Julius 132
Callow, Philip 130
Cather, Willa, *My Antonia* 172
characters 53, 56, 154–5, 169–71
Chaucer, Geoffrey 22
Churchill, Winston 153–4
computers 77–8, 119, 143
conjunctions 163
conversation 8–11
Cope, Wendy 102–3
Cornford, Frances, *Childhood* 104

D

Dahl, Roald
   The BFG 169
   Boy 44–5, 68, 164–5
   Charlie and the Chocolate Factory
     123–5
   Danny, The Champion of the World
     171
   George's Marvellous Medicine 170
   Matilda 125, 169
   The Twits 170
Desai, Anita 154
dialect 23–4

E

dialogue, plays 107–9
diaries 51, 73–6
Dickens, Charles 34–5
dictionaries 88–90, 107
discussion 11–12

Eliot, George 187–8
encyclopedias 84, 119
English
   accents 24–5
   change 22–3
   dialects 23–4
   history 20–3
   Standard English 22–3
environment, project 180–2
Exeter Book 29–30
experiences, speaking 13–14

F

Fanthorpe, Ursula 105
first-person narrative 50

G

games
   role-plays 19–20
   words 163–4
Gardam, Jane, *The Hollow Land* 51–2
Greene, Graham 142

H

haiku , poetry 151
handwriting 143
Henry, O, *Witches Loaves* 54–6
Hesketh, Phoebe, *Clown* 106
Hines, Barry, *Kes* 144–5
Hoggan, Neil, *Getting Home* 149
holidays, project 37–40
homework 130
Hughes, Ted, *Wind* 99–100

I

images, advertisements 113–17
information
   computers 119
   reading for 83–91
instructions 17–18
interests and hobbies, writing 151–4
interjections 163

J

Jenkins, Ray 8–9
Jintah, Soraya 155–6

Johnson, B S 99
Johnson, Dr Samuel 107
jokes 17
Jones, Terry, *Fairy Tales* 15–16, 60

K

Keyes, Daniel 143
Kilvert, Rev Francis 73–4
Kirkup, James 129–30

L

Lawrence, D H 79, 80–1
    The Collier's Wife 23–4
    Snake 94–6
learning, project 128–31
leisure 37–40
letters
    reading 77–82
    story-telling 50–1
    writing 156–8
Levi, Rosalind 149
Levine, Harriet 150
libraries, use 43–4
listening *see* speaking and listening
Lochhead, Liz 101–2

M

media 112–18
messages 17–18
Mortimer, John 109
Mudd, Andrew 150

N

National Curriculum
    attainment targets 5
    level descriptions 27–8, 121–2, 167–8
    skills 6
National Test
    Extension Paper 187–90, 192–3
    Paper 1 183–5, 191–2
    Paper 2 186, 192
    planning answers 191–3
    practice questions 183–93
Newby, Eric 136–7, 146
news, television 117–18
newspapers 112–18
Nichols, Grace
    autobiography 136
    The Dis-satisfied Poem 101
Norman, Frank, autobiography 66–7
notes 137–9
nouns 161

O

O'Flaherty, Liam 183–4
Olds, Sharon 137–8
omniscience, story-telling 50

onomatopoeia 96, 109, 196
orders 17–18
Owen, Gareth
    Boredom 40
    Half Asleep 100–1
    Make Believe 175
    Ping Pong 39
    Space Shot 176

P

paragraphs, writing 140–2
parts of speech 161–3
Patterson, Gavin 71–2
Pepys, Samuel 74–5
Pinter, Harold, *Last to Go* 107–9
planning
    National Test answers 191–3
    writing 137–42
plays
    acting 20
    reading 107–11
    writing 155–6
plots, stories 57
plurals, spelling 161
poetry
    haiku 151
    reading 91–107
    writing 137–8, 147–51
prefixes 159
prepositions 162–3
presentation, writing 143
projects
    environment 180–2
    holidays 37–40
    learning 128–31
    reading and television 123–7
    riddles 29–32
    Romans 132–4
    space 175–9
    stories 169–71
    transport 33–6
    Wild West 172–4
pronouns 161
proof-reading, writing 143
propaganda 112
punctuation, writing 164–5
puppets, role-plays 20

Q

questions, National Test 183–93

R

reading 41–134
    autobiography 62–8
    chart 120
    diaries 73–6
    information 83–91

letters 77–82
media 112–18
National Curriculum 6, 121–2
plays 107–11
poetry 91–107
record 61–2
story-telling 46–62
television 123–7
travel writing 68–72
types 42–6
reference books 83–91
rhythm, poetry 96–8
riddles, project 29–32
role-plays 19–20
Romans, project 132–4
Rosen, Michael 126
    Father Says 98

S
scanning 42–3, 44, 45
Scovell, E J, The Boy Fishing 38
Secombe, Harry 62–5
Shakespeare, William 22–3, 109–11,
    186, 192
signs, reading 41
simile, poetry 104
skimming 44, 45
slang 25
Smith, Iain Crichton 178
space travel, project 175–9
speaking and listening 7–40
    audience 14–15
    chart 26
    conversation 8–11
    difference from writing 25
    experiences 13–14
    first words 7
    instructions 17–18
    National Curriculum 6, 27–8
    story-telling 15–17
speech, punctuation 164–5
spelling 22, 158–61
sport 37–9
Standard English 22–3
stereotypes, advertising 116–17
Stevenson, Anne 104–5
stories
    characters 53, 56
    plots 57
    reading 46–8
    speaking and listening 15–17
    viewpoint 49–53
    writing 154–5
suffixes 160

Sutcliff, Rosemary 132, 134

T
Tawney, Clare, Bonfire 149
telephones 77–8
television 117–18, 123–7
thesauruses 90–1
Thomas, Dylan, Holiday Memory 37, 40
Thomas, Edward, Thaw 103
Thubron, Colin 69–71
Tokalulata, Discovery 173–4
transport, project 33–6
travel writing 68–72

V
Van der Post, Laurens 30–1
verbs 162
viewpoint, story-telling 49–53

W
Wainwright, Alfred 72
Waterhouse, Keith 75–6
White, E B 79
    Charlotte's Web 52–3
Wild West, project 172–4
Wilder, Laura Ingalls 172–3
Williams, John, Mac 148
word games 163–4
word processors see computers
Wordsworth, William 147
writing 135–82
    audience 139
    autobiography 144–7
    brainstorming 137–9
    characters 154–5, 169–71
    chart 166
    difference from speaking 25
    drafts 140–2
    interests and hobbies 151–4
    letters 156–8
    National Curriculum 6, 167–8
    paragraphs 140–2
    parts of speech 161–3
    plays 155–6
    poetry 137–8, 147–51
    presentation 143
    proof-reading 143
    punctuation 164–5
    spelling 158–61
    stories 154–5
    viewpoint 46–53

Z
Zephaniah, Benjamin 103–4